Hegel's *Phenomenology of Spirit*

READER'S GUIDES

Reader's Guides are clear, concise and accessible introductions to key texts in literature and philosophy. Each book explores the themes, context, criticism and influence of key works, providing a practical introduction to close reading, guiding students towards a thorough understanding of the text. They provide an essential, up-to-date resource, ideal for undergraduate students.

Reader's Guides available:

Aristotle's *Nicomachean Ethics*, Christopher Warne
Aristotle's *Politics*, Judith A. Swanson
Badiou's *Being and Event*, Christopher Norris
Berkeley's *Principles of Human Knowledge*, Alasdair Richmond
Berkeley's *Three Dialogues*, Aaron Garrett
Deleuze and Guattari's *Anti-Oedipus*, Ian Buchanan
Deleuze's *Difference and Repetition*, Joe Hughes
Derrida's *Writing and Difference*, Sarah Wood
Descartes' *Meditations*, Richard Francks
Hegel's *Philosophy of Right*, David Edward Rose
Heidegger's *Being and Time*, William Blattner
Heidegger's *Later Writings*, Lee Braver
Hobbes's *Leviathan*, Laurie M. Johnson Bagby
Hume's *Dialogues Concerning Natural Religion*, Andrew Pyle
Kant's *Critique of Aesthetic Judgement*, Fiona Hughes
Kant's *Critique of Pure Reason*, James Luchte
Kant's *Groundwork for the Metaphysics of Morals*, Paul Guyer
Kierkegaard's *Fear and Trembling*, Clare Carlisle
Locke's *Second Treatise of Government*, Paul Kelly
Mill's *On Liberty*, Geoffrey Scarre
Mill's *Utilitarianism*, Henry R. West
Nietzsche's *Beyond Good and Evil*, Christa Davis Acampora and
   Keith Ansell Pearson
Nietzsche's *On the Genealogy of Morals*, Daniel Conway
Nietzsche's *The Birth of Tragedy*, Douglas Burnham

Plato's *Republic*, Luke Purshouse
Plato's *Symposium*, Thomas L. Cooksey
Rawls's *A Theory of Justice*, Frank Lovett
Rousseau's *The Social Contract*, Christopher D. Wraight
Sartre's *Being and Nothingness*, Sebastian Gardner
Schopenhauer's *The World as Will and Representation*, Robert L. Wicks
Spinoza's *Ethics*, J. Thomas Cook
Wittgenstein's *Philosophical Investigations*, Arif Ahmed
Wittgenstein's *Tractatus Logico-Philosophicus*, Roger M. White

Forthcoming:
Deleuze and Guattari's *A Thousand Plateaus*, Eugene W. Holland
Deleuze and Guattari's *What is Philosophy?*, Rex Butler
Machiavelli's *The Prince*, Miguel Vatter
Nietzsche's *Thus Spoke Zarathustra*, Clancy Martin

A READER'S GUIDE

Hegel's *Phenomenology of Spirit*

STEPHEN HOULGATE

BLOOMSBURY
LONDON • NEW DELHI • NEW YORK • SYDNEY

Bloomsbury Academic
An imprint of Bloomsbury Publishing Plc

50 Bedford Square	175 Fifth Avenue
London	New York
WC1B 3DP	NY 10010
UK	USA

www.bloomsbury.com

First published 2013

© Stephen Houlgate, 2013

All rights reserved. No part of this publication may be reproduced or transmitted in any form or by any means, electronic or mechanical, including photocopying, recording, or any information storage or retrieval system, without prior permission in writing from the publishers.

Stephen Houlgate has asserted his right under the Copyright, Designs and Patents Act, 1988, to be identified as Author of this work.

No responsibility for loss caused to any individual or organization acting on or refraining from action as a result of the material in this publication can be accepted by Bloomsbury Academic or the author.

British Library Cataloguing-in-Publication Data
A catalogue record for this book is available from the British Library.

ISBN: HB: 978-0-8264-8510-6
PB: 978-0-8264-8511-3

Library of Congress Cataloging-in-Publication Data
Houlgate, Stephen.
Hegel's Phenomenology of spirit: a reader's guide/Stephen Houlgate.
  p. cm. – (Reader's guides)
Includes bibliographical references (p.) and index.
ISBN 978-0-8264-8510-6 (hardcover) – ISBN 978-0-8264-8511-3 (pbk.) –
ISBN 978-1-4411-8085-8 (ebook (pdf)) – ISBN 978-1-4411-3455-4 (ebook (epub))
  1. Hegel, Georg Wilhelm Friedrich, 1770–1831. Phänomenologie des Geistes.
  2. Spirit. 3. Consciousness. 4. Truth. I. Title.
  B2929.H68 2012
  193–dc23
  2012012761

Typeset by Deanta Global Publishing Services, Chennai, India

CONTENTS

Preface ix
Note on the text xi

1 Context 1
   Speculative logic and Kantian critique 2
   The role of phenomenology 5
   Phenomenology, immanence and scepticism 7
   Logic in phenomenology 8

2 Overview of themes 15
   Consciousness and its immanent criterion 15
   The experience of consciousness 18
   The object of experience 21
   The role of the 'we' 23
   The end and the beginning of phenomenology 29

3 Reading the text 31
   Consciousness 31
      Sense-certainty 31
      Perception 45
      Force and understanding 57
   Self-consciousness 83
      Desire and recognition 83
      The life and death struggle and master–slave relation 93
      Stoicism, scepticism and the unhappy consciousness 102

Reason 123
    Observing reason 123
    Active, self-conscious reason 134
    Individuality that is actual in and through itself 139
Spirit 145
    True spirit 146
    Self-alienated spirit 151
    Self-certain spirit 165
Religion 173
    Natural religion 174
    The religion of art 176
    Manifest religion 182
Absolute knowing 185

4 Reception and influence 191

Notes 195
Guide to further reading 203
Index 209

PREFACE

The purpose of this book is to provide a guide to reading Hegel's *Phenomenology of Spirit*. There are many fine commentaries that explore the historical background to, and philosophical relevance of, Hegel's text, but this guide aims specifically to help students follow the twists and turns of that text itself. My guiding principle is that the *Phenomenology* sets out a single, continuous, *logical* argument, whose details are to be taken seriously. It has to be admitted that this argument is, at times, horribly convoluted. I have made every effort, however, to present the argument as clearly as possible, and I hope that, with the help of this book, students will be able to understand and assess it for themselves.

Due to the considerable length of the *Phenomenology*, it is not possible in this guide to provide a detailed account of each stage of Hegel's argument. I have chosen, therefore, to give detailed accounts of the first four chapters of the book, which set out the development of consciousness and self-consciousness. These are the chapters with which most students are likely to start, and they also contain the famous analyses of sense-certainty, the master–slave relation and the unhappy consciousness. The remaining chapters on reason, spirit, religion and absolute knowing are also important and fascinating, but space is limited. My hope, therefore, is that students can learn from my account of the first four chapters to make headway in Hegel's text on their own, and that they will then be able to engage with the missing details from chapters five to eight by themselves.

My aim throughout this guide has been to explain how the argument of the *Phenomenology* proceeds and, by implication, why it might be deemed successful. I have not, therefore, considered specific criticisms of Hegel's ideas; nor, with rare exceptions, have I commented on the interpretations of other readers of Hegel. In view of this, I should like to express in this preface my gratitude to the many other readers, whose work, over the years, has helped me understand Hegel's *Phenomenology* better. A list of some of their works is provided in the 'Guide to Further Reading' at the end of this book.

NOTE ON THE TEXT

The translation used in this *Reader's Guide* is G. W. F. Hegel, *Phenomenology of Spirit*, trans. A. V. Miller (Oxford: Oxford University Press, 1977). This translation is divided into 808 paragraphs, and it has become common in much English-language secondary literature on the *Phenomenology* to make reference to these paragraphs. I have thus followed this convention in this guide. I have also made reference to the following German edition: G. W. F. Hegel, *Phänomenologie des Geistes*, ed. H.-F. Wessels and H. Clairmont (Hamburg: Felix Meiner Verlag, 1988). References to the *Phenomenology* are thus given in this guide in the following form (with the English text first, and the German text second): §90/69. Students who read German will find Hegel easier to read and understand in the original language, and I would strongly encourage them to consult the German edition, whenever possible.

Hegel is a striking stylist and Miller's translation also provides many memorable passages. There are times, however, when Miller's version needs correcting. I have thus amended his translation whenever this was necessary. I have not indicated that a change has been made, unless such a change means that students can no longer find the relevant passage in the translation. In this case, a note has been added giving Miller's wording. Translations of other works by Hegel have also been amended, where necessary.

CHAPTER ONE

Context

G. W. F. Hegel was born in Stuttgart in 1770 and died in Berlin in 1831. His *Phenomenology of Spirit* was published in the spring of 1807, 26 years after the first edition of Kant's *Critique of Pure Reason*, almost 18 years after the French Revolution, and in the middle of the Napoleonic Wars. The latter had an especially dramatic impact on the final stage of the *Phenomenology*'s birth and almost prevented it from seeing the light of day. At the time, Hegel was an unsalaried lecturer at the University of Jena, and, as he later told his friend, the philosopher F. W. J. Schelling, he 'actually completed the final draft in the middle of the night before the Battle of Jena' (which took place on 14 October 1806 and in which Napoleon's troops comprehensively defeated the Prussians).[1] Furthermore, Hegel had to entrust the last sheets of his manuscript to a courier who rode through French lines to take them to the publisher in Bamberg.[2] As Hegel notes with trepidation, if the manuscript were to fail to get through, 'my loss would indeed be all too great'.[3]

Hegel's manuscript did get through, however, and the *Phenomenology* went on to become perhaps Hegel's best-known work, exercising profound influence on a wide array of thinkers including Karl Marx, Alexandre Kojève and contemporary philosophers such as Judith Butler and Robert Brandom.

When the *Phenomenology* was first published, it was described by Hegel as the 'first part' of the system of philosophical 'science' (*Wissenschaft*).[4] This title was, however, dropped from Hegel's plan for a second edition in 1831, and this change highlights the ambiguity that characterized the book from the start.[5] On the one hand, the

Phenomenology is a work of systematic 'science' (§88/68); on the other hand, it does not form part of Hegel's philosophy proper – which comprises logic, philosophy of nature and philosophy of spirit – but serves as an introduction to that philosophy. Why, though, is such an introduction necessary? To answer this question we need to look at Hegel's philosophy proper, more specifically his logic, and its relation to Kant's 'critical philosophy'. Together these provide the context that explains why Hegel wrote his *Phenomenology*.

Speculative logic and Kantian critique

Hegel's logic is presented in its most developed form in the *Science of Logic* (1812–16, 2nd edn, 1832). Like Spinoza's *Ethics*, the *Logic* is a work of metaphysics or ontology: it discloses the nature of being through pure conceptual thought. Such 'speculative' logic, as Hegel calls it, shows being to entail various forms or ways of being, such as being finite and being quantifiable, that correspond to, and are articulated by, the categories of thought. Logic thus discloses the nature of *being* from within thought and finds the categories of *thought* – or their objective correlates – within being.[6]

In the *Logic*, Hegel states that this 'unity' of thought and being constitutes the 'element' or 'principle' of logic.[7] Logic thus starts from the idea that being is known *by* pure thought to be intelligible *to* pure thought. In this sense, Hegel's logic continues the tradition of *pre-Kantian* metaphysics. In Hegel's view, however, such metaphysics took for granted the categories through which it conceived of being. Spinoza and Leibniz, for example, simply presupposed their definitions of 'substance'; they did not investigate 'the peculiar content and validity' of the categories and concepts they used, and so, in Hegel's view, they 'employed these forms *uncritically* [*ohne Kritik*]'.[8] Kant's 'critical philosophy', by contrast, 'subjects to investigation the validity of the *concepts of the understanding* that are used in metaphysics', and Hegel confirms that doing so 'was without doubt a very important step'.[9] Hegel is a *post*-Kantian metaphysician, therefore, because he agrees with Kant that philosophy must adopt a thoroughly *critical* attitude to the categories of thought through which the nature of being is to be disclosed.

In Hegel's view, Kant is the father of the critical era in philosophy to which we all now belong. He contends, however, that Kant himself did not carry out a sufficiently profound critique of the categories. What Kant did, in Hegel's view, was – mistakenly – restrict their range of validity: he argued that they should be employed to understand only possible objects of experience, but not things 'in themselves'. He failed, however, to undertake a critical examination of the *content* of those categories, and retained a traditional, largely Aristotelian, understanding of such content. Kant's own critique of the categories was thus *insufficiently critical*.[10]

In Hegel's view, an uncritical, or inadequately critical, approach to the categories takes a certain understanding of them *on authority* – be it the authority of past philosophers, tradition, common sense or formal logic. A properly critical attitude, by contrast, takes nothing on authority. It begins by setting to one side all inherited assumptions about thought (and being) and taking *nothing* for granted. For Hegel, therefore, all truly critical philosophy in the wake of Kant is governed by the following imperative: all 'presuppositions or assumptions must equally be given up when we enter into science'. Science – that is to say, philosophy – should thus be 'preceded by *universal doubt*, i.e., by total *presuppositionlessness*'.[11]

At the start of his logic, therefore, Hegel suspends all previous assumptions about thought and being, and sets them to one side, in an act of radical freedom. The modern age, for Hegel, is not only the age of critique, but also the age of *freedom* – of Rousseau, Fichte and the French Revolution. Moreover, the twin imperatives of critique and freedom coincide in opposing the idea that human beings should simply take things on authority. The critical requirement of total presuppositionlessness in philosophy is therefore 'fulfilled by the freedom that abstracts from everything, and grasps its own pure abstraction, the simplicity of thinking – in the resolve [*Entschluß*] of *the will to think purely*'.[12] The starting point for speculative logic that results from this act of abstraction is thus devoid of any determinate presuppositions. Whereas Spinoza begins with contestable definitions of substance, attribute and mode, Hegel begins with the utterly *indeterminate* thought of pure 'being'.[13] From this initial category all other categories are to be derived, and in the process speculative logic will *discover* the true nature of thought and being without taking anything specific for granted about either.

Yet isn't the idea that pure thought can disclose the nature of being a mere assumption itself (and one that Kant, for example, would have rejected)? That is not how Hegel understands things.

In his view, it is Kantian reflective understanding that is guilty of making unwarranted assumptions about thought and cognition.

At the start of the Introduction to the *Phenomenology* Hegel draws attention to what he calls 'a natural idea' (*natürliche Vorstellung*) in philosophy. This is the idea that

> before we start to deal with its [philosophy's] proper subject-matter, viz. the actual cognition of what truly is, one must first of all come to an understanding about cognition, which is regarded either as the instrument to get hold of the Absolute, or as the medium through which one discovers it. (§73/57)

Hegel does not name those who embrace this idea, but his wording echoes a remark of Kant's in the *Critique of Pure Reason* (1781, 2nd edn, 1787):

> now it does indeed seem natural that, as soon as we have left the ground of experience, we should, through careful enquiries, assure ourselves as to the foundations of any building that we propose to erect, not making use of any knowledge that we possess without first determining whence it has come.[14]

The idea, then, is the one that underlies Kantian (and also Lockean) epistemology, namely that before we undertake the philosophical task of discovering what there is, we must make sure that our powers of cognition are up to the job. Embracing this idea might seem to be evidence of sensible caution or an understandable 'fear of falling into error' (§74/58); after all, who wouldn't want to test his tools before using them? Hegel points out, however, that such 'fear takes something – a great deal in fact – for granted as truth, supporting its scruples and inferences on what is itself in need of prior scrutiny' (§74/58). Kantian philosophical caution is thus not actually as cautious as it pretends to be, for it rests on *assumptions* that it takes for granted. Specifically, it takes for granted that cognition is an 'instrument' or 'medium', that 'there is a *difference between ourselves and this cognition*', and that, consequently, we can examine by itself, and set limits to, such cognition.

Note that Hegel here does not criticize this Kantian conception of cognition on the basis of his own alternative. He simply points out that it is assumed without 'prior scrutiny', that is, *uncritically*.

For that reason, he suggests, we should not trouble ourselves further with the idea that cognition is an instrument, but should just reject it as 'adventitious and arbitrary' (§76/59). If one bears in mind that Kant's critique of pure reason leads to the conclusion that thought, by itself, cannot know the true nature of things themselves, it is clear that Hegel's rejection of Kant's assumptions about cognition also entails the rejection of *that* Kantian conclusion. The free act whereby Hegel sets to one side what he regards as Kant's unwarranted *assumptions* about cognition must, therefore, leave us with the idea that thought *can* disclose the nature of being by itself (even though it leaves us with no determinate conception of either thought or being). For Hegel, then, the idea that thought can discover what there is, is not itself an assumption, but is the necessary result of freely and critically *suspending* the assumptions of Kantian reflection. Hegel thus understands his own speculative, ontological logic to take less for granted and to be more critical than Kantian reflection.[15]

The role of phenomenology

The direct way into speculative logic is through the free suspension of all inherited assumptions about thought and being, or what Hegel calls the simple 'resolve' to 'consider thought as such'.[16] This fulfils the promise of Kantian thought to be truly critical. Hegel recognizes, however, being free and critical does not give speculative logic credibility in the eyes of ordinary, natural consciousness. For Hegel, the ordinary, *non*-philosophical individual is the very opposite of a critical spirit: he is characterized, rather, by 'the *immediate certainty* of himself' (§26/20). Ordinary individuals live in the certainty that the world around them is as it appears and that their perception and understanding of that world is reliable. They do not, therefore, regard themselves as standing under an imperative to criticize or call into question their most basic assumptions about themselves and their world.

Natural consciousness also rejects the idea, from which speculative logic starts, that there is an immediate identity between thought and being. Such consciousness shares the view that the world is knowable, but it also insists that there is a clear distinction or 'antithesis' (*Gegensatz*) between what there *is* and our *knowing* of it. As Hegel writes, the standpoint of consciousness is one that 'knows objects in their antithesis to itself, and itself in antithesis to them' (§26/20). For consciousness, therefore, it is wrong to think, as philosophy does, that the nature of being can be discovered from *within* pure thought: for the world, *though knowable*, is clearly 'over there', not somehow also 'in here'. Indeed, natural consciousness regards the standpoint of speculative logic in this respect as the very 'antithesis' of its own, and feels that it is being *violated* when it is asked to enter philosophy.

Speculative logic considers natural consciousness to rest on the unwarranted assumption that the object known and the knowing of it are clearly distinct. Equally, however, natural consciousness considers such logic to rest on the mere assumption that there is an 'identity' between thought and being. Each, therefore, assures the other that *it* is in the right. Hegel points out, however, that *'one bare assurance is worth just as much as another'* (§76/60). He thus acknowledges that, from its own point of view, each position is *equally* valid. This is a remarkable admission by a thinker judged by many to assume that philosophy is unquestionably superior to every other human interest. Hegel insists, however, that philosophy, or 'science', may not expect the ordinary individual simply to give in to it. On the contrary, if 'science' expects the individual to rise up to its level, then 'the individual has the right to demand that science should at least provide him with the ladder to this standpoint, should show him this standpoint within himself' (§26/20). Hegel's *Phenomenology* will be that ladder. The role of the *Phenomenology*, therefore, is not to set out Hegel's own philosophy, but to lead natural consciousness from its own certainties to the perspective of philosophy, and so to *justify* such philosophy in the eyes of consciousness.[17]

Like Plato in the *Republic*, therefore, Hegel is interested not just in setting out his own understanding of the world, but also in educating the non-philosopher into the ways of philosophy. Hegel undertakes this task of education, however, acutely aware that in so doing he may not presuppose the validity of the philosophical perspective: for were he to do so, he would fail to respect the right of natural consciousness to be shown, starting from its *own* point of view, why the philosophical perspective is justified. This places a peculiar constraint upon philosophy that will determine the character of phenomenology: for it means that phenomenology must be a wholly *immanent* examination of the certainties of consciousness, in which the philosopher avoids begging the question against consciousness.

Phenomenology, immanence and scepticism

In the Introduction to the *Phenomenology* Hegel briefly considers two ways in which the philosopher can criticize non-philosophical consciousness and seek to persuade the latter of the merits of philosophy. The first is the direct approach: the philosopher simply maintains that the ordinary view of the world is mistaken and that philosophy alone understands the truth. This is the standard way in which philosophers try to dispose of their opponents: they argue (or assert) that they are in the right and their opponents in the wrong. The second approach is more indirect. The philosopher does not reject the ordinary view of the world outright, but rather 'appeals to the ordinary [*gemein*] view for the intimations it gives of something better' (§76/60). That is to say, the philosopher declares that contained in the ordinary view of things, but unbeknown to the latter, is the very understanding of things that *philosophy* puts forward.

In the *Phenomenology*, however, Hegel declares that both the direct and the indirect approaches to ordinary, natural consciousness are illegitimate. This is because in each case philosophy ultimately appeals to *itself* and its own insight and simply *assures* natural consciousness that the philosophical perspective is the right one. If, therefore, the philosopher is to persuade natural consciousness of the merits of philosophy, it cannot adopt either of these approaches. There remains, for Hegel, only one alternative: the *immanent* approach. Philosophy must show that the certainties of natural consciousness lead purely by themselves to the standpoint of philosophy. Only in this way can philosophy demonstrate to consciousness that the philosophical point of view is justified, without taking that point of view for granted. The task of carrying out the immanent examination of consciousness falls to *phenomenology*.

Phenomenology must start, therefore, from the certainties of consciousness itself, the most immediate of which is the certainty that *I* am conscious of *this* object, *here* and *now*. It must then show that these certainties transform themselves of their own accord into the insight that governs speculative philosophy, namely that being is intelligible from *within* pure thought. 'Pure science', Hegel writes (in the *Logic*), 'presupposes liberation from the opposition of consciousness';[18] to effect this liberation, phenomenology must bring about 'a state of despair about all the so-called natural ideas, thoughts and opinions' (§78/61). Furthermore, phenomenology must show that consciousness actually brings about this state of despair *by itself*, by holding on to its *own* certainties and experiencing the destructive consequences of so doing. In this way consciousness will be led from its own point of view to that of philosophy, but it will not be forced *by philosophy* along this path of transformation. Consciousness is thus subjected to no 'violence' (*Gewalt*) from philosophy; but it suffers 'violence at its own hands' and 'spoils its own limited satisfaction' (§80/63). Simply by adhering to its own point of view, it *loses* the very certainties it holds dear.

Phenomenology can thus be regarded as an exercise in *scepticism*: it casts doubt on, and liberates us from, all the cherished certainties of ordinary, natural consciousness. Indeed, Hegel's *Phenomenology* could perhaps be regarded as his equivalent of Descartes' first *Meditation*, as his general demolition of the opinions of natural consciousness. In this sense, phenomenology serves a similar purpose to the 'resolve' of the will to think purely, which is the direct route into speculative philosophy: both undermine the presuppositions that 'bar the entrance to philosophy'.[19] They do so, however, in different ways: the resolve is the free act of simply setting all presuppositions aside, whereas phenomenology shows in painstaking detail how the certainties of natural consciousness undermine themselves. Phenomenological scepticism is thus not the work of free thought (or of the Cartesian I), but it is carried forward by natural consciousness itself. For that reason Hegel calls phenomenology thoroughgoing or 'self-actualising scepticism' (*sich vollbringender Skeptizismus*) (§78/61).

Logic in phenomenology

Hegel's immanent examination of consciousness is also reminiscent of Socrates' approach to his interlocutors (or at least of the ideal 'Socratic' approach). In both cases, the aim is to let one's opponent undermine his own position. Unlike Socrates, however, Hegel does not engage in a dialogue with his opponent, but undertakes a systematic, *logical* analysis of the latter's position. Hegel does not, therefore, examine the actual experience of people in concrete situations, but he analyses the experience that, logically, consciousness *must* make – or *should* make – given its own particular certainties. The development of consciousness that Hegel describes in the *Phenomenology* is thus a necessary one. Indeed, this necessity is what makes 'the way to science' traced in that book 'scientific' itself in Hegel's distinctive sense: the 'science of the *experience of consciousness*' (§88/68). It is also, Hegel claims, what guarantees the 'completeness' of that phenomenological science (§79/62).

In the eyes of some commentators, however, this logical necessity means that Hegelian phenomenology is subject to a vicious circularity. It is the attempt to lead consciousness to the standpoint of philosophy – or speculative logic – without presupposing the legitimacy of that standpoint; yet it is itself a *logical* enterprise and so surely presupposes the philosophical standpoint after all. Stanley Rosen spells out the problem nicely: on the one hand, he says, we are to understand 'phenomenological experience as the preparation for logic', but, on the other hand, 'the *Phenomenology* is not genuinely intelligible without a knowledge of the *Logic*'.[20] If this is the full story, then the *Phenomenology* clearly fails in its endeavour, since it presupposes what it is meant to justify. In my view, however, it is not the full story.

Hegelian phenomenology is certainly a systematic, 'scientific' examination of consciousness. It sets out *in thought* the experience that, logically, consciousness must make, given its certainties. This is not to deny that many of the shapes of consciousness analysed in the *Phenomenology* emerged in history; what is examined by phenomenology, however, are not the historical shapes themselves but these shapes 'reduced to abbreviated, simple determinations of thought' (§29/24). In the section on 'absolute freedom', for example, Hegel describes the logic, at work in the French Revolution, that leads such freedom to death and terror; but he omits anything not directly produced by that logic (such as the Revolutionary Wars).

Hegel notes in the Preface to the *Phenomenology* that 'the *study* of *science*' requires 'attention to the concept [*Begriff*]' and to logical determinations, such as 'being-in-itself, being-for-itself, self-identity, etc.' (§58/43).[21] Hegel's 'scientific' phenomenological examination of consciousness will thus employ *categories* of thought that are derived and analysed in the *Logic*. He also makes this clear in the *Logic* itself, when he states that the development set out in the *Phenomenology* 'rests solely on the nature of the pure essentialities [*Wesenheiten*] which constitute the content of logic'.[22]

It is important to note, however, that Hegel does not *presuppose* that the experience of consciousness is guided by certain categories. The categories are not presupposed in logic either, but are derived immanently in the course of logic itself. The same is true, in my view, of phenomenology: the latter *discovers* the categories to be at work in the experience of consciousness. Hegel's account of natural consciousness certainly employs categories that such consciousness is unlikely to use itself. Sense-certainty, for example, thinks of its object as *this*, *here*, *now*, but it does not think of it explicitly as this 'individual' that proves in experience to be a 'universal'; similarly, perception is not aware of the 'simple essentialities' that hold sway over it (§131/91). Nonetheless, such categories are shown by phenomenology to be immanent in the experience of consciousness: the 'universal' is the name Hegel gives to the form that the object comes to have for sense-certainty *itself* through its *own* experience (§96/71).[23]

Hegel's examination of consciousness is clearly a logical one. He insists, however, that it must also be immanent. It may not, therefore, presuppose that consciousness will be forced by logical categories to develop in a particular direction. Of course, Hegel *aims* to show that the certainties of consciousness lead to the standpoint of philosophy, but he may not assume in advance that logic will ensure this happens. He must simply think through with an open mind the experience that consciousness undergoes and wait to discover where, if anywhere, it leads.

In the Preface to the *Phenomenology* Hegel contrasts 'scientific cognition' (which includes philosophy and phenomenology) with what he calls 'formal understanding'. Such understanding, he writes, 'is forever surveying the whole and standing above the particular existence of which it is speaking, i.e. it does not see it at all' (§53/40). To approach consciousness by presupposing that categories move consciousness in a predetermined direction would be to form a conception of the *whole* prior to encountering the individual shapes of consciousness themselves, and so would be equivalent to 'surveying the whole'. Scientific cognition, however, 'forgets about that general survey' and does not presuppose a determinate conception of the whole. On the contrary, it 'demands surrender to the life of the object, or, what amounts to the same thing, confronting and expressing its inner necessity' (§53/40). Phenomenological thought must thus immerse itself in the content at hand, namely consciousness, 'letting it move spontaneously of its own nature' and simply 'contemplate this movement' (§58/44).

Phenomenology, like philosophy, is thus in this sense passive: its role is to follow in thought the immanent development of its object. Such passivity, however, itself involves a high degree of activity and effort, for it requires us to exercise 'restraint' and not to 'intrude into the immanent rhythm of the concept' which belongs to the *object* (§58/44). In phenomenology we immerse ourselves in our object by 'lingering' over each shape of consciousness and focussing on its 'distinctive character' (*Eigentümlichkeit*) (§29/23).[24] Phenomenology is, indeed, an enterprise carried out by thought; but this does not conflict with the demand for immanence, for, unlike feeling and imagination, thought can *abstract* from its preconceptions and immerse itself in the 'inner necessity' of its object (§53/40). Indeed, only by so doing will it be able to persuade natural consciousness that it is being led by its *own* certainties alone to philosophy.

In phenomenology, philosophical thought not only refrains from imposing its categories on consciousness, but it also suspends its philosophical conviction that pure thought discloses the true nature of being. Phenomenology is thus not itself a straightforward *philosophy* or *ontology* of consciousness (or spirit). It thinks through the *experience* that consciousness undergoes, but it does not claim thereby to disclose what consciousness *is*. Indeed, phenomenology does not aim to disclose directly what there *is* at all, and so is to be distinguished from both pre-Kantian and Hegel's own, post-Kantian, ontology, as well as from twentieth-century 'phenomenological ontology'. (It is also to be distinguished from *epistemology* and *transcendental* philosophy that both seek a *philosophical* understanding of cognition and its conditions.)

Phenomenology does not reveal what there is, but examines the experience that consciousness makes of what *it takes* there to be. This does not mean, though, that phenomenology treats consciousness as if it were cut off from being altogether and confined to its own mental world. Phenomenology cannot think of consciousness as limited in this way, because it may not presuppose any independent 'being', from which consciousness could be 'cut off'. Phenomenology immerses itself in the perspective of consciousness. It has no choice, therefore, but to accept, without further comment, consciousness' claim to be aware of what there *is*, and it must confine itself to examining the experiences that consciousness is led to have by making this claim.

At the end of phenomenology, consciousness is led by its experience to the standpoint of 'absolute knowing' or philosophy. Philosophy, however, does not disclose a world that is distinct from that known by consciousness.[25] It knows the very world that consciousness takes itself to know, but it knows that world as it is in truth: it knows it *in the right way*. That is to say, it now knows *being* to have the form of *thought* and so to be knowable from *within* thought itself.

At this point, the standpoint of philosophy is justified in the eyes of consciousness because the very certainties of consciousness itself have made that standpoint necessary. Philosophy *can* begin with the free act of suspending all presuppositions, and proceed directly to think being. This is what happens in Hegel's *Logic*. Yet the conviction that pure thought can know from within itself what there is, is itself rejected by natural consciousness; and, in Hegel's view, consciousness is within its rights to reject philosophy in this way. If philosophy is to persuade consciousness of its merits, therefore, it has no choice but to suspend its own ontological pretensions and undertake a phenomenological examination of consciousness itself. It thus has to lose itself to consciousness. In the course of phenomenology, however, consciousness loses its own certainties and is led on to the standpoint of philosophy. At that point, philosophy receives its justification, and so receives itself back, from consciousness.

As we will see later in this guide, the 'absolute knowing' achieved at the end of the *Phenomenology* is actually the unity of 'substance' and 'subject' (§797/522). As such, it does not coincide exactly with the thought of sheer *indeterminate being*, with which the *Logic* begins. Thought, at the end of the *Phenomenology*, thus still has to perform a further act of abstraction before the *Logic* can get underway.[26] Nonetheless, the *element* of philosophy – the identity of thought and being – has received its justification through phenomenology. Speculative logic can thus begin with the blessing, as it were, of natural consciousness.

CHAPTER TWO

Overview of themes

The themes dealt with in Hegel's *Phenomenology* are as many and varied as the shapes taken by consciousness in the course of the book. They include the relation between desire and recognition, the limits of observing reason, the necessary self-alienation of spirit, the intimate connection between abstract freedom and death and the importance of sacrifice to religion. A proper overview of the themes in the *Phenomenology* would thus have to summarize the whole work, and would overlap with much of the next chapter of this *Reader's Guide*. There is, however, one theme that runs throughout Hegel's text: that of the *education* (*Bildung*) of consciousness (§78/61). What the *Phenomenology* is ultimately *about* is the way in which natural consciousness is educated by its own experience and thereby transformed into 'absolute knowing'. Different shapes of consciousness are, of course, educated in different ways; but in his Introduction, Hegel provides an account of the general pattern of such education. This chapter, therefore, will not present my overview of all the themes in the *Phenomenology*, but will be devoted to Hegel's own 'overview' of its principal theme: how consciousness is educated by its experience.

Consciousness and its immanent criterion

Consciousness is educated, we are told, in the course of our phenomenological examination of its claim to be 'real knowledge' (§78/60). From the perspective of philosophy, natural consciousness is at most 'apparent' or 'phenomenal' knowledge (§77/60). From its own perspective, by contrast, its knowledge is real and sound. The phenomenologist may not assume in advance that consciousness is mistaken in this claim. He must, therefore, take seriously the standpoint of consciousness and examine with an open mind the *'reality'* of its cognition (§81/63).

Hegel notes, however, that such an examination would appear to require a 'criterion' (*Maßstab*) of judgement: for how can one determine whether consciousness knows the truth without an independent standard against which to assess what consciousness knows (§81/63)? Yet in phenomenology no such independent standard is available, since we are not permitted to endorse any understanding of things other than that of natural consciousness. The difficulty is removed, Hegel points out, when we recognize that consciousness has within *itself* a standard or criterion against which to assess what it knows. This is because consciousness itself distinguishes between its knowing of something and the thing it knows, and so is able to compare the one with the other.

In the Introduction Hegel writes the following:

> In consciousness one thing exists *for* another, i.e. consciousness regularly contains the determinateness of the moment of knowing; at the same time, this other is to consciousness not merely *for it*, but is also outside of this relationship, or exists *in itself*: the moment of truth. (§84/64–5)

These lines do not present Hegel's philosophical theory of consciousness: they do not tell us what he thinks consciousness *is*. They tell us how, in his view, consciousness understands *itself*. It is true that Hegel's language here is somewhat abstract. Nonetheless, that language is meant to capture in abstract, formal terms the structure that consciousness takes itself to have.

There are three principal features to consciousness, as Hegel describes it. First, it understands itself to be conscious of something that is distinct from it. Second, it takes that something to be '*for*' it, that is, to be known by it. Third, it takes the thing it is conscious of to have a character of its own – *in itself* – and in that sense to fall 'outside' consciousness. This does not mean that the thing is in fact hidden from consciousness, like a Kantian 'thing in itself', but simply that it is taken to have an independent existence. Consciousness thus understands the thing not just to exist *in being known*. Yet it also takes itself to *know* things in their independence; in that sense, things do not fall completely 'outside' consciousness. As Hegel puts it, 'consciousness is, on the one hand, consciousness of the object, and on the other, consciousness of itself', but 'both are *for* the same consciousness' (§85/65).

Note that in distinguishing between its knowing of an object and the object or 'truth' that is known, consciousness supplies its own criterion of examination, for its knowledge of the object can be measured against whatever *it* takes the object in itself to be. 'Thus in what consciousness affirms from within itself as *being-in-itself* or the *True* we have the standard which consciousness itself sets up by which to measure what it knows' (§84/65). Phenomenology may make reference only to this standard that is immanent in consciousness itself. The question it must consider, therefore, is not whether consciousness knows objects as *philosophy* knows them to be, but whether consciousness knows, quite as it thinks it does, the very object that it takes *itself* to be aware of.

Hegel maintains that we can call our knowledge of the object our 'concept' (*Begriff*) of it, and we can call the object, as we take it to be in itself, the 'object' (*Gegenstand*). Alternatively, we can call the object, as we *know* it to be, the 'object', and the object, as we take it to be in itself, the 'concept' (i.e. the object as it is in its very concept). Either way, the phenomenologist considers whether 'concept' and 'object' match one another and so undertakes a wholly *immanent* examination of consciousness (§84/65).

Or, rather, the phenomenologist observes while *consciousness* undertakes the examination. Consciousness is aware both of what it takes its object to be *in itself* and of what it *knows* its object to be, and 'since both are *for* the same consciousness, this consciousness is itself their comparison; it is for this same consciousness to know whether its knowledge of the object corresponds to the object or not' (§85/65). Since consciousness examines its own knowledge, the phenomenologist in fact has no active role to play. 'All that is left for us to do' as phenomenologists, therefore, is 'simply to look on' (*das reine Zusehen*), as consciousness does all the work (§85/65). We are, indeed, active in our passivity, since we present the experience of consciousness in categories that consciousness itself would not employ (and, as we shall see below, are active in other ways). Nonetheless, the claim that our role is simply to 'look on' gives vivid expression to the idea that in phenomenology consciousness examines *itself*.

As Hegel continues with his introductory overview of the education of consciousness, it becomes clear that consciousness does not *set out* to put its knowledge to the test. It starts by simply taking its object to be such and such. It is, however, *brought* to the point at which it can examine its knowledge by comparing the latter with its 'criterion', with what it takes the object *itself* to be. What brings it to that point is its own *experience*.

The experience of consciousness

Certain lines in the Introduction make it look as though consciousness is able to compare its knowledge with its object from the start. In fact, it must first undergo a process of experience. Consciousness thus compares what it *initially* takes its object to be with what it *comes to know* that object to be. The process in which it comes to examine its knowledge and comes to be educated is described in §85 of the Introduction. There is, however, a difficulty in this paragraph that needs to be addressed.

Hegel notes that when, in phenomenology, knowledge of an object does not match the object concerned, one might expect consciousness to change and correct its knowledge, so that it matches the object after all. 'If the comparison [of knowledge and the object] shows that these two moments do not correspond to one another, it would seem that consciousness must alter [*ändern*] its knowledge to make it conform to the object' (§85/66). This, at least, is what often happens in everyday experience: I see a small cat on my lawn; its behaviour makes me think that it is actually a squirrel; I look again more closely and realize that it is a cat after all; I thus change what I have come to know the object to be, to bring my knowledge *back in line* with the original object.

Hegel then makes the following claim:

> But, in fact, in the alteration of knowledge [*Veränderung des Wissens*], the object itself alters [*ändert sich*] for it too, for the knowledge that was present was essentially a knowledge of the object: as the knowledge changes, so too does the object, for it essentially belonged to this knowledge. (§85/66)

These lines are important to Hegel's argument. As they stand, however, they are more problematic than commentators have recognized. The problem is this: the word 'alteration' in these lines appears to refer back to the alteration that Hegel said 'it would seem' we should make, if our knowledge and object don't match.[1] If this is the case, however, Hegel's claim does not make complete sense. His argument would run as follows: (1) I take the object to be X; (2) I come to know the object to be Y; (3) my knowledge thus does not match the object; (4) it would seem, therefore, that I should alter my knowledge to make it conform to the object, that I should revert to knowing it to be X; (5) in altering my knowledge in this way, however, the *object alters* for me, too, and so becomes something different. This last point is the one that does not make sense: for why should the object alter for me when I bring my knowledge *back in line* with that object?

This problem can, however, be avoided if the word 'alteration' in the indented passage above is understood to have a different referent. That word, I suggest, refers *not* to the alteration that 'it would seem' consciousness should make to bring its knowledge *back* in line with its object, but to the alteration through which the knowledge *first* came to *diverge* from the initial conception of the object. This reading of the word 'alteration' makes more sense of Hegel's argument and, indeed, is supported by lines in §86 of the Introduction. There Hegel states: 'as was shown previously, the first object, *in being known*, is altered for consciousness'.[2] This suggests that the object alters, not when I *revert* to seeing it as I originally did, but *in the very process of being known in the first place*. Hegel's words also indicate that this is the point that was made 'previously' in §85.

Hegel's argument in §85 should therefore be understood as follows: (1) I take the object to be X; (2) I come to know it to be Y; (3) my knowledge thus does not match the object; (4) it would *seem*, therefore, that I should alter my knowledge to make it conform to the object, that I should revert to knowing it to be X; (5) I cannot revert to that initial conception of the object, however, because in the alteration of my knowledge that has *already taken place* the object itself has been altered in my eyes: the object has proven not just to be X, but to be Y; (6) this alteration of the object is *irreversible*, because the knowledge we have come to have of that object is not erroneous, but genuine knowledge of the object. As

Hegel puts it in lines quoted above, 'in the alteration of knowledge, the object itself alters for it too, for the knowledge that was present was essentially a knowledge *of the object*' (§85/66).

The knowledge to which consciousness comes through its experience is genuine knowledge *of* the object because it is generated *by* the object as it is initially taken to be. In this respect the process of learning described in the *Phenomenology* is different from the process of learning and self-correction we go through in everyday life. In life we might see what we think is a squirrel, but discover that it is in fact a small cat. In such a case, our understanding alters because we replace one object with *another*: our realization that the object is a cat is not generated *by* the initial thought that it is a squirrel. The process described in the *Phenomenology* is different: one object does not replace another, but the object, as we initially take it to be, leads *by itself* to its being known to be different from what it is initially taken to be. The object is initially taken to be X, and precisely in being known *to be X*, it proves *not* to be X (or not just X), but to be Y. This is the *dialectical* element in the process Hegel describes: the object turns out, in simply *being* what it is, *not* just to be what it is, but to be something different.

Recall that the object, as it is initially taken to be, constitutes the *criterion*, set up by consciousness itself, against which its knowledge is to be measured. Note, however, that when knowledge and its object fail to match, this occurs, not because the knowledge is deficient, but because the initial conception of the object fails to hold out in face of the knowledge of it. This means that the criterion against which knowledge is to be measured from this point on is *itself* altered. Phenomenology, as Hegel conceives it, is thus the process in which consciousness compares its knowledge with its immanent criterion, but comes to acquire a *new* criterion, as the first – the object as initially conceived – alters in the very knowing of it. In phenomenology the 'object' is what a particular shape of consciousness *takes* or *conceives* it to be. In acquiring new knowledge and a new *conception* of its object, therefore, consciousness acquires a new *object*. Thus, in the course of phenomenology, consciousness acquires new criteria, new conceptions of its object, and new objects at the same time, because these are in fact all the same thing.

The process in which a new object arises for consciousness, as it comes to know its initial object properly, is what Hegel calls *experience* (*Erfahrung*) (§86/66). Such experience is the process in which the true character of the object of consciousness is progressively revealed. What emerges in the experience of consciousness counts as the *truth*, not because it matches what philosophy judges to be the truth, but because it is what the object *necessarily* proves to be in being known by consciousness. The experience described in the *Phenomenology* is thus not the empirical experience of historical individuals or communities. It is the experience that is made necessary *logically* by the object of consciousness – the experience that consciousness *must* make, or *should* make, given the way it conceives of its object. Since this experience involves the continuous disclosure of the true nature of the object of consciousness (and, as we have seen, is irreversible), it is of necessity *progressive*. The *Phenomenology* traces the progress of consciousness towards absolute knowing, therefore, not because Hegel is an incurable optimist, but because the experience he describes is one in which the object of consciousness necessarily transforms itself into a newer, richer form of itself.

This, then, is the overall theme of the *Phenomenology*: consciousness is brought by its experience to know its object to be such and such; on examining its new knowledge, it sees that the latter differs from its initial conception of the object; it also sees, however, that this new knowledge reveals the true character of the object and that there is thus no going back; in this way, consciousness is educated by its experience. This education is completed, in absolute knowing, when the object of consciousness proves to be not just the *object*, or *Gegen-stand*, of consciousness, but the *identity* of being and thought.

The object of experience

Note that what Hegel understands by the 'object' of consciousness is not a particular empirical object, but a particular *form* of object. The alteration he describes is the alteration of that form in the experience of it. Sense-certainty, for example, takes its object to be something simple and immediate: *this, now*. In the experience it makes, however, this simple object changes its form and becomes something complex: 'an absolute plurality of nows' (§107/75). This new form is then affirmed by perception as the true object of consciousness. More specifically, the complex object is understood by perception to have the form of a *thing* with many *properties*. In the experience of perception, the thing then mutates into a dynamic play of moments that understanding conceives of as *force*. Sense-certainty, perception and understanding may encounter the same range of sensory material – colours, shapes and so on – but sense-certainty will think of each colour simply as *this*, whereas perception will regard it as the property of a thing and understanding will take it to be the expression of a certain force. Each shape of consciousness conceives of the sensory material in a different way, therefore, and takes itself to be confronted by a different *kind* of object. Later shapes confront even more radically different kinds of object, including other selves, the state, wealth and duty.

The alteration of the form of the object – and thus of the *object* that consciousness takes itself to be aware of – occurs in the experience that consciousness makes of it, in the *knowing* of it. In being known, the object proves to be different from what it is initially taken to be. Furthermore, it proves to be different *because of* what it is initially taken to be. The new object that emerges in experience is thus not something separate from the first object, but is simply what consciousness has come to know that *first object* to be. The first object is what consciousness takes to be the object *in itself* (*an sich*). The new object that emerges is thus 'our knowledge of the first object, or the being-*for*-consciousness of the first in-itself' (§87/67).

In the process in which the new object emerges, the original object – what the object is initially taken to be – is shown not to be the true object of consciousness after all. The object as initially conceived turns out not to be the object as it is in truth or *in itself*, but only what *consciousness* first understood the object in itself to be. Thus, as Hegel puts it, 'it comes to pass for consciousness that what it previously took to be the *in-itself* is not an *in-itself*, or that it was only an in-itself *for consciousness*' (§85/66).

Hegel's wording in these lines and in those cited at the end of the preceding paragraph leave room for confusion on the part of the reader, for both the new object *and* the initial object of consciousness are described as being the object '*for* consciousness'. Confusion can, however, be avoided if we keep a clear focus on what Hegel is claiming: the new object is what the first *has come* to be *for* consciousness, and as the new object emerges the first turns out to be merely what the object *was for* consciousness. In this way, the experience of consciousness exposes the limits of its own initial certainty. As we are about to see, however, there is a limit to the extent to which any shape of consciousness really recognizes the limits of its own certainty.

The role of the 'we'

Hegel now proceeds subtly to amend the picture he has been painting. It remains the case that the new object emerges in the knowing of the first object; but Hegel adds the following significant qualification: 'the new object shows itself to have come about through a *reversal* [*Umkehrung*] *of consciousness itself*' (§87/67). The new object emerges, therefore, as one shape of consciousness turns into a new and different shape. In this way, Hegel maintains, a necessary sequence of shapes is generated by the experience of consciousness.

Hegel further complicates this picture, however, with the following claim: the idea that the new object emerges in and through a 'reversal' of consciousness 'is something contributed by *us* [*unsere Zutat*]', but 'it is not known to the consciousness that we are observing'. 'The *origination* [*Entstehung*] of the new object,' in other words, 'proceeds for us, as it were, behind the back of consciousness' (§87/67–8). So, too, does the emergence of a new *shape* of consciousness: a given shape is not itself conscious of becoming a new shape, as a new object emerges in its experience. Our role, as phenomenologists, is to think through the experience that consciousness is required to make by its own conception of the object. Yet it turns out that we are also actively involved in generating the necessary *sequence* of shapes of consciousness. This raises the following three questions: (1) Who are 'we'? (2) What do 'we' know and do? (3) What exactly does consciousness experience?

Hegel gives us little help in answering the first question. The answer, however, would seem to be that 'we' comprise the philosopher (acting as phenomenologist) and the readers of the *Phenomenology*. Since phenomenology is undertaken in order to justify the standpoint of philosophy to natural consciousness, one would expect the intended readers of Hegel's book to be attached to such consciousness in some way. The *Phenomenology*, however, is not just a *book* to be read, but it sets out a *science* with which we must think along. Like the philosopher, therefore, the readers of Hegel's book must also be phenomenologists. Hegel's readers, however, come to the phenomenological study of consciousness from a different perspective to that of Hegel himself. He must first suspend his *philosophical* conviction that thought can think being before he can do phenomenology.[3] His readers, by contrast, come to phenomenology to discover whether the latter will dislodge their '*natural* ideas, thoughts and opinions' (§78/61).

If Hegel's phenomenology is successful, his readers will be educated by it and shown the necessity of the philosophical way of knowing. These readers will be educated, however, by being shown how the shapes of natural consciousness that are the subject of phenomenology are *themselves* educated by their experiences and transformed into new shapes (and eventually into absolute knowing). Hegel's readers are concrete individuals with identities formed within families, societies, states and history. The shapes that are examined by phenomenology constitute either aspects of individual consciousness (such as perception) or abbreviated versions of historical (and literary) shapes that form the context in which Hegel's readers have grown up. Hegel's intended readers will thus be wedded to a certain degree to the certainties embodied in those shapes (though they must also be open to what phenomenology might disclose, otherwise there is no point in their studying it). By thinking through the experience of the shapes of consciousness under examination, Hegel's readers will thus see their *own* natural certainties progressively undermined.

What, then, do 'we' know and do, and what exactly does the consciousness under examination experience? We can answer these questions by distinguishing between the 'micro-transitions' within a given shape of consciousness and the 'macro-transitions' that take us from one shape to another (such as from sense-certainty to perception). It is clear from the Introduction that all macro-transitions require *our* contribution, which will be further explained below. Many micro-transitions, by contrast, do not appear to require our contribution, but are experienced by the shape of consciousness concerned. The changes in their objects experienced, for example, by sense-certainty and absolute freedom, fall into this category (see §§103, 592/73, 391).[4] There are some micro-transitions, however, that are not experienced by consciousness itself. For example, the transition from the first to the second shape of the unhappy consciousness is described by Hegel as occurring only 'for us' (§218/150).[5] What makes the difference between these micro-transitions is the fact that in some cases a change *within* a shape of consciousness effectively amounts to a change *to* a new shape.[6] One of the things that readers of the *Phenomenology* should look out for, therefore, is whether a given shape of consciousness experiences its micro-transitions or not. It is clear that no shape experiences such changes in the explicitly *logical* terms employed by the phenomenologist.[7] In some cases, however, consciousness experiences for itself the changes that such logic articulates, whereas in others it does not.

To get a clearer idea of the difference between micro- and macro-transitions, let us look briefly at the transition from sense-certainty to perception. Sense-certainty passes through three subtly different conceptions of the object, and Hegel makes it clear that it is taken by its own *experience* from one conception of the object to another: 'sense-certainty thus comes to know *by experience* [*erfährt also*] that its essence is neither in the object nor in the "I"' alone (§103/73). Indeed, Hegel states that the whole 'dialectic of sense-certainty is nothing else but the simple history of its movement or of its experience' (§109/76). The micro-transitions that occur within the chapter on sense-certainty are thus ones of which sense-certainty itself is aware: it knows that its own experience takes it beyond its initial conception of the object.

Prior to the conclusion of its experience, however, these changes do not take sense-certainty forward to a completely new object; they take it on to a modified version *of* its original object (which is simply *this*, *here*, *now*). At the conclusion of that experience, a more dramatic change in the object then occurs: the object proves to be not just a *simple 'this'* at all, but a unified *complex* or *plurality* of different moments, or concrete 'universal'. The experience of sense-certainty concludes, therefore, when a *new* object arises that goes radically beyond what it initially takes its object to be. Hegel notes, however, that sense-certainty does not affirm or take up this new object, but seeks to cling to its own object (even if in a modified form): 'immediate certainty does not take over the truth, for its truth is the universal, whereas certainty wants to apprehend the this' (§111/79). Sense-certainty thus loses its initial object, and so loses its own certainty, as a new truth emerges *for it* in its *own* experience;

but such certainty refuses to accept this loss and disavows the new truth in favour of its familiar object.

This refusal to take up the new object that has emerged in its experience means that sense-certainty does not actually become anything other than the certainty it is: it remains what it is and does not mutate into a new shape of consciousness. Rather, *we*, the phenomenologists, move on to the new shape that takes up the truth that has emerged for sense-certainty. This new shape is *perception*, which in German is called *Wahrnehmung* or 'true-taking'. Unlike sense-certainty, Hegel notes, perception 'takes what is present to it as a universal' (§111/79). This macro-transition from sense-certainty to perception prefigures – *more or less* – all such moves in the *Phenomenology*. A new object emerges, with greater or lesser explicitness, in the experience of a given shape of consciousness and so is something of which that shape is more or less conscious. However, that shape does not *itself* take up and affirm this new object and new truth. Rather, we, the phenomenologists, move on to the shape that does take it up and affirm it. The macro-transition from one shape to another – the *'reversal of consciousness'* (§87/67) – is thus a move that *we* undertake and is one of which the shape from which we move remains unaware.

Looked at broadly, we can say that consciousness in the *Phenomenology* transforms *itself*, or mutates, into new shapes of itself. Strictly speaking, however, no shape of consciousness in the *Phenomenology* turns directly into the following shape: sense-certainty does not become perception, the slave does not become a stoic, and the sceptic does not become the unhappy consciousness. In each case, we are the ones who effect the transition from one shape to another. No shape is conscious, therefore, of becoming something other than itself. Nor is any shape aware of having emerged from a previous shape. Perception does not regard itself as the result of sense-certainty's experience, but just takes itself to be what it is, and the same is true of all other shapes. None is aware that its object has *emerged* through the experience of its predecessor, but each knows the object simply to be *its* object:

> Thus in the movement of consciousness there occurs a moment of *being-in-itself* or *being-for-us* which is not present to the consciousness comprehended in the experience itself. The *content*, however, of what presents itself to us does exist *for it*;

we comprehend only the formal aspect of that content, or its pure origination. *For it*, what has thus arisen exists only as an object; *for us*, it appears at the same time as movement and a process of becoming. (§87/68)

The experiences of the different shapes of consciousness thus form a single, continuous development of consciousness *for phenomenological thought* only. Thought allows this continuous development to emerge by moving from one shape to a subsequent one in which what is implicit in the experience of the first is rendered explicit.

We phenomenologists not only effect the transition from one shape to another, but in many cases, though not necessarily all, we also play a role in working out what the new object must be for the new shape of consciousness. The chapter on perception, for example, begins with §111, but the account of the *experience* of perception does not begin until §117. Before that account can begin, Hegel states, the 'object must now be defined more precisely, and the definition must be developed briefly from the result that has been reached' (§112/79). The new object that emerges in the experience of sense-certainty is a complex plurality of moments, rather than a simple *this*. In §§113–15, however, Hegel shows that such a complex plurality must be conceived by perception as a *thing* with many *properties*. It is the experience of this thing that Hegel then begins to trace in §117. Prior to tracing this experience, Hegel does not present his own philosophical understanding of perceptual objects but sets out what the object must be *for perception itself*. Nonetheless, he is the one, in his capacity as phenomenologist, who works out more precisely what the object must be taken by perception to be.[8]

Yet does not this activity of the phenomenologist undermine the claim that phenomenology is a strictly *immanent* account of the experience of consciousness? No, because the macro-transition from one shape to another is not engineered by the phenomenologist, but is made necessary by what emerges in the *experience* of that shape. The new object is fully present for the succeeding shape, but it first emerges as a new object – more or less explicitly – in the preceding one. Furthermore, in working out 'more precisely' what that new object must be for the next shape of consciousness, all the phenomenologist is doing is rendering explicit what is implicit in that object; he is not giving his own philosophical account of that object.[9] The immanence of the phenomenological account of consciousness is thus preserved, even though the phenomenologist plays a more active role in presenting that account than is suggested by Hegel's claim that all we do is 'look on'.

It is clear, therefore, that the development of consciousness presented in the *Phenomenology* is not historical, but logical. Phenomenology sets out the experience that consciousness *must* make, given the way it conceives of its object. The logic of such experience has not always been, and will not always be, followed by historical individuals and communities, but it is the logic that should be followed by them if they are true to themselves. The life and death struggle, for example, leads logically to the master–slave relation, but such struggles in history often continue unresolved for generations or end with the death of the protagonists.

Many of the shapes of consciousness considered by Hegel have obvious historical parallels, such as 'enlightenment' and 'absolute freedom'; others, such as sense-certainty and perception, are aspects of the consciousness of individuals who themselves live in history. The story told in the *Phenomenology* can thus be understood as a reconstruction in thought of the 'enormous labour of world history' in which shapes of consciousness were born and then surpassed to a greater or lesser degree (§29/23; see also §§295, 808/199, 530). The sequence of shapes presented in the *Phenomenology* does not, however, directly match that of history, since Hegel discusses the unhappy consciousness that finds expression in medieval Catholicism *after* the understanding embodied in Newtonian physics, and examines ancient Egyptian and Greek religion *after* the French Revolution. More importantly, Hegel is interested in the logically necessary transition from one shape to another, not in whatever historical connection there may be between them. Indeed, it is solely such logically necessary transitions that justify the standpoint of philosophy and so fulfil the aim of phenomenology.

Having said all this, there turns out in practice to be more *variety* in the transitions, and in the ways in which each shape develops, than is apparent from the Introduction. It is important to bear in mind, therefore, that what Hegel sets out in the Introduction is only a general account or overview of the way in which, in phenomenology, consciousness is educated by its experience. It does not lay down a hard and fast method to be followed rigidly by each shape of consciousness. The differences in the ways in which shapes develop are due to the character of the shapes concerned. In some shapes, such as observing reason and self-alienated spirit, the experiences they undergo are long and complicated. In the first form of natural religion, by contrast, the changes that occur in its object are slight: all that happens is that the 'light-being' sends forth 'torrents of light', and then, as the lord or power over them, dissolves them back into itself (§§686–8/452–3). Some shapes have an acute sense that they have *lost* their original object or self-understanding: pleasure-seeking reason, for example, feels that it has seized hold of death, where it sought life, and faith explicitly 'mourns over the loss of its spiritual world' (§§364, 573/243, 378). In other cases, the sense of loss is more muted: stoicism, we are told, is simply 'perplexed' by its inability to point to any intrinsic content in its thoughts of the true and the good (§200/139). The slave, indeed, experiences the loss of its initial self-understanding as a *gain*: for in his work, in which he seemed to have only 'an alienated existence', he in fact 'acquires a mind of his own' (§196/136). And in scepticism, the constant change and contradiction it experiences is deliberately engendered by it and so is not felt to be a *loss* of its freedom at all. What remains constant throughout the *Phenomenology*, however, is the fact that each shape of consciousness experiences some change in its object or in itself (or both), and that the phenomenologist then moves from this shape to another that renders explicit what is implicit in the experience of the first. This ensures that what we are doing is phenomenology, rather than speculative philosophy, throughout (though readers will note that the chapters on reason and spirit contain more Hegelian *obiter dicta* than they probably should).

The end and the beginning of phenomenology

The goal of phenomenology, for Hegel, is the point at which the experience of consciousness no longer leads beyond the conception that consciousness first has of its object but coincides with it (see §80/62). At this point, knowledge and the object known match one another, because they are both understood to have *the same form*. Note that Hegel's claim is not that consciousness now catches up with particular insights that philosophy presupposes as true all along. His claim is that it now enters into the distinctive *way of knowing* that characterizes philosophy. This way of knowing is the one in which the clear *distinction* between the knower and the known – between certainty and truth – is dissolved or 'overcome' (§ 37/29). Precisely what that way of knowing will disclose the world to be remains to be discovered by philosophy. Phenomenology, however, has justified the philosophical way of knowing to natural consciousness by showing how the element of philosophy – the *identity* of thought and being – is made necessary by the experience of consciousness itself.

At the end of phenomenology, therefore, the consciousness that is thematized in it *becomes* philosophical consciousness or thought (albeit via the transition from religion to absolute knowing effected by the phenomenologist). At the same time, both the philosopher-qua-phenomenologist and the reader see that the standpoint of philosophy is justified by the certainties of natural consciousness itself. The perspectives of all three – phenomenologist, reader and thematized consciousness – thus converge and philosophy can begin.

Thus ends phenomenology; but how does it begin? It must begin, Hegel contends, with the simplest and most immediate form of natural consciousness. Such consciousness will not be the oldest historically, but the simplest structurally or logically. It will thus be the immediate awareness of what is immediately given to us, what is immediately *there* before our eyes and for our other senses. Such *sensuous certainty* forms the starting point for phenomenology because it is the least that *natural* consciousness can be. More advanced shapes of consciousness cannot form the starting point of phenomenology, precisely because they are *advanced*. On the other hand, anything less than sense-certainty – any form of mindedness that does not at least entail an *I* knowing *this*, *here*, *now* – would not count as a form of natural *consciousness* at all, either in its own eyes or the eyes of the philosopher.

Unlike twentieth-century phenomenologists, such as Husserl and Heidegger, therefore, Hegel does not begin with developed, concrete human experience, but with the simplest shape of consciousness conceivable. His task is then to think through, with a genuine openness of mind, the experience of such certainty and to discover where, *if anywhere*, that experience leads to.

CHAPTER THREE

Reading the text

The *Phenomenology* is meant to show how the experience of consciousness takes it from the standpoint of sense-certainty to that of absolute knowing. Hegel understood this development to be driven forward by the *logic* that is inherent in the experience of consciousness. In what follows, I have concentrated on trying to make this logic as clear as possible. I have thus said very little, indeed almost nothing, about the historical phenomena that correspond to the various shapes of consciousness that emerge. I hope, however, that my approach will help readers of the *Phenomenology* understand why Hegel thought the development he describes is *necessary*. They will then be in a position to assess for themselves whether the *Phenomenology* succeeds in fulfilling the specific task Hegel set for it.

Consciousness

Sense-certainty

Sense-certainty, in Hegel's view, is natural consciousness in its simplest and most immediate form. It takes its object to be there before it immediately and thinks that nothing of the object is hidden from view: it believes that it has before it the sheer *being* or unalloyed *immediacy* of the thing. It takes itself in turn to *know* such immediacy immediately. It does not know its object by means of concepts, but takes itself to be directly acquainted with it. Sense-certainty, Hegel writes, is 'immediate knowledge itself, a knowledge of the immediate or of what simply *is*' (§90/69).

Such certainty is *sense*-certainty because it takes its object to be immediately given to the senses in space and time. It sees and hears many different things, indeed it confronts an 'infinite wealth for which no bounds can be found' (§91/69); but it takes each thing to be given to it *here* and *now* in its immediacy. Accordingly, sense-certainty always has something quite *specific* in view. It sees this night, this day, this house or this tree.

Yet it does not identify its object explicitly *as* a 'house' rather than a 'tree', for to do so would be to understand it *by means of* a contrast with something else, and the object would thus not be known *immediately*. Sense-certainty sees this house and is aware that it is not this tree, but it does not focus on the difference between the two things. It attends directly to the immediacy of the thing before it. It thus does not say 'this is a house, not a tree' or even merely 'this is a house'. 'All that it says about what it knows is just that it *is*; and its truth contains nothing but the sheer *being* of the thing' (§91/69). Indeed, sense-certainty not only *says* no more than this, but also *has in mind* no more than this.

Such immediate consciousness of the specific is something we are familiar with in our everyday experience. We share in it whenever we say or think we are conscious of *this*. In ordinary usage, the word or thought 'this' is meant to focus the mind on a specific individual, as in: 'look at *this*'; but it is meant to do so directly, without the interference of mediating concepts or descriptions. Sense-certainty, which claims to be immediate consciousness of the specific, thus necessarily thinks of its object as simply *this*. More precisely, since it takes its object to be given in space and time, it thinks of it as *this, here* or *this, now*. Furthermore, such certainty takes *itself* to be no more than *this* immediate consciousness or *this I*. It takes itself to be a specific individual – one I among many – but it does not differentiate itself explicitly from other Is by giving itself a name. It thinks of itself simply as *this* I that is immediately aware of *this* object. In Hegel's own words, 'consciousness is *I*, nothing more, a pure *this*; the individual consciousness knows a pure this, or *the individual*' (§91/70).

In the Introduction to the *Phenomenology* Hegel writes that 'in what consciousness affirms from within itself as *being-in-itself* or the *True* we have the standard which consciousness itself sets up by which to measure what it knows' (§84/65). We can now see clearly what sense-certainty affirms as the 'true', what it first takes its object to be. That object is not the play of forces or the world of spirit, but simply *this*, *here*, *now*, in its immediacy, specificity and uniqueness. The task of phenomenology is to trace the experience that is generated by this object and to discover whether this object is preserved in the experience of it.

The first experience of sense-certainty: the now

In his *Science of Logic*, Hegel maintains that 'there is nothing, nothing in heaven or in nature or mind or anywhere else which does not equally contain both immediacy and mediation'.[1] Yet – unlike, for example, Adorno – Hegel does not draw on his philosophical insight in order to challenge the idea that one can be *immediately* aware of the *immediacy* of what is before one.[2] Phenomenology, in Hegel's view, must set all philosophical convictions to one side and undertake an immanent examination of the experience undergone by sense-certainty. It must seek to discover, therefore, where such certainty is led by its *own* conviction that it beholds the immediacy of *this* specific thing.

At the start of his examination of sense-certainty Hegel proposes a simple experiment. He asks sense-certainty *what* it is aware of: 'What is the this?', or more precisely 'What is the now?'. To this question, Hegel says, we ourselves answer, for example, 'now is night'. We have to give this answer on behalf of sense-certainty, because it does not identify its object *as* the night, but takes it simply to be *this*, *now*. We then write down this 'truth' and keep it until it is daytime. We then look at it again and see that it is no longer true, since it is now no longer night but day. We are forced to conclude, therefore, that this 'truth' 'has become stale [*schal*]' (§95/71).

This experiment seems curious, since it does not initially appear to demonstrate anything that sense-certainty would find problematic. After all, sense-certainty never claimed that it would be true to say it is night during the *day*! It becomes clear from §96, however, that Hegel's real aim is to show, not just that what was written down becomes stale over time, but that, as night gives way to day, sense-certainty actually remains conscious of the very *same* thing.

Sense-certainty is conscious of *this*, *now*, without further qualification. It sees the night and thinks it has *this* in mind in all its specificity; but it does not further identify its object *as* the night – to itself or anyone else. All it has explicitly in mind is the thought: '*this* is now before me'. This means, therefore, that it is explicitly conscious, not of its object's being the *night* (as opposed to the day), but simply of its object's *being now* before it. This consciousness, however, remains, as night gives way to day: for in the day, just as at night, sense-certainty is conscious of its object's *being now* before it. Indeed, this remains the case, *whatever* sense-certainty encounters. What sense-certainty is explicitly conscious of, therefore, proves to be wholly universal. It is, of course, not meant to be universal, because, in being conscious of *this*, *now*, sense-certainty thinks it has in view the unique specificity of the thing. Through the simple passage of time, however, sense-certainty learns that it has nothing specific in view after all, but something quite indeterminate and universal: the *being-this-now*-before-me that can belong to anything.

The result of Hegel's analysis is not, by the way, that we can never be conscious of specific things. Hegel's claim, in the words of Robert Stern, is that 'nothing we can know about the object is unique to it, if we stick just to sense-certainty'.[3] The specificity of things eludes sense-certainty because it refuses to identify them explicitly, but thinks of each purely as *this*, *here*, *now*. And it does that because it thinks that, in so doing, it will have in view the undiluted immediacy of the thing. Sense-certainty's concern for *immediacy* is thus what consigns it to utter *indeterminacy*.

Language or time?

In 1839 – eight years after Hegel's death – the Young Hegelian, Ludwig Feuerbach, accused Hegel of playing 'a verbal game' in his analysis of sense-certainty. All Hegel shows, Feuerbach claims, is that the *words* 'here' and 'now' do not specify the objects to which they refer. In Feuerbach's view, this shows the limitations of language, but not of sense-certainty itself: even if words fail us, sense-certainty is perfectly conscious, as *sense-certainty*, of the specific character of things.[4] Feuerbach's charge appears to gain support from Hegel's claim that, in sense-certainty, 'we do not envisage [*vorstellen*] the universal this or being in general, but we *utter* the universal' (§97/71). In my view, however, this appearance is misleading. Language is not itself responsible for the indeterminacy and universality that comes to afflict sense-certainty, but it reveals the indeterminacy and universality in the very *consciousness* of *this*, *here*, *now*. Hegel maintains that 'the universal is the truth [*das Wahre*] of sense-certainty and language expresses this truth alone' (§97/72). This suggests, not that language causes the problem besetting sense-certainty, but that it *expresses* the truth that emerges below the level of language in sense-certainty itself.

In my view, the object of sense-certainty proves to be universal, because such certainty is immediate *sensuous* certainty and so takes its object to be spatio-temporal. As such, the latter is understood to be a *now* or a *here* connected to *other* moments and points. If, *per impossibile*, there were only one moment for sense-certainty, then the consciousness of *this*, *now* would clearly hold in view that moment alone. For sense-certainty, however, one moment in time (and one point in space) leads to another. Yet sense-certainty always takes itself to be conscious of *this*, *now*, of its object's *being now* before it. Accordingly, as one moment gives way to the next, '*this*, *now*' continues to be the object of consciousness: as Hegel puts it, the *now* 'preserves itself' (§96/71). It is in *continuing* to be the object of consciousness – in being *preserved* – that the *now* becomes something *universal*. The now first comes to be a universal, not in being uttered in language, but in the passage of time from one now to another.

The now is initially taken by consciousness, not to be universal, but to be something quite specific: *this*, *now* before me. As one now gives way to another now, however, the now is preserved as the object of consciousness and so *comes to be* something universal – something that is encountered not just *now*, but also *now* and *now* and *now*. The universality displayed by the now thus has a distinctive character. Since it emerges in and through the vanishing of one moment into another – the vanishing of night into day, and day into night – the now is 'not immediate but mediated'. This is because 'it is determined as a permanent and self-preserving now *through* the fact that something else, viz. day and night, is *not*' (§96/71). At the same time, it remains a *simple*, indeterminate object of consciousness: *this*, *now*, with no further qualification or complexity. As such it remains the object of consciousness, whatever 'example' is at hand: as Hegel puts it, the now is 'indifferent to what happens in it [*was noch bei ihm herspielt*]', indifferent to whether it is night or day (§96/71). Note that this simple now does not transcend the individual 'nows' that vanish and arise, but continues in and through them. The now, in Hegel's words, is thus 'a simple thing' which '*is* through negation, which is neither this nor that, a *not*-this, and is with equal indifference this as well as that', and this structure marks it out as a *universal* (§96/71). It is, moreover, an *abstract* universal because it is utterly indeterminate.

Before we move on to consider the second experience of sense-certainty, two further points need to be made. First, although §95 suggests that sense-certainty undergoes its first experience only because *we* write something down and show it to such certainty later in the day, this act of writing is not central to that experience. We do not bring about the dialectical transformation of the object of sense-certainty into an actual universal by our act of writing down what sense-certainty is aware of. As becomes clear in §96, the work of writing is done, without any activity on the part of the phenomenologist, by *time* itself. All the writing down achieves, therefore, is to show sense-certainty the consequences of the temporality to which it knows itself to be subject. The first experience of sense-certainty thus remains quite immanent. Indeed, in my view, the whole experiment of writing could be dropped without detriment to Hegel's account. The paragraph on writing could be deleted and all one would need to say is this: sense-certainty is aware of *this*, *now*, but time moves on for sense-certainty itself; the now is nonetheless preserved as the object of sense-certainty and so proves in the experience of consciousness itself to be universal.

Second, it is we phenomenologists who call the emergent object of sense-certainty a 'universal'; that technical term is not employed by such certainty. Nonetheless, the object comes to have the structure *of* a universal *for* sense-certainty itself: 'sense-certainty has demonstrated in its own self [*an ihr selbst*] that the truth of its object is the universal' (§99/72). Sense-certainty itself, therefore, experiences the transformation of its object and the loss of the object as it initially takes it to be. In this way, both sense-certainty and the reader are *educated* by this first experience of consciousness. Both see that the object, as initially conceived, itself generates the experience in which it proves *not* to be what it is first taken to be. The initial object is not, however, simply replaced by a new object: the object *remains* '*this*, *now*'. But that very object – *this*, *now* – proves in the experience of it to be indeterminate and universal, rather than specific, and so proves to be other than it is first taken to be. The analysis of sense-certainty, to begin with at least, thus conforms to the method of phenomenology set out in the Introduction: for the initial conception consciousness has of its object is undermined, and subjected to an immanent critique, by its own experience.

By the way, though I have concentrated on the now, consciousness of *this*, *here* is subject to a similar dialectic. Hegel describes this dialectic in these lines, which I shall leave to speak for themselves:

> 'Here' is, e.g., the tree. If I turn round, this truth has vanished and is converted into its opposite: 'no tree is here but a house instead'. 'Here' itself does not vanish; on the contrary, it abides constant in the vanishing of the house, the tree, etc., and is indifferently house or tree. Again, therefore, the 'this' shows itself to be a *mediated simplicity*, or a *universality*. (§98/72)

The second experience of sense-certainty: the dialectic of the I

In the experience of sense-certainty, as we have seen, the object of such certainty – *this*, *here*, *now* – comes to diverge from what it is initially taken to be. At this point, Hegel notes, we can compare the former with the latter. Such a comparison could not be undertaken at the outset, but becomes possible through the experience of sense-certainty. We now see, therefore, that 'the universal which the object has come to be is no longer what the object was supposed essentially to be for sense-certainty' (§100/72). Sense-certainty sees this, too, and its awareness of this disparity drives it back into itself. It knows that its object is not meant to be indeterminate and universal, but something wholly specific. It now looks to itself, therefore, to preserve its consciousness of the specific in face of its experience.

Accordingly, sense-certainty now claims that it is conscious of something specific, not because its *object* is simple and immediate, but because its *own certainty* is immediate. For sense-certainty, the specificity and immediacy of the object before me are held in view by the 'immediacy of my *seeing*, *hearing*' (§101/73), by the immediate certainty of the *I*. This means that the object I take myself to be certain of is itself subtly transformed: it is no longer merely *this*, *here*, *now*, but what *I* mean by this, what *I* know to be immediately present before me. Hegel notes, however, that 'in this relationship sense-certainty experiences the same dialectic acting upon itself as in the previous one' (§101/73).

The problem, put simply, is this: if all I am aware of is 'what *I* mean by this', I do not actually have anything *specific* in mind, for another I is equally conscious of 'what *I* mean by this'. 'What *I* mean by this' is thus just as vague and indeterminate as 'this, here, now': it *remains*, beyond me, what other Is are certain of, and indeed what I myself am certain of at other times and in other places (and so when I am myself another I than the one I am now). By thinking of what *I* am immediately certain of, I think I have in mind something utterly specific *to me*; but the truth is that 'when I say "I", this singular "I", I say in general all Is; everyone is what I say, everyone is "I", this singular "I"' (§102/73). Like *this*, *here* and *now*, therefore, the unspecified *I* proves to be an abstract, indeterminate universal.

The second experience thus shows sense-certainty that it is no more certain of something specific when it takes its object to be what *I* mean by this than when it takes its object to be simply *this*. 'Sense-certainty thus comes to know by experience that its essence is neither in the object nor in the "I"' (§103/73).

The third experience of sense-certainty: pointing

The result of this second experience leads sense-certainty to adopt a new strategy in order to secure for itself the immediate consciousness of *this* specific thing. In the first and second experiences what turned 'now', 'here' and 'I' into universals was the fact that they preserved themselves, beyond *this* now, *this* here and *this* I, in *other* 'nows', 'heres' and 'Is'. To prevent its object becoming a universal, therefore, sense-certainty turns its back on all other 'nows', 'heres' and 'Is' and focuses exclusively on *this* specific thing that is before *me* here and now. Sense-certainty takes itself thereby to bring to mind *this*, *here*, *now* in all its immediacy; but it secures such immediate consciousness of immediacy by explicitly *excluding* everything else from view. Such immediate consciousness is thus grounded no longer just in the immediacy of the object or of my certainty, but in the unity of the two, that is, in *this* I focussing on *this*, here, now *alone*. As Hegel puts it, 'it is only sense-certainty as a *whole* which stands firm within itself as *immediacy* and by so doing excludes from itself all the opposition which has hitherto obtained' (§103/74). Hegel emphasizes this act of exclusion in a series of related expressions: I 'do not turn around', 'I take no notice', and 'I, for my part, stick to the fact' (§104/74).

Since sense-certainty now pays no attention to other 'heres', 'nows' and 'Is', it does not allow itself to be directed by us – or by space and time – beyond this, here, now before it. We phenomenologists must, therefore, adopt a new strategy towards sense-certainty. Taking the case of the 'now' first, we must simply approach such certainty and 'have the now that is asserted pointed out to us' (*lassen uns das Itzt zeigen*) (§105/74). Miller renders Hegel's German as follows: we will 'let ourselves point to the now that is asserted'. Hegel, however, uses a German construction with the verb *lassen* (to let) that means 'to have something done': 'ein Haus bauen lassen', for example, means 'to have a house built'. We do not, therefore let *ourselves* point to the now, but 'we must have it *pointed out* to us' by sense-certainty, and we must do so because sense-certainty must show us *which* of the many 'nows' it is directly conscious of. Indeed – though Hegel does not note this explicitly – sense-certainty must point to the now it is aware of for its own benefit, too. It confines itself to one now among many and so must pick out *for itself* the one that captures its attention. In pointing out to us what it is aware of, sense-certainty thus also points this out to itself.[5] Hegel notes, however, that what is pointed out changes its character for sense-certainty in the very process of being pointed out and *ceases* being the simple, immediate now that sense-certainty aims to bring to mind.

The problem for sense-certainty is this: it has to point out what it is conscious of *now*, but *as* it points out that *now* the latter recedes into the past and so is no more. In being pointed out, therefore, the now vanishes. What comes to be pointed out is thus a now that no longer *is* but that *has been*. Hegel presents the process of the now's disappearance, with a degree of drama, in these lines: 'The now is pointed to, *this* now. "Now"; it has already ceased to be in the act of pointing to it. The now that *is*, is another now than the one pointed to' (§106/75).

From the start sense-certainty takes itself to be aware of *this* specific thing in its unalloyed immediacy and being: for such certainty, 'the thing *is*, and it *is*, merely because it *is*' (§91/69). In order to prevent its object – *this, now* – turning into an empty universal, however, sense-certainty has to confine itself to one among the many 'nows' with which it is surrounded. That in turn means that it has to pick out, or *point out*, from that many the one that it is directly aware of. We have seen, however, that in being pointed out that now vanishes. It is pointed out and brought to mind, therefore, as a 'now that *has been*' and so no longer *is*. As Hegel puts it, the now that has been pointed out no longer has 'the truth of *being*', but 'it was with *being*' – with what *is* now before us – 'that we were concerned' (§106/75). In confining itself to and pointing out *this* now, rather than any other, sense-certainty thus loses the very now it wants to bring to mind: it deprives itself of that now precisely *by* pointing it out. Yet it has to point out and isolate that now, if it is not to slip into consciousness of abstract, indeterminate universality. Sense-certainty is thus caught in a double bind: either way it loses the object of its certainty.

Yet this is only half the story, for in losing the object of its certainty, sense-certainty also gains a radically new object. The act of pointing, as Hegel describes it, takes time: it brings forth what we are conscious of *now* at a later point in time, namely . . . *now*. What is pointed out *now* is thus actually a now that no longer *is* but that lies in the past. Yet what is pointed out *now* cannot simply be that which is past. After all, it is that which *has* been pointed out and so *is now* present to consciousness. In the process Hegel describes, the now that sense-certainty has in mind *is*, indeed, pointed out and *is*, therefore, *now* before the mind. Yet what is *now* before the mind is not a pure and simple *now*, precisely because it is a now that *has been* pointed out and in that respect *is no longer*.

What is brought to mind in the act of pointing comes before us *now*: it comes to be present to mind. At the same time, it comes to be present to mind *as having a past*. What comes to presence through pointing, therefore, is never sheer, immediate presence, but always a presence that incorporates its past, its *having-been*. That is because it comes to presence as a now that *has been* pointed out. This fusion of presence and 'pastness', of being-now and having-been – that is, of being and *not* being – is what emerges through the experience of pointing as the new object or 'truth' of sense-certainty. It is the positive result of that experience. (Similarly, the *here* is pointed out as *not* just *here*, but as a here that is also distinguished from, and so related to, *there*, that is, as 'a before and behind, an above and below, a right and left' (§108/75).)

The object or 'truth' that emerges in the experience of sense-certainty is not, therefore, the pure being or immediacy that such certainty first took its object to be, but a complex fusion of being and *not-being* or *negation*. This moment of negation will be a central feature of all subsequent shapes of consciousness in the *Phenomenology*. By being this fusion of being and negation – of presence and 'pastness' – the newly emergent object of consciousness is necessarily a unity of *different* moments. It is, in Hegel's own words, a 'now which is an absolute plurality of nows' (§107/75) or 'a simple complex of many heres' (§108/76). In this sense, the object of sense-certainty turns out not simply to be *this* after all, but to be a unity of *this* and *not*-this, of now and then, or here and there.

Yet the emergent object of consciousness does not cease altogether to be *this*, for it remains that which is brought to mind *here* and *now*. As such, as Hegel puts it, it remains a 'simple entity' (*Einfaches*) (§107/75). The paradoxical result of the third experience of sense-certainty, in Hegel's view, is thus that the object of consciousness proves to be complex *in its very simplicity*, and simple in its complexity. It is for this reason that Hegel says that the spatial object of consciousness is the 'simple complex' (*einfache Komplexion*) of many heres. Hegel is not playing verbal games, but making an important point. The truth that emerges through the activity of pointing does not completely replace what sense-certainty first took to be the truth. That emergent truth is what the *simple this* itself turns out to be when it is pointed out by sense-certainty and in this way is picked out from other 'thises'. Through the activity of pointing, sense-certainty succeeds in bringing *this*, *now* to mind *now* as something simple and immediate. It is brought to mind, however, as being complex in its simplicity, since it incorporates both itself – its being-*now* – and its negation – its *having-been*. The object of consciousness, Hegel states, is thus a simple entity 'which, in its otherness, *remains* what it is' (§107/75).

It is this structure of *remaining-itself*-in-its-negation that marks the object of sense-certainty, at the end of its third experience, as a *universal*. This universal is, however, different from the universals that arise in the first two experiences. Those two universals are utterly abstract: they consist in nothing but the continuous, *indeterminate* now, here or I that remain the objects of sense-certainty, whatever *example* the latter turns to. By contrast, the universal that emerges at the end of the third experience is internally complex and differentiated, rather than abstract and indeterminate, since it consists in the unity of this *and* its negation, the 'not-this'. Indeed, one might call it a 'concrete universal'. Its concreteness is still fairly minimal, but nonetheless it constitutes an advance on the abstract universals that arise earlier in the experience of sense-certainty.

This new, complex universal also differs from the earlier two abstract ones by leaving sense-certainty (logically, at least) with nowhere to go and nothing to cling on to. After *this*, *here*, *now* proved in its first experience to be an abstract universal, sense-certainty took refuge in 'what *I* mean by this'; and after the I proved to be abstractly universal in its second experience, sense-certainty took refuge in 'what I mean by this to the exclusion of everything else'. By excluding all other objects and points of view and retreating wholly into itself, sense-certainty sought finally to bring to mind the simple immediacy and sheer being of *this* that is its focus from the start. Yet that very retreat into itself, and the accompanying act of pointing out to itself what it is aware of, are precisely what turn the object of consciousness into a *complex universal*. In seeking to be purely itself, therefore, sense-certainty brings about the very opposite of what it intends and deprives itself of the object it seeks to cling on to: 'it spoils its own limited satisfaction' (§80/63). By clinging on to itself, in other words, it *loses* itself and suffers the *dialectic* that is inherent in it. Furthermore, at this point, sense-certainty has run out of options, for there is nowhere else for it to retreat to. It thus has no alternative but to accept the result of its experience *or* to repeat those experiences endlessly, like a hamster caught in a wheel.

The transition to perception

Sense-certainty starts out as consciousness of simple immediacy. After each of its first two experiences it tries to cling to this simple immediacy by modifying it slightly: its object changes from being 'this, here, now' to being 'what *I* mean by this' and then to being '*this* (not that, or that, or that)'. The third experience, however, produces an altogether *new* object of consciousness, one that is no longer *simple* and immediate, but a 'simple *complex*' of different moments. This new object is the *truth* that emerges in the experience of sense-certainty. It counts as the truth, not because it matches what philosophy tells us about the world, but because it is made necessary *by* the experience of consciousness. Indeed, it is what the original object proves to be *in* the experience of it, what that original object comes to be for consciousness itself. In the words of the Introduction, therefore, the new object is simply 'the being-*for*-consciousness of the first in-itself' (§87/67).

With the emergence of this new object, sense-certainty learns that its initial conception of the object is unsustainable. Readers who may be wedded to the position of sense-certainty learn this lesson, too, and so are *educated* by the experience of consciousness. These readers will presumably not find it hard to give up the perspective of sense-certainty, since it is so primitive. Sense-certainty, by contrast, cannot let go of itself so easily. Like all shapes of consciousness examined in the *Phenomenology*, it is characterized above all by the *'immediate certainty'* of itself (§26/20). It cannot, therefore, just give up its certainty and cease being what it is. In that sense, it cannot learn from its experience in the profound way the reader can; it cannot become a new shape of consciousness.

For sense-certainty, the object is meant to be pure *being* – the pure now and pure here – and it simply cannot admit *non*-being, difference and complexity into its object. It thus disavows the truth that emerges in its experience and refuses to take it up. Or rather, as Hegel puts it, sense-certainty learns from experience what its truth is, 'but equally it is always forgetting it and starting the movement all over again' (§109/76). The shape of consciousness that does take up this truth is *perception* (*Wahrnehmung*) or *'true-taking'*. As Hegel writes, 'immediate certainty does not take over the truth, for its truth is the universal, whereas certainty wants to apprehend the this. Perception, on the other hand, takes what is present to it as a universal' (§111/79). Perception, however, does not see this universal as the result of a previous experience, but simply takes it to be the *given* object of consciousness.

Sense-certainty, therefore, does not itself mutate into perception, but *we* phenomenologists make the transition to perception ourselves (see §87/67). There is thus a difference between the micro-transitions from one conception of the object to another *within* sense-certainty and the macro-transition *from* sense-certainty to perception. Sense-certainty experiences those micro-transitions, but it does not experience the macro-transition – we do. We do so, however, by moving to a new shape of consciousness that simply affirms the truth that emerges in the experience of sense-certainty itself. That macro-transition is made necessary by nothing other than sense-certainty, therefore, even though we are the ones who undertake it. The 'reversal of consciousness' that produces the new shape of perception is thus 'something contributed by *us*, by means of which the succession of experiences through which consciousness passes is raised into a scientific progression' (§87/67); but this succession nonetheless arises immanently through the experience of consciousness itself.

Two problems

Before leaving sense-certainty behind, a few words of clarification are needed concerning two problems that might worry readers. The first problem concerns time. Hegel argues that in the act of pointing out the now, that now is brought to mind at a later now. Does this not presuppose, however, that time is divided into discrete 'nows', and is this not an illegitimate presupposition for Hegel to make in phenomenology? This problem disappears when we recall that it is sense-certainty, *not* Hegel, that thinks of time as divided into discrete moments. Phenomenology, for Hegel, is not ontology and does not set out his philosophical understanding of time or of anything else; rather, it sets out the experience that consciousness makes of its own objects. In the chapter on sense-certainty, we see that such certainty thinks of the now (like the here) as *this* now among many other 'nows'. In this way, such certainty itself divides time into discrete moments. It is sense-certainty, therefore, that is ultimately responsible for the peculiar expressions, '*the* now' and '*this* now', that have bothered some readers of Hegel's text. 'Now' is an adverb, but Hegel turns it into a noun in order to capture sense-certainty's view that its object is something specific and individual: *this* now. Hegel distorts ordinary language, therefore, in order to give voice to the distinctive perspective of natural consciousness in its most immediate and primitive form.

The second problem is this: the third experience of sense-certainty shows that its consciousness of what is present also involves consciousness of what is past. Unlike Kant, however, Hegel says nothing about the transcendental (and empirical) *condition* that enables consciousness to hold together the present and the past, namely the reproduction of a past moment in the present through the work of imagination.[6] This problem dissolves when we recall that Hegel's aim in the *Phenomenology* is precisely to *avoid* making claims of his own about the conditions of consciousness. In that text Hegel is doing *phenomenology*, not transcendental philosophy. He thus restricts himself to setting out what emerges in the experience of consciousness, and says nothing about the roles *he* thinks are played by attention, imagination or memory in making experience possible. Hegel discusses such topics in his *Encyclopaedia Philosophy of Spirit*,[7] but that philosophical discussion has no place in the phenomenological study of what arises *in and for* consciousness itself.

It should be noted, by the way, that perception is not itself to be understood as the *condition* of sense-certainty, and understanding is not the condition in turn of perception. Later shapes of consciousness take up and affirm the truth that emerges in the preceding shape, but they are not necessarily the conditions of those earlier shapes. Otherwise, the 'absolute freedom' embodied in Revolutionary France would have to be understood as the condition of the Enlightenment that preceded it, which would be somewhat bizarre. This is not to deny, however, that all shapes of consciousness, self-consciousness and reason prove in the course of the *Phenomenology* to be moments of the concrete whole that Hegel calls 'spirit', which can thus be regarded as their condition and 'presupposition' (§440/289). Spirit first arises, however, *as* that which takes up the *truth* of those shapes, rather than *as* their condition.[8]

Study questions

1 Why does the *now* prove to be a universal in the first experience of sense-certainty?

2 How does pointing out the *now* change its character?

Perception

The thing with properties

The chapter on perception does not start directly with the *experience* of perception. It begins by setting out in greater detail how the object of perception must be understood. Hegel's opening remarks (in §113) are somewhat abstract. They become comprehensible, however, if one bears in mind that *negation* belongs essentially to the object of perception.

The object of perception is still simple and immediate: a *this*. Indeed, it is still a *sensuous* immediacy. In this sense, perception has the same object in view as sense-certainty. In the latter's experience, however, the simple, immediate *this* proved *not* just to be simple and immediate – *not* just to be *this* – but to be the unity of being and not-being. For perception, therefore, the object explicitly combines *being* this with *not* just being this. As Hegel puts it, in a rather concentrated formulation, 'the this is thus posited as *not this*' (*Das Dieses ist also gesetzt als nicht dieses*) (§113/80). This does not mean that the object of perception is in fact nothing at all. The object is still *this*; but it is also not-this, and so is no longer *simply* this. The object is, say, *this* red, and yet it is *not just* this red. Does that mean that red has been mixed with another colour, say, green? No. Hegel does not say that perception's object is *this* together with *something else*; he says it is *this* 'posited as not this'. The very *this* of which perception is aware is *itself* 'posited as not this' and so is not just the this that it is. For perception, therefore, the object is *this* red insofar as it is itself *not just* the red it is.

Yet how can this red be more than just this red? It can be such, if it extends beyond its own specificity. This gets us to the heart of what Hegel has in mind here. The object of perception is a sensuous immediacy – *this* red – that is not reducible to *this* red but continues beyond itself where its specificity is no longer to be found, namely in *that* red and *that* red and so on. Such a this that continues beyond itself in its negation Hegel calls a 'universal'. The object of perception is thus a sensuous universal – red, green, hot, cold and so on. Note that the *truth* as it is first conceived by 'truth-taking' consciousness *must* take the form of what is universal. This is not because Hegel is here in thrall to a lingering Platonism. It is because the very *form* of truth, understood as that which is *not* simply immediate, incorporates the moment of negation. The truth is something universal because it is a *this* that preserves itself in *no longer* being this.

This moment of negation is initially contained *within* the simple self-identity of the universal. Negation is explicitly *expressed* in the universal, however, when the latter is understood to be this universal, *not that one*, that is, when it is understood to be different from one or more other universals. If perception is to take explicit account of the idea that the universal has 'the negative within it', as well as the positive – that it is *not* such and such, just as much as it *is* such and such – it must regard its object as a '*differentiated, determinate*' universal, as one of many (or at least one of two) (§113/80).

Yet each of these universals remains the *universal* that it is: each retains its own continuing identity. They differ from one another, therefore, not by opposing or excluding one another, but by simply being what they are. As such, Hegel writes, they are 'related to themselves' and are 'indifferent to one another': 'each is on its own and free from the others' (§113/80). Since they are not mutually exclusive, they can coexist in the *same* object of perception, the same 'this, here, now'. Indeed, they are simply different 'determinations' *of* one and the same object. That object is thus to be understood as the '*medium* in which all these determinacies are'. In this medium, the different universals 'interpenetrate' since they occupy the same space; but they do not come '*into contact* with one another' since they are mutually indifferent. This medium, Hegel writes, is thus the '*simple togetherness* of a plurality', or 'thinghood' (§113/80). It is what perception (as opposed to sense-certainty) necessarily takes to be present before it: a this, such as salt, that incorporates a manifold of different properties in one here and now:

> this salt is a simple here, and at the same time manifold; it is white and *also* tart, *also* cubical in shape, of a specific gravity, etc. All these many properties are in a single simple here, in which, therefore, they interpenetrate. (§113/81)

Since the properties coexist in this way in the same here and now, or medium, Hegel calls the latter the 'also' (*Auch*) that holds the properties together (§113/81). This 'also' is what the 'absolute plurality of nows' and the 'simple complex of many heres', that emerge in the experience of sense-certainty, prove to be for perception.

Hegel notes, however, that the moment of negation in the object so construed still has not been given its proper due. If the sensuous universals contained in the 'also' remain merely indifferent to one another, then they are not understood to be genuinely *negative* and properly *determinate*. They are perceived to be properly determinate – to be this, *not* that – only 'in so far as they *differentiate* themselves from one another, and *relate* themselves *to others* as to their opposites' (§114/81). If they oppose and exclude one another, however, they cannot coexist in the same medium. Rather, they must belong to different media that thereby also exclude one another. When the medium or 'also' is understood in this way to be an *exclusive unity* – a unity that is explicitly *not* another unity – it ceases to be a mere medium or 'also' and takes the form of a distinct and separate, self-enclosed *thing*. When they are understood to be contained within such a thing, the sensuous universals become 'properties' (*Eigenschaften*) in the full sense of the word: determinations that are proper to this thing, rather than that one.

The form that the object must take for perception has now been fully determined:

> It is (a) an indifferent, passive universality, the *also* of the many properties or rather 'matters' [*Materien*]; (b) negation, equally simply; or the *one*, which excludes opposite properties; and (c) the many *properties* themselves. (§115/82)

Note that Hegel has reached this conception of the object of perception not by reflection on our everyday perceiving, but by rendering explicit what is implicit in the truth that emerges in the experience of sense-certainty. What he has disclosed, therefore, is the truth, not as he takes it to be, but as perception must take it to be, given the experience of sense-certainty.

Joachim Hagner maintains that, through the analysis of perception, Hegel examines in an idealized form philosophical problems in the thought of Plato, Aristotle, Hume and Kant.[9] While this is no doubt correct, it is important to recognize that Hegel's *derivation* of the object of perception is wholly immanent: the truth for perception must take the form of things with properties because this is what is implicit in the very form of emergent truth. If you spell out what it means for the truth, as object of consciousness, to be that-which-is-*not*-just-the-object-of-immediate-certainty, what you get first are things with properties.[10] This, then, is the conception that *necessarily* governs perception, the consciousness that first takes up the truth.

The first experience of perception

Hegel now turns to examine the *experience* of perception. The experience he traces is not the empirical experience that people may have in their everyday lives. It is made necessary, logically, by the very form of the perceptual object, the thing with properties. The twists and turns that arise in this experience are due to the fact that the object of perception is still marked by a certain immediacy and simplicity. The immediacy to which sense-certainty tries to hold on is pure, relationless immediacy. By contrast, the distinctive immediacy that holds sway in perception is evident in the *differences* that characterize perception's object. Properties differ from one another by simply being themselves and so being indifferent to one another, but also by excluding one another. In both cases, properties are thus immediately what they are and not something else. Similarly, the things of which perception is aware are immediately what they are and not another thing. Perception will also see an immediate difference between the different *aspects* of the thing, that is, between its being an 'also' – a manifold – and its being an exclusive unity, between its being a many and a one. In its experience perception will be taken from one such aspect to another and be invited to think of both as belonging to the same thing; but it will also seek to preserve the *immediate difference* between them. The character of its experience will be determined by this tension between needing to combine, and endeavouring to keep apart, the different aspects of the thing.

Not only is the object of perception characterized by both immediacy and non-immediacy (see p. 46, above), but so also is the relation of perception *to* that object. On the one hand, perception thinks that all it has to do to get the truth is take up what is there before it, without acting or reflecting on it. In this sense, it takes its knowledge of the truth to be immediate (§116/82). On the other hand, perception knows that its knowledge is not simply immediate. This is because the truth contains the moment of negation, difference, or 'otherness', and so can differ from what we perceive (or take ourselves to perceive). In other words, perception knows that, if it is not careful, it can get things wrong, and so, unlike sense-certainty, it 'is aware of the possibility of deception' (§116/82). In the eyes of perception, therefore, to know the truth is also to know that one can be in error.

How, then, does perception know whether it has got things right? The answer is clear. Perception takes the object to be a '*simple complex*' – a *simple* universal that is and remains what it is. More specifically, the object of perception is the self-identical *thing* that is itself and not another thing. Perception's criterion of truth, therefore, is 'self-identity' or 'self-equality' (*Sichselbstgleichheit*) (§116/82). Provided there are no incompatibilities or contradictions in its object (and that it takes up only what is there before it), perception can thus rest assured that it knows the truth. If, however, perception comes upon any such contradictions in what it perceives, it will conclude that it has gone astray. These contradictions will thus not be put down to the object itself but will be seen as the mark of error on the part of consciousness. Consciousness will not consider such contradictions to be 'an untruth of the object – for this is the self-identical – but an untruth in perceiving it' (§116/83). Accordingly, consciousness will alter its perception so that it can avoid the contradiction and take up the truth properly. For Hegel, therefore, perception is governed by the *conception* that there are *things* out there that *are* what they *are* and lack all contradiction.

In the first perceptual experience Hegel describes (in §117), however, consciousness comes upon several incompatibilities or contradictions in its object and so is forced continually to alter its perception of that object. Consciousness starts from the view that the object is a simple unity or 'one': the single, separate, self-identical thing. It soon notices, however, that the properties of this thing are universal and extend beyond the confines of the thing to other things. The universality of its properties conflicts with the separateness and singularity of the thing because it turns that thing into a member of a community of things with shared properties. For perception, however, there can be no such conflict in things themselves: things are either one thing or the other. Perception thus concludes that its initial apprehension of the object was incorrect and now takes the object to be this *community* of similar things.

Perception goes on to note, however, that the properties of things are determinate and exclude other properties. Things do not, therefore, form a community with shared, continuous properties, but, by virtue of the exclusive properties they possess, actually constitute distinct things that exclude one another. Each thing, therefore, is an *exclusive* unit, rather than a member of a continuous community.

Perception then notices that the properties *within* the thing do not exclude one another, but coexist in indifference to one another. The thing is thus not an exclusive unit after all, but simply a *medium* in which properties are gathered together. Indeed, the real objects of perception are actually those *properties* themselves; there is thus in fact no distinct 'thing' there, but just a collection of sensuous universals. Each such universal is indifferent to the others with which it coexists and is simply and immediately what *it* is. As such, it is no longer truly a 'property' of a 'thing', but is simply a sensuous *immediacy* or '*sensuous being*' that is there before me (§117/83). At this point, however, the object ceases to be a proper object of perception, and perception reverts to being the immediate sensuous certainty of *this*, *here*, *now*.

Yet perception is aware that such immediate certainty does not disclose the truth about *things*. It recognizes that such certainty is a *subjective* view of things that fails to perceive what they actually are. Through its first experience, therefore, perception learns that, in perceiving what is there, it also withdraws into itself and its own merely *subjective* perspective. Indeed, it learns that it is led into that subjective perspective, and so led into error, *by* the very process of perceiving. This insight transforms perception's conception of itself: for it can now no longer be sure that it will get the truth by simply avoiding contradiction and taking up or 'apprehending' what is there before it. It can no longer be sure of this, because it knows that '*in its apprehension* [it] is at the same time *reflected out of the True and into itself*' (§118/84). Its perceiving is thus much more intimately entangled with subjective error or 'untruth' than it initially thought.

In describing the first experience of perception, Hegel shows that perception switches from one conception of its object to another for two reasons. On the one hand, it detects different aspects of the object that, in its view, conflict with one another. On the other hand, it insists that the object itself – the truth – cannot contain contradictions. For perception (initially, at least), the object cannot be both one and many, discrete and continuous, at the same time. Consciousness thus has to alter its perception successively to accommodate each new aspect of the thing. This, remember, is not an empirical experience that we would go through in precisely this form. It is the experience that Hegel thinks is made necessary *logically* by the way perception takes its object – its truth – to be.

At the end of this experience, perception learns that it is not just *capable* of error but that it is always *in* error in some respect. Perception believes, however, that its errors are due to itself, not to the object. As far as perception is concerned, it is not deceived by the object, since the object is the truth and is simply what it is. Perception is subject to error because its apprehension of the truth is not as pure and unadulterated as it initially thought, but is always mixed with its own subjective view of things.

Perception recognizes, however, that it can secure the truth if it remains reflectively aware of what is due to its own perspective and keeps that perspective at bay. In this way, it can 'correct' (*korrigieren*) its erroneous view of things and so allow the truth to be perceived after all. Perception thus no longer takes itself merely to *perceive* and *apprehend* what there is, but it 'is also conscious of its reflection into itself, and separates this from simple apprehension proper' (§118/84).

To recapitulate: perception initially thinks of itself as open to the truth, though capable of error. Now perception realizes that it always has a twofold view of things: its own 'untrue' subjective view and an objective view that gets things right. It also knows that it can secure the truth if it distinguishes clearly between these two points of view. Perception's *criterion* of truth thereby remains the same: it takes the truth to be non-contradictory. If, therefore, perception comes upon something that contradicts what it perceives to be the truth, it will attribute this to its own perspective and claim that it does not belong to the thing itself.

The second experience of perception

In the second experience it undergoes, perception first perceives the thing to be *one* thing. Yet it also sees that the thing appears to have various *different* properties. Since this diversity of properties conflicts with the unity of the thing, perception attributes that diversity to its own subjective perspective. It thus maintains that the thing itself is *one*, and that it 'is white only to *our eyes*, *also* tart to *our* tongue, *also* cubical to *our* touch, and so on' (§119/85). We become the 'medium', therefore, in which properties are artificially kept apart as different items. By regarding ourselves as this medium in this way, we avoid contradiction and 'preserve the self-identity and truth of the thing, its being a one'.

As we saw in §114, however, the thing is *one* single, separate thing only because it *excludes* other things. It excludes those other things because it has distinctive *properties* of its own that do not belong to the others. These properties must, however, coexist in the thing, and that in turn means that the thing itself, not the perceiving consciousness, must now be understood to be the *medium* or 'also' that contains the different properties that strike our eye. Yet this means that the thing itself is no longer perceived to be *one* single thing after all, but is now taken to be a manifold or 'bundle' of different properties. Since that is the case, the *unity* that the thing appears to have must now be due to *our* perception. 'Thus we say of the thing: *it is* white, *also* cubical, and *also* tart, and so on'; by contrast, 'positing these properties as a oneness is the work of consciousness alone' (§121/86). Perception keeps these properties apart in the thing itself by means of the 'in so far as': in the thing itself, so perception claims, the thing is white *in so far as* it is not cubical, and vice versa. *We*, on the other hand, see all these properties as forming a single *unified* thing.

This second experience, like the first, is one that consciousness is forced to undergo by its own commitments. Yet it brings about a much more significant change in the way perception regards its object or truth. Indeed, a crack begins to emerge in that truth. Hegel points out that in this second experience 'consciousness alternately makes itself, *as well as the thing*, into both a pure, many-less one, and into an also' (or bundle of properties) (§122/86). Consciousness thus not only confirms that *it* has a twofold view of things – one subjective, one objective – but it also accepts that the *thing* itself has two sides to it, that it is both one *and* many. This latter insight does not cause perception to abandon the distinction between the way the thing appears to consciousness and what it is itself. Yet perception now believes that the disparity between the two can be due as much to *the thing* as to perception. Perception knows that it is still capable of error, but it now believes, too, that the thing presents *itself* to consciousness in a way that differs from what it is for itself. The thing for itself is the thing in so far as it is reflected back into itself and relates to itself alone. In this respect, the thing is *one* single, self-identical, self-relating thing. The *diversity* of properties the thing displays must, therefore, belong to the side of itself that the thing presents to consciousness. The thing itself is thus indeed one and many, but not in one and the same respect.

This is what introduces a crack into the truth as perception conceives it: for the thing is now no longer regarded as simply 'self-identical'. Rather, it is divided into what it is for itself and how it shows itself to consciousness, the way it presents itself to another.

The thing, for perception, is certainly *one* thing and is what it is 'for itself'; but it is also 'for another; and, moreover, it is other for itself than it is for another' (§123/87).[11]

The problem for perception is that its second experience thereby renders the thing itself contradictory. On the one hand, 'the thing is for itself and *also* for another', and so has *two* sides to it (§123/87). On the other hand, the thing is understood to be *one* single thing. Perception thus holds the thing *both* to be doubled *and* to be one thing at the same time. Yet these two aspects of the thing contradict one another. Perception resolves this contradiction in the following way. It claims that the thing is indeed doubled and does differ in itself from the way it relates to and presents itself to others. This doubled character is quite independent of consciousness and in *that* sense belongs to the *thing*. However, since the thing itself is *one* unified thing, the disparity it exhibits between what it is for itself and what it is in relation to others cannot be produced by that thing alone, but must be caused by *other things* to which it relates. 'In and for itself,' therefore, 'the thing is self-identical, but this unity with itself is disturbed by other things' (and so the thing comes to exhibit many different properties in *relation* to other things) (§123/87). In this way, perception preserves both the objective unity *and* the objective doubling of the thing. Yet perception's success comes at a heavy price.

The third experience of perception

This relation *between* things generates the third experience of perception. For perception, each thing considered by itself, or as it is for itself, is one single, separate, self-identical thing. Each thing is also different from the other things that 'disturb' its self-identity. The truth, for perception, therefore, comprises *'different things'* (*verschiedene Dinge*) that exist *'for themselves'* (*für sich*) and so are quite *separate* from one another (§124/87).[12] Since each thing is a separate thing for itself, it must have 'in its own self' (*an ihm*) that which makes it the thing it is, that which distinguishes it from other things. This is the thing's *own* distinguishing feature or 'essential character' (§124/87–8). This essential character, however, is deeply problematic. On the one hand, it makes the thing the *separate* thing it is; on the other hand, it *differentiates* the thing from other things and so sets it in *relation* to them. In doing the latter, however, it *connects* the thing to other things and so undermines its separateness: for a thing 'is only a *thing*, or a one that exists for itself, in so far as it does not stand in this relation to others' (§125/88). Paradoxically, therefore, the thing's separateness or 'being-for-itself' is undermined by the very feature that is meant to guarantee it.

At this point the object of perception becomes *intrinsically self-contradictory*: what makes it a separate thing for itself differentiates it from other things and so sets it in relation to them; and yet what differentiates the thing from others, and so relates it to them, is precisely what makes it a separate thing for itself. The object of perception is thus '*in one and the same respect the opposite of itself: it is for itself, so far as it is for another*, and *it is for another, so far as it for itself*' (§128/89) (where being '*for* another' simply means standing in *relation* to it.) The truth as perception conceives it is thus transformed in the experience of perception itself into a fundamentally self-contradictory truth.

From the conditioned to the unconditioned universal

As we saw earlier, the truth, as perception conceives it, is not simply immediate but takes the form of something universal. It is a universal, however, that is *conditioned* by the immediacy from which it has arisen (§129/89). First, it is a sensuous universal: it is *this* sensuous immediacy, not just as *this*, but as that which continues beyond its own specificity. Second, this universal is immediately different from other universals, by virtue of either being indifferent to them or excluding them. Third, the universal 'here and now' that contains these sensuous universals takes two immediately different forms: it is one thing but also a manifold or 'also'. Whether we focus on the properties of things or the thing itself, therefore, the universal of perception shows itself to be one that is immediately different from another such universal. It is thus a *one-sided* universal.

The truth that emerges in the experience of perception, however, is that the different one-sided aspects of the thing – its being for itself and its being related to others (and thus its being one and being many) – *prove to be their own opposites*. In this way, these aspects lose their one-sidedness, for each proves to be the other as well as itself and both thereby reveal themselves to be the *unity* – indeed, the same unity – of opposing moments.

This unity of opposing moments is one in which the immediate difference between the aspects of the thing is undermined. Furthermore, this unity does not stand in relation to any other universal, from which it would be immediately different. This unity is thus one that is no longer *conditioned* by any immediate difference. It is rather what Hegel calls the 'unconditioned absolute' universal (§129/89). This unconditioned universal is thus not itself something *other* than the one-sided, conditioned universals that make up the thing of perception. Rather, it arises through the self-undermining or self-negation *of* those one-sided, conditioned universals. That is to say, it emerges in the experience of the *dialectic* that is made necessary by the multiply one-sided object of perception.

The unconditioned universal, therefore, is a *dynamic* unity of opposites. It is a wholly self-relating *unity* that has nothing outside it; but it emerges through, and so incorporates, the dialectical *slippage* of one aspect of the thing into its very opposite. This unconditioned universal emerges in the experience of perception: it is the result to which perception is led, logically, by its own conception of truth. Perception, however, does not affirm this result but seeks to avoid the contradiction at the heart of its truth by means of what Hegel calls the 'sophistry' of the 'in so far as'. Perception insists on keeping things clear and distinct: the thing is, indeed, one and many, separate and related to others, but in so far as it is one, it is not the other, and vice versa. As Hegel writes, 'the sophistry of perception seeks to save these moments from their contradiction, and it seeks to lay hold on the truth, by distinguishing between the *aspects*, by sticking to the "also" and to the "in so far"' (§130/90). Logically, however – if not in the eyes of perception itself – this sophistry proves to be 'empty' and futile. Perception may disavow the result of its experience, just as sense-certainty does, but this does not prevent its own experience leading necessarily to that result.

Perception, Hegel writes, takes itself to be a 'solid, realistic consciousness' of the world (§131/90). It has in mind not the indeterminate immediacy of sense-certainty, but the concrete realm of things with manifold properties. Nonetheless, in Hegel's view, perception is governed by abstract, *one-sided* universals that it seeks to hold apart, such as one and many, indifferent difference and exclusive difference, being for self and being for another. Perception is at the mercy of such abstract universals throughout its experience: it is, Hegel says, the 'play of these *abstractions*' (§131/90). These abstract universals or 'categories' are not imported into perception by an overly logicizing phenomenologist, but are inherent in the way perception takes up the truth and are *discovered* by the phenomenologist in the experience of perception.

Due to the presence of these abstractions in perception, and to the fact that perception endeavours to preserve the self-identity and non-contradictoriness of things, Hegel refers to perception at the end of his account as 'perceptual understanding' (*wahrnehmender Verstand*) (§131/91). By contrast, the understanding that follows perception in the *Phenomenology* will not merely be perceptual, but will take up and affirm the unconditioned universal that emerges in the experience of perception.

In the *Phenomenology*, perception is the first shape of consciousness that distinguishes between the *truth* and the object of immediate certainty. Perception endeavours to keep that truth as free of contradiction as possible; indeed, it is led to do so *by* its conception of the truth, and so has no choice in the matter. The lesson that emerges from the experience of perception, however, is that *contradiction* proves to be intrinsic to truth. The idea that truth can be kept free from contradiction thus proves to be a *deception* – one from which perception is unable to free itself. By contrast, understanding will be governed by a different conception of truth. Its task will be not to avoid contradiction at all costs, but to discover, in a way that perception cannot comprehend, what a world that *incorporates* contradiction actually looks like.

Study questions

1 How does perception differ from sense-certainty?
2 Why does the object of perception prove to be contradictory in perception's third experience?

Force and understanding

The object for sense-certainty is immediate being: *this*. By contrast, the object of perception combines being with its *negation*, and thereby proves to be a one-sided, conditioned universal. The unconditioned universal is a unity that arises through the *self-negation* of those one-sided universals. This unconditioned universal is what the understanding takes to be the truth. Our first task as phenomenologists is to render explicit what this truth involves, what the object must be for the understanding itself.

The concept of force

Hegel first reminds us that the unconditioned universal unites the two aspects of the perceivable thing. Indeed, it is nothing but 'the unity of being-for-self and being-for-another', of the thing's self-identity and its other-relatedness (§134/94). These two aspects form a *unity* because they *pass over* into one another in the experience of perception.

Perception itself turned its back on this unity. For the understanding, however, the unity of the two aspects is explicit and thoroughgoing. They thus constitute both the *content* of the unconditioned universal and the *form* that they take in that universal. On the one hand, 'being-for-self and being-for-another are the *content* itself' (§134/94) – the moments that constitute the unconditioned universal. On the other hand, these moments are present in that universal both *as* they are for themselves and *as* they are in relation to one another. The unconditioned universal thus unites the being-for-self (or independence) and the other-relatedness of the perceivable thing in such a way that each aspect of the thing is what it is *for itself*, even as it relates to and passes over into its opposite. Understanding focuses first on this 'passing over' or 'transition' (*Übergehen*) (§135/95), since that is what first distinguishes the unconditioned from the conditioned universal, and it then takes account of the fact that each moment is also 'for itself', and so really different and separate from the other.

For perception, the thing for itself is *one* unified thing; in its relations to other things, however, it exhibits a *manifold* of different properties (see p. 54, above). The unconditioned universal must thus itself be the unity of the oneness *and* the manifold character of the perceivable thing. It is, however, a *dynamic* unity in which one aspect of the thing negates itself and *passes over* of its own accord into its opposite. Understanding is still conscious of perceivable things with manifold properties, therefore, but it discerns in them a dynamism from which perception itself shrinks back.

So how, precisely, does understanding conceive of the different aspects of the thing? Understanding starts, in Hegel's account, from the idea of the thing as 'medium'. As such a medium, the thing is simply a collection of many 'independent matters [*Materien*]' or properties and in this respect lacks genuine unity or being-for-self. From this point of view, therefore, there is nothing to the thing over and above the matters that make it up: 'the *independence* of these matters is nothing else than this medium' (§136/95). At the same time, the matters are not just disconnected from one another, but together constitute *this* collection of matters: they co-exist in *this* space rather than that one. In so doing, these matters all occupy the *same* 'here and now': they 'are each where the other is'. As such, however, they are no longer wholly *independent* of one another; rather, as Hegel puts it, they 'mutually interpenetrate' one another (and in that sense are 'absolutely porous'). Now the thing lacked unity and being-for-self precisely because it was merely a collection of *independent* matters; to the extent that the independence of those matters is *negated* or 'sublated' (*aufgehoben*), therefore, the thing must be *one* unified thing after all. Through their co-existence, therefore, the independent matters that constitute the thing-as-medium, or thing-as-bundle, reduce themselves to a unity and thereby constitute *one* thing that exists 'for itself' (§136/95).

The thing is one thing, however, only because the *matters* that make it up occupy the same 'here and now'. The unity of the thing, in other words, is nothing beyond the *co-existence* of those matters. This means that the thing is not really one unified thing after all, but is in truth a collection of matters and properties that are *independent* of one another. Yet, as we have seen, by co-existing in the same space, those independent matters immediately reduce themselves to moments of one unified thing.

In this way, Hegel argues, each aspect of the thing passes over directly into its opposite: 'the matters posited as independent directly pass over into their unity, and their unity directly unfolds its diversity, and this once again reduces itself to unity' (§136/95). Perception would try to keep these two aspects of the thing distinct by saying that 'in this respect' the thing is one and 'in that respect' it is a manifold. Understanding, by contrast, affirms the dynamic *transition* of each aspect into its opposite and sees that transition as the true character of its object. For the understanding, therefore, a perceivable thing is not just a *thing*, but a site of *movement* – a movement in which the many matters in a thing are unfolded and 'dispersed' at the same time as they reduce themselves to moments of a fundamental *unity* in the thing. This movement, Hegel writes, 'is what is called *force* [*Kraft*]' by the understanding (§136/95). Note that this derivation of the concept of 'force' is wholly immanent. Force is discussed in the *Phenomenology*, not because it is a popular scientific concept, but because it is the necessary correlate of the understanding that affirms the result of perception's experience.

The movement in which the manifold matters in the thing manifest themselves is conceived by the understanding as the '*expression* of force'. By contrast, the unity to which those matters reduce themselves is conceived as 'force *proper*, force which has been *driven back* into itself' (§136/95). For the understanding, therefore, force must express itself: it must burst forth and display itself for all to see. In so doing, however, it must also draw back 'into itself' (*in sich*) and establish its own unity as a force. Note that these two aspects of force are moments of *one* process. Force is thus not something separate from its expression: it proves to be one unified, self-contained force *in* the movement of expressing itself.

For the understanding, therefore, there is no real difference – in the *object* – between force proper and its expression: force is one simple process or movement of self-expression. The difference between the moments of this process thus exists 'only in thought' (§136/95). For this reason, Hegel remarks, understanding at this stage is conscious only of the 'concept of force, not its reality'. This is not to deny that understanding regards force as something *objective*, as *there* in the things we perceive; but it regards objective force as a *unity* and does not see the difference between force and its expression as something real.

This understanding of force cannot, however, be sustained, since, as we noted above, the unconditioned universal is the unity of moments that are what they are *for themselves*, independently of one another, even as they pass over into one another and form a unity. This is what makes the unconditioned universal so contradictory: it is the unity of genuinely *different* moments that vanish into one another. Force, which is what the unconditioned universal has now proven to be, must, therefore, exhibit this genuine difference explicitly in itself. The difference between force and expression thus cannot exist 'only in thought', but must belong to *objective force* itself. For the understanding, therefore, there must be a *real difference* between force proper and its expression: 'force as such, or as driven back into itself, thus exists on its own account as an *exclusive one*, for which the unfolding of the matters is *another* subsisting essence; and thus two distinct independent aspects are set up' (§136/96). If the two aspects of force are to be genuinely different and independent of one another, however, the expression of force must be due to – or, as Hegel will say, be *'solicited'* by – something *other* than the force itself. Yet, at the same time, force is force proper only in expressing *itself*. We now have to consider the experience that is generated by this contradictory conception of force.

The first experience of understanding: the play of forces

Real, objective force, as the understanding now conceives it, is one unified force that is *'reflected into itself'* (§137/96). As such, it is self-contained and quite *separate* from the dispersed matters in which force finds expression. Such dispersed matters are in turn 'something other than force'. Yet, as we have seen, force must express itself. Since, however, the dispersed matters in which force finds expression are separate from force, they must approach force from the outside and *'solicit'* (*sollizitieren*) it to express itself (§137/97). Nonetheless, through such solicitation by something *else*, force expresses only *itself*.

Once force has expressed itself, it takes the form of a collection of independent matters, and so is no longer a single, unified force. Indeed, being such a self-contained unity is something quite *separate* from being a collection of matters. Yet in expressing itself, force must draw back into itself and establish itself as a unified force. Since, however, self-contained unity is separate from the dispersal of matters, such unity must approach dispersed, expressed force from the outside and solicit it to draw back into itself. And yet, even though it is solicited by another to do so, it is force *itself* that draws back into itself and establishes its unity as a force.

Force thus expresses itself and in so doing establishes itself as a unified force; but it must be *solicited* to do so and so cannot express itself and draw back into itself purely by itself. Force is force precisely in expressing itself, but it can be what it is only with the help of something else. This is because, even though force *must* express itself, there is now a real *difference* for the understanding between force proper and its expression.

Hegel goes on to note that what solicits force to express itself is itself a *force*. This is because it is first a collection of dispersed matters separate from force proper and then a self-contained unity separate from expressed force, and 'in such a way that each of these forms at the same time appears only as a vanishing moment' (§138/97). That is to say, that which is separate from and other than force is itself the *movement* from one state to another: the movement in which dispersed matters draw back into their unity and are then once again dispersed. As this movement, the other is itself a force. This second force performs its work of solicitation, therefore, by expressing itself and in so doing drawing back into its unity and self-containment.

The force animating perceivable things thus cannot be the force that it is all by itself, but must be solicited by *another* force to be itself. But, of course, since the second, soliciting, force is itself a force, it is subject to the same logic as the first and so must be *solicited* by the first in turn to express itself and thereby do its work of solicitation. Indeed, Hegel insists, each force 'solicits only in so far as the other solicits it to be a soliciting force' (§139/98). This reciprocal solicitation constitutes what Hegel calls the 'play' (or 'interplay') (*Spiel*) of forces.

Hegel notes that in this play each force, and each aspect of force, loses its separate identity and ceases being simply and immediately what it is: each passes over or 'vanishes' into its opposite. Force in its self-containment ceases being self-contained and *expresses* itself, but in so doing it immediately draws back *into* itself again. Furthermore, each force expresses *itself* only in so far as it is solicited to do so by the *other* force. Neither force, therefore, is simply itself, but each is itself only through the help of the other. In Hegel's own words, 'each *is* solely through the other, and what each thus is it immediately no longer is in being it' (§141/99).

In the play of forces, therefore, the separate aspects of force, and the two forces themselves, are 'only vanishing moments' – 'an immediate transition of each into its opposite'. This is not just how the phenomenologist conceives of force, but 'this truth becomes apparent to consciousness in its perception of the movement of force' (§140/99). Hegel's use of the term 'perception' (*Wahrnehmung*) here is significant. Strictly speaking, perception proper is incapable of discerning the movement of force, but sees only *things* before it. The understanding, by contrast, is conscious of force, rather than mere things. But understanding discerns the movement of force *in* perceivable things; indeed, it understands the matters or properties that constitute such things to be the expression of the force within them. In that respect, therefore, understanding remains an advanced form of perception. At the end of chapter two of the *Phenomenology*, Hegel describes perception as 'perceptual understanding' because it is governed by the abstract thoughts of the one and the many (or being-for-self and being-for-another) (§131/91). Now Hegel describes understanding itself as 'perception' because it sees force at work in perceivable things. It is clear, therefore, that in so far as understanding is aware of the play of forces, it does not yet have before it an object that belongs to the *understanding alone*. Hegel now points out, however, that through the play of forces understanding comes to be aware of a purely *intelligible* object.

The inner being of things

In the *concept* of force – force as it is initially understood – the difference between the moments involved – force proper and its expression – is undermined as each moment passes into, and so becomes one with, its opposite. In this way, force proves to be 'an immediate unity' of its two moments (§136/95). Yet this difference is also preserved in that unity, because force and expression become one by passing into *one another*. The *unity* of force is constituted by the *transition* of each moment into its other, but this transition into *one another* preserves their difference. The two moments of force and expression are, however, not really and substantially distinct, but differ only as moments of a single, *unified* self-expressing force. As Hegel puts it, therefore, the difference between them exists 'only in thought' (§136/95).

In the play of forces, by contrast, the difference between the elements involved – force and expression, soliciting and solicited force – is a real and substantial difference. The elements, initially at least, are separate from one another: each is what it is *for itself* (§141/99). The play of forces undermines the difference between the elements, since the functions of soliciting and being-solicited pass into one another. Yet the unity that emerges in this way is significantly different from the unity exhibited by the concept of force. In that unity, as we have just seen, the difference that is undermined is preserved in the transition of one into *the other*. In the play of forces, however, the transition of one element into its opposite means that the *real, substantial* difference between them disappears *altogether*. The distinct functions of soliciting and being-solicited become so thoroughly confused that there is no longer any *real* difference between them, or between the two forces involved, *at all*. The real difference between the elements in the play of forces is thus *not* preserved in the unity constituted by their transition into one another. As Hegel puts it, 'the realization of force is at the same time the loss of reality' (§141/100). The unity in the *concept* of force is a unity *of* different moments; by contrast, the unity that arises through the play of forces is one in which real difference vanishes altogether. Such unity is thus the thorough *negation* of real difference and independence.

In Hegel's view, the understanding cannot experience the play of forces except as their collapse into a unity or 'universality' (*Allgemeinheit*) (§141/100). In the process, however, the distinctive difference involved in that play – the *real* difference between the forces – vanishes altogether. The unity into which the forces collapse must, therefore, be one in which this difference is wholly absent: they 'collapse unresistingly into an *undifferentiated* unity' (§141/100). Such a unity *without difference* cannot, however, manifest itself *in* the play of forces itself. This is because that play is the interplay between forces that are, initially at least, really distinct and separate. By collapsing into an undifferentiated unity, therefore, the play of different forces collapses into something wholly other than itself. Such unity is thus necessarily located by the understanding *beyond* the play of forces itself.

For the understanding, then, the play of forces points towards a fundamental unity that is not manifest *in* that play. Forces are held by the understanding to be active within perceivable things; by locating unity beyond the play of forces, the understanding thus locates it beyond the realm of the perceivable. Undifferentiated unity thus constitutes 'the *inner* being of things' (*das Innere der Dinge*) that is beyond perception altogether and evident to the understanding alone (§142/100). Force is the first object of understanding, but it belongs to understanding that is still closely tied to perception; the inner being of things, by contrast, is a purely intelligible object and so the first object that belongs to the understanding exclusively.

This inner being is taken by the understanding to be the true object of its experience. It is the 'true essence of things' (§143/100) or, rather, what the play of forces within things is in truth. This truth is *not* manifest in that play of forces itself, but is what Hegel calls 'the *negative* of sensuously objective force' (§142/100). There is thus a sharp distinction for the understanding between the play of forces and the 'inner being of things'. Whereas the play is restless and dynamic – the perpetual vanishing of differences – the inner being of things is a simple undifferentiated unity *without* movement and dynamism. As Hegel puts it, 'what is *immediate* for the understanding is the play of forces, but what is the *true* for it is the simple inner world' (§148/103). In the initial concept of force, the two aspects of dynamism (or vanishing difference) and unity are perfectly fused, since force and expression constitute a unity *by* passing into one another; through the experience of the play of forces, however, those two aspects have come apart and are now held to be quite different – indeed, separate – from one another. The one characterizes the sensuous, perceivable world that is immediately present to consciousness; the other characterizes the 'supersensible', intelligible world that lies *beyond* what is perceivable (§144/101).

Note that Hegel does not endorse this division of the world into a 'here and now' and a 'beyond'. He simply shows how the understanding is led to divide the world in this way by its experience. For Nietzsche, the idea of a 'true world' is the product of a *'ressentiment'* against the world, or of a life-denying nihilism.[13] For Hegel, by contrast, understanding embraces the idea of the 'true world' quite simply because it is *understanding*.

Study questions

1 Why is force the object of understanding?
2 Why does the play of forces point back to the 'inner being' of things?

The second experience of understanding: appearance and law

The understanding takes the play of forces to be immediately present (even if it sees more in 'things' and 'forces' than mere immediacy).

It does not, however, take the inner being of things to be immediately present, but understands it to come to mind through the *mediation* of the play of forces: the understanding '*looks through this mediating play of forces into the true background of things*' (§143/100).

This play of forces, as we know, is more than the mere concept of force as such. It is the play of real forces that are really different from one another; but it is equally the interplay in which those differences undermine themselves and disappear before our very eyes. In Hegel's words, the play of forces is 'the developed *being* of force which, *for the understanding itself*, is henceforth only a *vanishing*' (§143/100). Through the play of forces, therefore, the differences between the forces and their various aspects turn out to be merely *apparent* differences, and the whole play itself proves to be a realm of '*appearance*' (*Erscheinung*). This does not mean that the understanding now completely denies the empirical reality of the world before it: it still takes itself to be confronted by perceivable things animated by forces. Yet it now believes that such things and forces are not simply what they first appear to be. Furthermore, they point back to a realm of intelligible 'inner being' which is different from them but also what they are *in truth*.

It is, however, only *by means* of the sphere of appearance that the inner being of things beyond appearance comes to consciousness. This fact directly determines the manner in which the understanding experiences that inner being. On the one hand, since the latter is taken to lie *beyond* appearance, it is understood to lack the moment of difference that characterizes appearance itself, indeed to lack all the different determinations that belong to the play of forces. In the inner of being of things there are *no* things and forces: 'it is merely the nothingness of appearance'. As such, the inner being of things is quite 'empty'. It is nothing but the bare inner unity or 'the simple universal' beyond appearance to which appearance itself points back (§146/102).

On the other hand, this inner being cannot be wholly other than, and separate from, the sphere of appearance, since 'it *comes from* the world of appearance'. Indeed, it is what the sphere of appearance *itself* is in its innermost being: 'the supersensible is the sensuous and the perceived posited as it is *in truth*' (§147/103). It is appearance *once again*, but this time understood as 'undifferentiated unity' (§141/100). In the inner being of things, therefore, the true nature of appearance itself becomes explicit. The sphere of appearance is the sphere in which differences disappear; they *truly* disappear, however, in the undifferentiated unity that constitutes the inner being of things; in that inner being, therefore, the true nature of appearance as the disappearance of difference becomes fully *manifest and apparent*.

This, I think, helps us comprehend Hegel's otherwise bewildering claim that the supersensible is '*appearance qua appearance*' (*Erscheinung, als Erscheinung*) (§147/103). The supersensible inner being of things is simply the sphere of appearance, understood fully and consistently *as* what it is, *as* the complete disappearance of differences. In this sense, it is the fully explicit 'appearance' *of* appearance, or appearance itself *as* appearance. Hegel is not indulging in deliberate paradox at this point (or, indeed, anywhere in the *Phenomenology*). He is drawing attention to a fundamental ambiguity in the understanding's conception of inner being: that being is the truth *in contrast* to appearance and also appearance *itself* as it is in truth. This ambiguity has a significant further consequence.

The understanding takes the inner being of things to be an empty 'undifferentiated unity' beyond appearance. What is prominent in this idea is the thought that the inner being is *different* from, and the *negation* of, appearance. By contrast, the thought that it is appearance *itself* as it is in truth – that there is some degree of identity between the inner being and appearance – is merely implicit. How can the understanding build this latter thought *explicitly* into its conception of inner being? It can do so by conceiving of inner being as explicitly manifesting within itself the distinctive feature of appearance itself.

What, then, is the distinctive feature of appearance (or the play of forces), the one that distinguishes it from the unity of inner being? It is, of course, *difference*. Various differences are undermined in the sphere of appearance, including that between soliciting and being-solicited and that between the two independent forces. The most general feature of appearance, however, is that it is the sphere of difference as such, difference that undermines itself whatever form it takes. As Hegel writes, 'what there is in this absolute flux is only *difference* as a *universal* difference, or as a difference into which the many antitheses have been resolved' (§148/104). By building the idea of *difference* into the inner being, therefore, the understanding 'fills out' its otherwise empty conception of the latter. Moreover, this allows it to think of the inner being explicitly as not just beyond appearance, but appearance *once again*.

The inner being of things is thus now to be understood to incorporate *difference* within itself. This newly conceived inner being remains something intelligible and retains the character of unity and universality. Yet it is now understood explicitly as appearance itself *in its truth*, as appearance itself as an *intelligible* unity. The name that Hegel gives to such an intelligible unity is *law* (*Gesetz*). The understanding thus takes the play of forces to point back, not just to an empty inner being, but to a supersensible realm of law that governs that play (§148/104).

Several things should be noted about the understanding's conception of law. First, law is introduced because the experience of the understanding makes it logically necessary (though Hegel draws his *examples* of laws of the understanding from history). Second, the idea of law combines the thoughts of unity *and* difference. A law, as the understanding conceives it, expresses the simple unity of different terms – a simple or 'universal difference' (§149/104). Another way to put this is to say that a law, as conceived by the understanding, expresses a simple, constant *relation* between different terms. This can be seen, for example, in Galileo's law of falling bodies to which Hegel later refers: according to this law, the *distance* travelled by a falling body is always proportional to the square of the *time* elapsed (so if a body falls y metres in 1 second, the distance it travels in 2 seconds is not $2y$, but rather $y \times 2^2$ or $4y$).[14]

Third, since law expresses a constant *unity* of different terms, it constitutes the *inner being* of things beyond the play of forces itself. In law we encounter, not the dynamic flux of appearance itself, but 'the *stable* image of unstable appearance' (§149/105). Yet, fourth, since law is precisely *appearance* in its truth, law cannot simply transcend such appearance, but must also be discernible *in* the play of forces itself. Inner unity can thus be found in the play of forces after all, but only in the form of law, which Hegel describes as the '*simple element [das Einfache] in the play of force itself*' (§148/104). The idea of law emerged for the understanding because the inner being of things had to be understood both as lying beyond appearance *and* as appearance once again, and the ambiguous status of law is expressed nicely in these lines: 'the *supersensible* world is an inert *realm of laws* which, though beyond the perceived world – for this exhibits law only through incessant change – is equally *present* in it and is its direct tranquil image' (§149/105).

Law and the concept of law (or simple force)

The second experience of the understanding leads to the idea that the true object of understanding is *law* that is both beyond and present in appearance. This, however, is only part of the story: for the understanding recognizes that, although law is present *in* appearance, there is more to the latter – and so to the play of forces – than law. Law is the constant unity of, or the regular relation between, different elements that governs appearance. Yet appearance is also the realm in which nothing is constant, because differences undermine themselves and everything turns into its opposite – the space of 'absolute flux' (§149/104). Accordingly, 'appearance retains *for itself* an aspect which is not in the inner world' (§150/105).

Yet the law is precisely the law *of* appearance; it is not a free-floating, wholly transcendent principle, but the intelligible unity found *in* the play of forces. The law cannot, therefore, preserve its own identity unalloyed, but must reflect the character of the realm of appearance to which it belongs. It must reflect the fact that appearance is distinguished by *change*, not just unity and stability. Accordingly, Hegel writes, 'the law always has a different actuality in different circumstances' (§150/105). There cannot, therefore, just be *one* simple, stable law governing appearance, but there must be 'indefinitely *many* laws' governing the different circumstances that arise (including Galileo's law that governs falling terrestrial bodies and Kepler's laws that govern the motion of planets).[15] We saw above that a single, unified force must express itself in a multiplicity of different properties. Now we see that the unity of law must be broken up into many different laws, because law is present in, and gives expression to, a sphere that is not itself stable and unified. Each of these laws, however, governs a different *stable* feature of that changing world.

Yet this is not the end of the story, either: for the plurality of laws 'contradicts the principle of the understanding for which, as consciousness of the simple inner world, the true is the implicitly universal *unity*' (§150/105). The understanding seeks to restore the unity of law by reducing the plurality of laws to a single, thoroughly *universal* law that governs all phenomena equally – a law that governs the movement of the planets *and* falling bodies on earth. Just as the play of *forces* points back to the undifferentiated unity of inner being, therefore, so, too, the many different *laws* governing that play point back to a single, universal – and in that sense, undifferentiated – law. The many laws do not, however, vanish of their own accord into the one law underlying them, because, unlike forces, they are *stable* and *unified* in themselves (even though they are different from one another) and so do not undermine or 'negate' themselves. It is the understanding, therefore, that reduces them to a simple unity.

The understanding thus sees the truth as a simple unity for a *second* time. The universal law that is thereby formulated by the understanding is the law of *'universal attraction'* or gravitation (§150/105).[16] Hegel points out that this law is unlike any other, because it expresses what he calls *'the mere concept of law itself'* (§150/106). What exactly does this mean? It means that this law is not just one law in contrast to *other*, more limited laws, but expresses the very idea or 'concept' that all things and forces are subject to law *at all*. This is due to the utter generality of the law.

The law of universal attraction states that everything is connected by attraction to, and in that sense forms a unity with, everything else, but in such a way that everything preserves its difference from everything else, too. As Hegel puts it, *'everything has a constant difference from other things'* (§150/106). Yet this is to say that everything has a constant relation to everything else. To say that all things have a *constant relation* to one another, however, is precisely to say that the relations between them all *conform to law*. The law of universal attraction is thus unlike any other, because, as well as stating its own principle, it also states that everything is *'in its own self* conformable to law [*gesetzmäßig*]' as such.

By formulating the law of universal attraction the understanding recovers the unity that was lost in the idea that there are many laws. At the same time, it gains a new understanding of the 'inner being' of things: for it now understands that inner being to be the *lawfulness* of things that finds expression *in* law. Such inner being is distinguished by the understanding from, and indeed placed *beyond*, the law in which it finds expression. Accordingly, Hegel argues, the understanding attributes a *unity* to that inner being that exceeds that found in law itself. Law is the unity, or constant relation, between *different* things. The inner being of things, by contrast, is now conceived by the understanding as the 'absolutely *simple*', or '*simple unity*', to which the differences present in law point back, but in which they are not present as such (§151/106). This unity is understood to be the true inner being that expresses itself in law as the relation between different elements. As we have seen, the understanding has to understand the play of forces to be governed by the law of universal attraction. We have now also seen that this law is itself the expression of a more fundamental inner being. That inner being can thus be regarded as what grounds the law and makes it necessary. As Hegel puts it, 'this unity is the inner *necessity* of the law' (§151/106).

This inner unity expresses itself in law in which *different* elements are related. As we know, however, unity that expresses itself as difference is conceived by the understanding as *force*. The understanding thus takes the law governing appearance to be grounded in, and to be the expression of, force that is purely intelligible (§152/107). It is thanks to such force that things behave lawfully. This force, however, lacks the dynamism that has been associated with force so far. Force, conceived as the dynamic expression of itself in an interplay with another force, is now regarded as belonging – with perceivable things – to the realm of appearance. The *true* inner being of such appearance, by contrast, is a quite abstract force characterized by simplicity, unity and, as we shall see, utter *indifference* to the law in which it is expressed. When the understanding generalizes this new conception of force and law, and conceives of all laws, not just the law of universal attraction, as grounded in abstract force, it becomes the activity of *explanation* (*Erklären*).

Hegel's account of law is certainly complicated and tortuous. There is, however, a clear logic to it that, with patience, is not too hard to understand. The thing to bear in mind is that the idea of law combines two thoughts: (a) that intelligible inner being lies *beyond* appearance; and (b) that such inner being is appearance *itself*, as it is in truth. The first thought brings with it the idea of unity, the second the idea of difference. The concept of law arises by simply combining these two thoughts: law is a simple, stable, intelligible *unity* of the *different* moments in the play of forces (such as space and time). Since law remains different from appearance, appearance retains an element of dynamism and change that is at odds with the constancy of law. Yet, since law is also present *in* appearance, it must itself be affected *by* that very element of change. Law must, therefore, take several *different* forms, according to different circumstances. Consequently, the *unity* of law is lost. It is recovered in the idea of a single universal law that supersedes all the different laws. At this point, we have not just a unity beyond appearance, but a unity beyond the many different *laws* that are present in appearance. This universal law is, however, itself ambiguous, since it is, on the one hand, a law, and, on the other, the expression of the very 'concept of law', the very idea that things conform to law at all. Such inner conformity to law, or lawfulness, is then itself understood as the true inner being of things. As such, it is placed beyond the law and construed as the simple unity that makes the law necessary. Since this unity expresses itself in law, which itself connects *different* terms, it is conceived as the simple abstract *force* that grounds the law. Such force renders things lawful in their behaviour and is expressed in the law that governs them.

The understanding arrives at this point by pursuing the idea of the *unity* of inner being above all. Such unity is placed first beyond the play of forces, then beyond the many laws, and then beyond the difference within law itself. In this way, the understanding works its way through different conceptions of inner being until it reaches one that is *utterly simple and unified*, namely simple abstract force. Such force is thus the logical outcome of understanding's quest for *undifferentiated unity*, a quest to which it was committed by the complete disappearance of real differences in the play of forces. As we are about to see, however, this quest for simplicity and unity leads to the idea that the dynamic *vanishing of differences* actually belongs to the intelligible 'inner being' of things itself.

Explanation

Abstract force, for Hegel, is the most distinctive object of the understanding. It blends the first object of understanding – *force* – with the second – inner, undifferentiated *unity*. The activity in which the idea of such abstract force is employed is thus itself the most distinctive activity of understanding, namely *explanation* (*Erklären*). The understanding takes explanation to render *laws* fully intelligible. In Hegel's view, however, such explanation renders nothing intelligible at all. The problem is that the concept of force that has now emerged in the experience of the understanding is too abstract to do any real explanatory work.

Understanding takes such force to be completely *simple*, but conceives of law as a relation between *different* elements: '*simple electricity*, e.g., is *force*; but the expression of difference falls within the *law*' (§152/107). Since the force itself is simple and undifferentiated, however, the difference expressed in the law is not contained in the force itself. This means that, although force is held to ground the law and make it necessary, nothing in the force itself requires the law to connect *these* different elements in *this* specific way. Consequently, 'necessity is here an empty word'. Force contains the inner necessity of the law, but it is impossible to say why; all one can say is that 'force *must*, just *because* it *must*, duplicate itself in this way' (§152/107).

The first forces that understanding discerns in things are understood to be dynamic and to express themselves immediately. By contrast, the simple, abstract force that understanding now has in view is utterly inert: it does not differentiate itself *into* the elements contained in the law, but simply underlies that law as its ground. As such, '*simple force* is indifferent to its law' (§152/107). As a consequence, the different elements that are related in the law are also indifferent to one another. This is because they show no sign of having originated in *one* force (and cannot do so, because no connection between them is evident in the force that expresses itself in the law concerned). Accordingly, in the laws governing motion, 'space is thought of as able to be without time, [and] time without space' (§153/108). The two are not understood to be intrinsically connected, in contrast to what Hegel will argue in his philosophy of nature.[17]

There is a further problem with the process of explanation: force is so simple and abstract that it has no *content* of its own beyond what is expressed in the law that it grounds. How, then, can one force (such as electricity) be distinguished from another (such as gravity)? Only through the difference between the *laws* that the two forces ground. Thus, all that can be said about the force grounding a law is that it is the simple unity that expresses itself *in that law*. The understanding thus distinguishes force from law in order to explain the law, but immediately undermines that difference by holding both force and law to have 'the *same* content, the *same* constitution' (§154/109).

The understanding acknowledges that force and law have the same content – that a force takes its content from its law – and so accepts that the difference between them is not a substantial difference in the matter at hand. As Hegel puts it, understanding distinguishes between a force and its law, but 'at the same time *expressly states [ausdrückt]* that the difference is not *a difference belonging to the thing [Sache] itself*' (§154/109). Nonetheless, understanding thinks that a law *is explained* by the force that grounds it. For Hegel, however, nothing is explained in this way, but such 'explanation' is purely 'tautological': understanding just thinks one and the same object twice, once as law and once as force. By grounding a known law in an underlying force, understanding 'pretends to say something different from what has already been said, [yet it] really says nothing at all but only repeats the same thing' (§155/109–10). The scientist who explains the law of gravity by reference to the simple force of gravity, therefore, does not actually *explain* anything at all.

Yet Hegel may not, and does not, simply dismiss the activity of explanation out of hand. Rather, he points out that it exhibits a *movement* that has been missing from both the understanding and its intelligible object since the latter first emerged as the 'inner being of things'. The play of forces is the dynamic sphere in which differences undermine themselves and so turn into their opposites. By contrast, the inner being of things is characterized by 'undifferentiated *unity*', found in its purest form in the simple force that underlies law. Hegel now points out, however, that by explaining law through force, but at the same time declaring them to have 'the *same* content', the understanding *itself* becomes the movement of drawing distinctions that are not distinctions and so are immediately their own opposites. The 'movement' (*Bewegung*) of understanding 'posits a difference which is not only *not* a difference for us, but one which the movement itself cancels as a difference' (§155/110).

We phenomenologists thus now discern *in the understanding* the dynamic undermining of differences, or 'change' (*Wechsel*), that was earlier taken to characterize the realm of appearance. Furthermore, the understanding itself comes to share the conception we now have of it: 'our consciousness . . . has passed over . . . into the *understanding*, and it experiences change there' (§155/110). Understanding initially takes itself merely to be explaining why there are laws; but it proceeds to recognize in such explanation the *movement* of drawing and undermining distinctions that it had previously seen only in appearance.

Understanding does not, however, just acquire a new conception of itself; it also sees in that new conception – or 'concept of the understanding' – the key to a new understanding of the *'inner being of things'* (§156/110). More precisely, it sees in that conception the key to understanding the *true* inner being, or law, of *appearance*. The first laws were at odds with the flux of appearance, since they presented a *'stable* image of unstable appearance' (§149/105). In the movement of drawing and undermining distinctions, however, the understanding now has a new conception through which to comprehend the law of appearance. This new conception of inner being builds dynamic flux *into* law itself and thereby produces a law that accounts for the *instability* of appearance.

Through its experience of explanation, therefore, understanding is led to a deeper comprehension of the law of appearance. As Hegel puts it, the understanding *'learns* that it is the *law of appearance itself* that differences arise which are no differences' (§156/110). This new law goes beyond the simplicity, constancy and unity that the understanding has so far taken to be its true object. Nonetheless, this new law is itself the true object of understanding, because it renders explicit what is implicit *in* that simplicity and unity.

The initial inner being is not just a truth beyond appearance, but what appearance itself is in truth. Yet conceived as law and then as simple abstract force, that inner being conspicuously *lacks* the dynamism and flux of appearance. In this sense, it is not fully and explicitly appearance *once again*, appearance *qua appearance*. In the new law of appearance, by contrast, the dynamism and flux characteristic of appearance are explicitly built into the law, for the law makes it necessary that 'differences arise which are no differences' and so *undermine themselves*. What the first inner being is implicitly, therefore, the new law is explicitly; or, as Hegel puts it, in the new law 'the inner world is completed as appearance' (§157/111).

This new law is no longer simply a principle of constancy, but accounts for the *flux* and *dynamism* of appearance. It is, indeed, still a principle of constancy, since it is an intelligible, supersensible object of understanding, like all law; but it accounts for the 'constancy of inconstancy' in appearance (§156/111).[18] In this new law, therefore, the *dynamism* that characterizes the first object of understanding – force as self-expression – and the intelligible *unity and constancy* that characterize the second object – 'inner being' – are brought together explicitly in one thought. This new law is what Hegel calls the law of 'the *inverted* world' (§157/111).

Study questions

1 Why is the play of forces governed by law?
2 In what respect is explanation tautological?

The third experience of understanding: the inverted world

Hegel's account of the inverted world is notoriously complex and full of strange examples. The idea of the inverted world is, however, one to which understanding is taken by the logic of its own experience. It is not the fanciful object of an understanding gone astray, but the object that *genuine* understanding must come to recognize.

The law of the inverted world states that 'differences arise which are no differences' (§156/110). Indeed, this law dictates generally that *all* things turn into, or prove to be, their own *opposites*. This new law is clearly opposed to, and the inversion of, the first law governing appearance. That first law dictates that there is a *constant* difference or relation between phenomena (e.g. the distance travelled by a falling body is always proportional to the square of the time elapsed). The new law, by contrast, dictates that everything in the realm of appearance is *inconstant and unstable*. 'The law was, in general, like its differences, that which remains selfsame'; now, however, the law states that 'the selfsame' and 'what is not selfsame' are both 'really the opposites of themselves' (§157/111).

According to the new law, therefore, that which is stable and self-identical under the *first* law must turn into, or prove to be, its opposite. Hence, 'what in the law of the first world is sweet, in this inverted in-itself [*Ansich*] is sour, what in the former is black is, in the other, white' (§158/112). These particular examples are somewhat obscure, but another example shows that the law of the inverted world is the product of a more *profound* understanding of things than we have encountered so far, rather than a more *absurd* understanding. According to the first law, Hegel writes, revenge on an enemy is 'the supreme satisfaction of the injured individuality'.

I have been harmed by another, so I meet like with like and seek to harm, or even destroy, the other in return. According to the new law, however, this first law *'turns itself* . . . into its opposite': 'the reinstatement of myself as essential through the destruction of the alien individuality is turned into self-destruction' (§158/112). In other words, I bring about my own downfall by the pursuit of revenge. Through its insight into the law of the inverted world, therefore, the understanding discovers what Hegel himself (in his lectures on aesthetics) will declare to be the principle of *tragedy*.[19] Indeed, such understanding begins to glimpse the principle of *dialectic* at work in the world.[20] This new understanding thus not only takes itself to be more profound than any other, but is recognized by Hegel, too, to be insightful.

Note that this new understanding no longer draws a clear distinction between law, which is intelligible and supersensible, and appearance. The first law was present in appearance but also clearly distinct from it, since the dynamism of appearance was at odds with the constancy of law. Nothing in appearance is at odds with the new law, however, since that law grounds the very dynamism and inconstancy of appearance itself. In that sense, the new law undermines the previous distinction, or opposition, between appearance and the intelligible inner being of things. Nonetheless, the new law remains opposed to *the first law*, since it is precisely the inverting of that law. The new law states that a thing's identity under the first law will always prove to be the opposite of itself. It is in this way, indeed, that the new law grounds the dynamism and change in the realm of appearance. Thus, even though the new understanding no longer sees a clear distinction between law and appearance, it does not encounter a *single, unified* world, because it understands appearance to be governed by *two* laws, one of which is the opposite of the other.

Hegel points out that this distinction between the laws can also be understood 'superficially' as the distinction between two quite *separate* spheres, one of which – the inverted world – is the true, inner world that lies *beyond* the other. According to this superficial understanding, therefore, the inverted world would be one in which things are *truly* or *inwardly* what they are, as opposed to what they merely *appear* to be in the world governed by the first law: 'what tastes sweet is *really*, or *inwardly* in the thing, sour', or 'an action which in the world of *appearance* is a crime would, in the *inner* world, be capable of being really good (a bad action may be well-intentioned)' (§159/112–13). By understanding the two laws in this way, however, consciousness would reintroduce the very opposition that is undermined by the law of inversion: for, as we have just noted, 'such antitheses of inner and outer, of appearance and the supersensible, as of two different kinds of actuality, we no longer find here' (§159/113). Indeed, consciousness would fall back into a way of thinking that is reminiscent of *sensuous perception*, since it is perception that typically seeks to keep things separate from one another. This explains Hegel's otherwise puzzling injunction that we should eliminate from the idea of inversion 'the *sensuous* idea of fixing the differences in a different sustaining element' (§160/114).

We should avoid such a superficial 'sensuous' separation of the two laws and worlds because, as we have seen, the law of inversion itself undermines the clear distinction between the spheres of inner truth and appearance. Indeed, the law of inversion undermines the very idea that there are *two* opposed laws *at all*. This is because the law of inversion actually encompasses the first law within itself. After all, the law of inversion does not simply put the first law out of order, but states that whatever something is, *according to the first law*, turns itself into its opposite. The world governed by the law of inversion thus *includes* the world governed by the first law. Accordingly, the inverted world is at the same time the opposite or 'inversion' of itself: 'it is itself and its opposite in one unity' (§160/114). There is in truth, therefore, just *one* world. This world is a world of law, and so is an intelligible, inner world, known only by the understanding; yet it is one in which 'all the moments of appearance are taken up into the inner world' (§161/114), that is, in which the *movement* of appearance is enshrined in law itself. Indeed, this intelligible world of law coincides with and incorporates the realm of appearance. The dynamic structure of this world is that of change and contradiction: the 'repulsion of the selfsame, as selfsame, from itself, and the likeness of the unlike as unlike' (§160/114).

If we are to be true to the experience of the understanding, therefore, we must move beyond the idea that there are *two* laws, one of which is the *inversion* of the other, and we must take the object of consciousness to be *one* simple process in which differences arise and immediately undermine themselves. As Hegel puts it, 'we have to *think* pure change' or '*contradiction*' as such (§160/114). When we do so, he writes, we think of the object of consciousness as '*infinity*' (*Unendlichkeit*). Infinity thus proves ultimately to be the *true* object of understanding.

From consciousness to self-consciousness

Over two pages Hegel gives a detailed account of infinity, which he describes as 'the absolute concept' and also as 'the simple essence of life' (§162/115). The core of the idea, however, is set out at the start of §163: infinity is 'this absolute unrest of pure self-movement, in which whatever is determined in one way or another, e.g. as being, is rather the opposite of this determinateness' (116). Yet infinity is not just the *vanishing* of different determinations into their opposites, but also the *unity* that is thereby constituted. In infinity, therefore, the idea of a dynamic unity of opposed moments, which characterized 'unconditioned absolute universality' (§129/89), and then took the form of force, becomes the *intelligible* object of consciousness. Dynamism and unity were fused in the concept of force; they then fell apart with the distinction between appearance and inner being (or law); they were then brought back together again in the law of inversion, which captures the 'constancy of inconstancy' in appearance (§156/111). When the law of inversion is itself conceived as the unity of itself and its opposite (namely the first law), it is conceived as intelligible 'infinity'. The idea of infinity thus renders fully explicit what was present in the idea of force at the start of the chapter and is the proper object of *true understanding*. Note, however, the significant difference between such force and infinity. Force came to be understood as one of *two*, each of which solicits the other to express itself; by contrast, infinity is the *single*, autonomous process of generating and undermining differences and thereby integrating them into a unity, or 'pure self-movement' (§163/116). This, indeed, is why infinity, but *not* force as such, constitutes 'the essence of life'. (It goes without saying that the simple force that grounds law cannot be equated with life, since it is so abstract.)

Hegel points out that, implicitly, infinity has been 'from the start the soul of all that has gone before' (§163/116): it was implicit in the very concept of force and was then displayed by the play of forces, too. In neither case, however, was it an explicitly *intelligible* object. Hegel maintains that infinity frees itself from the play of forces, and so 'first freely stands forth', in and as the movement of *explanation*. Explanation exhibits the structure of infinity, because it is the movement of drawing a distinction between force and law, and then *undermining* it again by declaring force to have the same content as its law. In this case, however, infinity is not the object of understanding, but the movement of understanding itself. Infinity finally becomes the intelligible *object* of consciousness when the latter recognizes that there are not two laws and two worlds but just one world in which differences arise and immediately negate themselves into a unity. And at that point, Hegel claims, consciousness is no longer consciousness *tout court*, but *self-consciousness* (§163/116).

Why should this be? The answer is clear: when consciousness knows its object to be infinity, it sees in that object the very movement that, as explanation, it already knows *itself* to be. Hegel noted earlier that understanding does not recognize itself in its initial object (which proves to be force) (§133/93) or in the inner being beyond appearance (§146/102). It does, however, recognize itself in the infinity that confronts it; indeed, it sees in that object *nothing but* the process of producing and undermining distinctions that it knows itself to be. In the inner world as it is now conceived, therefore, 'the understanding experiences only *itself*' and so is *self-conscious* (§165/118). There is an element of self-awareness in both sense-certainty and perception, and a degree of self-enjoyment to be found in explanation taken by itself (§163/117).[21] Neither, however, constitutes self-consciousness proper. Self-consciousness proper is achieved only when I see nothing but *myself* in the *object* that confronts me.

Note that self-consciousness is *itself* the movement of infinity, insofar as it is the distinguishing of two items – itself and the object – that it knows not to be distinct: 'consciousness is for its own self, it is a distinguishing of that which contains no difference, or *self-consciousness*' (§164/117–18). Self-consciousness arises, therefore, when consciousness first knows *itself* to be the movement of infinity, and then comes to know the object to be the very same movement, and in so doing sees the difference between its object and itself disappear. This means that self-consciousness is possible, at least in the *Phenomenology*, only for a consciousness that has thoroughly generalized the idea that *differences undermine themselves*. Thus, neither sense-certainty, nor perception, nor the understanding that is conscious of a difference between forces, between appearance and 'inner being' or between laws, is capable of self-consciousness. Self-consciousness arises only when understanding has *infinity* as its object and sees only *itself* therein.

At this point, however, we need to notice a tension in the final paragraphs of chapter three that I have ignored so far. As I have argued, if understanding is true to its experience and its own law of inversion, then the object of consciousness should be understood as infinity. Moreover, when infinity is 'finally an object for consciousness, as *that which it is*, consciousness is thus *self-consciousness*' (§163/116). This suggests that consciousness *becomes* self-consciousness, as it gains a clear conception of the nature of infinity. That is how I have presented the transition to self-consciousness above. Yet Hegel also suggests very strongly that understanding does *not* actually become self-consciousness itself. This is because 'the understanding falls short of [*verfehlt*] infinity as such' (§164/117). This in turn can only be because it preserves the *difference* between the law of inversion and the first laws, and so fails to embrace fully what is stated by that law of inversion, namely that 'differences arise *which are no differences*' (§156/110).

Hegel does not comment further on why the understanding should fail in this way, but the reason, in my view, is this: for all its insight into the vanishing of differences, understanding proper remains tied to the idea of *difference* as such. Understanding initially differs from perception by affirming the dynamism in things, the passage of opposites into one another. It acquires a purely intelligible object, however, when it formulates the idea of 'inner being' that lies beyond the dynamic play of forces. Understanding becomes understanding *proper*, therefore, by looking beyond one point of view to a *different* one that it takes to be more profound. Indeed, this act of distinguishing what is more profound and true from what is less so defines proper understanding.[22] Accordingly, such understanding preserves the distinction between its *two* laws, even when it has undermined the distinction between law and appearance, and so falls short of infinity as such.

Hegel suggests that the understanding also slips into that 'superficial' conception of the law of inversion that he earlier warned us to avoid, and so takes this law to mean that the *inner* nature of things is the inversion of their *apparent* character. Insofar as it does so, it apportions the differences between the first and the second laws to 'two substantial elements' and in this way invests those laws with a separateness that is reminiscent of sensuous perception. Accordingly, Hegel writes, infinity is present to the understanding, not as such, but 'in a sensuous covering' (*in sinnlicher Hülle*) (§164/117).

If it is the case, however, that understanding never has unadorned infinity as its explicit object, but that consciousness is self-consciousness only when infinity is the 'object of consciousness, *as that which it is*' (§163/116), then it follows that understanding itself *never becomes self-consciousness*. How then does self-consciousness become the explicit topic of phenomenology? The answer, I think, is that the *phenomenologist* takes us forward from understanding proper to the *true* understanding, which is conscious of infinity '*as that which it is*'. He does so by rendering explicit what is implicit in the law of inversion and heeding the injunction to '*think contradiction*' (§160/114). Once understanding has 'become' true understanding in this way, it immediately proves to be self-consciousness for the reasons we have seen. Understanding proper does not, therefore, turn *directly* into self-consciousness (just as sense-certainty does not turn into perception). Self-consciousness is made necessary, however, by the immanent development of understanding's *own* experience.

We can, therefore, say that consciousness becomes self-consciousness, provided we bear in mind that this happens with the assistance of the phenomenologist. In this transition, there emerges a wholly new shape of consciousness, for which the true object is now no longer something *other* than consciousness, but consciousness *itself*. As Hegel puts it, whereas 'in the previous modes of certainty what is true for consciousness is something other than itself', for self-consciousness 'consciousness is to itself the truth' (§166/120). The next chapter of the *Phenomenology* will thus be concerned with '*what consciousness knows in knowing itself*' (§165/119).

Study questions

1. What is the difference between the first laws of the understanding and the law of inversion?
2. How is the transition made from understanding to self-consciousness?

Self-consciousness

Desire and recognition

Consciousness is certain of something *other* than it: a simple *this*, a perceivable thing, or a realm of forces subject to law. Experience then takes it to the point at which its object proves to be 'the absolute unrest of pure self-movement' or 'infinity', albeit 'in a sensuous covering' (§§163–4/116–17). Implicit in this consciousness of veiled infinity is the consciousness of infinity 'as *that which it is*', in which consciousness sees the movement it already knows *itself* to be. Implicit in consciousness, therefore, is *self*-consciousness (§163/116).

The phenomenologist now takes us forward to *explicit* self-consciousness. Yet he also has a further role to play, for he has to render explicit what is implicit in such self-consciousness itself. This task is carried out in §§166–84 and leads to the insight that self-consciousness must confront *another* self-consciousness. In §185 Hegel then starts to examine the experience that self-consciousness undergoes in its relation to another self.

Desire and life

Self-consciousness is intrinsically two sided, though it does not know why this is the case. We, however, do know: it is because self-consciousness is *consciousness* that has mutated – with our help – *into* self-consciousness. As self-consciousness, it sees itself, and itself alone, as the truth: it takes itself to be pure *self*-consciousness (§166/120). As consciousness, however, it remains conscious of the objects of sense-certainty, perception and understanding. It is thus not pure *self*-consciousness after all, but 'the whole expanse of the sensuous world is preserved for it' (§167/121). This places self-consciousness in a contradictory position: for it can enjoy pure *self*-consciousness only in relation to what is *other* than it.

How can self-consciousness resolve this contradiction? How can it be conscious of itself alone while also relating to something else? It can do so, Hegel maintains, only by starting with the other, actively removing it and in so doing *turning back* to itself. Self-consciousness, therefore, must be the 'return from *otherness*' (§167/121). As such, it proves to be not simply a state, but a *movement* – the movement that Hegel calls 'desire' (*Begierde*). As Judith Butler points out, Hegel's account of desire in the *Phenomenology* exercised enormous influence on twentieth-century French thinkers, such as Kojève, Sartre and Lacan.[23] That account itself, however, is remarkably brief. Hegel describes the movement of desire as follows.

Self-consciousness faces an other that belongs to the 'sensuous world'; but it regards this other as subordinate to it. That is to say, it sees that other as having no independent being of its own, but as being there *for* the self. Hegel expresses this idea by saying that the other, for self-consciousness, is a mere 'appearance' (*Erscheinung*) (§167/121). The other is not something illusory, but is a real perceivable thing; nor is it an appearance in contrast to 'inner being'. It is a mere 'appearance' because it is known to be there only for the sake of the *self*.

The 'truth' for self-consciousness – in contrast to this appearance – is self-consciousness itself, or what Hegel describes as the simple 'unity of self-consciousness with itself'. Desire, Hegel maintains, is the movement in which self-consciousness supplants appearance with this truth, the movement in which it actively *negates*, and does away with, the other and thereby returns to the simple identity or 'equality [*Gleichheit*] of itself with itself' (§167/121–2). Desire starts from what is other than the self, and ends, after the removal of this other, with the affirmation by the self of itself alone. It is thus the self's 'pursuit of identity' through the destruction of a given object.[24]

Insofar as it is conscious of itself alone self-consciousness is the 'motionless tautology of: "I am I"' (§167/121). This, however, is merely one moment of self-consciousness, because self-consciousness proper is the *movement* of returning to itself from – and through the negation of – what is other than it. Self-consciousness must be this movement because it is inextricably connected to *consciousness*. Self-consciousness is desire, therefore, not simply because it is a self-relating I – and not, as Terry Pinkard claims, because desires are given to it by *life*[25] – but because it is *self*-conscious in being *conscious* of what is other than it.

Although desire itself is not rooted in life, the *object* to which desire relates must be – or, rather, include – life. Desire thus takes itself to encounter not just inanimate but also living things. Self-consciousness does not know why this should be, but *we* do; it is thus '*for us*' that the object of self-consciousness *proves* to be life (though the object *is* life for self-consciousness itself) (§168/122). We know that, given the logical history of self-consciousness, the object that it confronts must include infinity as well as things and forces. Such infinity, Hegel says, is itself 'the simple essence of life' (§162/115). We see, therefore, that desire must confront *life*, as well as things.

Yet why does Hegel equate infinity with life? There are, I think, two reasons. First, unlike the expression of force, which is solicited by *another* force, infinity is 'pure self-movement' (§163/116) – the autonomous process of generating and undermining differences and thereby integrating them into a unity. In this sense, it has a 'life of its own'. Second, the differences within infinity are 'organic'. Organic differences are those that subsist only within their unity. Think of Aristotle's example of the hand in the *Politics*. The hand is different from the eye or ear; but it is the *distinct* organ it is only within the *unity* of the body: 'separate hand or foot from the whole body, and they will no longer be hand or foot except in name'.[26] Similarly, infinity is 'every difference, as also their supersession' into a unity (§162/115), so differences are 'present as *differences* in this *simple universal medium*', in this unity (§169/123). These two reasons are connected. The differences generated by infinity are organic *because* they belong to the latter's self-movement.

Since life is the autonomous process of *self*-movement, it exhibits a certain independence that desire does not encounter in mere perceivable things. Such independence mirrors that of self-consciousness: 'to the extent, then, that consciousness is independent, so too is its object' (§168/122). Yet self-consciousness does not fully affirm the independence of life, and so regards the latter as only implicitly independent. This is because it remains *desire* and continues to seek an unalloyed consciousness of itself through *negating* the life it encounters. Hegel goes on to note, however, that desire will be forced to affirm the independence of its object by its own *experience* (§168/122); but in so doing it will come to see in the object more than just life.

Recognition

Whether 'desire' is the best translation for the German '*Begierde*' is open to question. *Begierde* in the *Phenomenology* is not the feeling of wanting something I lack – it is not the desire for an *object* – but is more akin to greedy consumption that feeds my sense of self. (Contained within *Begierde* is the German word for greed, '*Gier*'.) *Begierde* also encompasses the activity of wantonly destroying things, for no other reason than to affirm one's sense of self. As Hegel puts it, desire is the movement through which self-consciousness 'destroys the independent object and thereby gives itself the certainty of itself' (§174/125). He now points out, however, that desire is not the be all and end all of self-consciousness, but is required by its own experience to mutate into a new shape.

Self-consciousness seeks to be certain of itself alone, but it can achieve such certainty only through negating something *other* than itself. This act of negation is not just a means to an end, a means that can be forgotten once the end is achieved, but it is inseparable from that end. This is because self-consciousness enjoys a large part of its sense of self in actually *carrying out* that act of negation: it knows that much of its identity consists *in* negating the other, *in* the very movement of desire itself. When self-consciousness completes the movement of desire, therefore, it both gains *and loses* its sense of self. It regains what it has lost, however, by carrying out another act of negation, and another, and so on. In this way, desire reproduces itself endlessly and moves from one other to another in search of that sense of self that comes only through actually negating something else.

In the process, Hegel argues, self-consciousness learns that the presence of something other is the *ineliminable* condition of its own sense of self. It can destroy this object, and this one, but it cannot do away with what is other and objective altogether, because it always needs an *other* in order to be and to satisfy itself. In this sense, Hegel writes, 'self-consciousness, by its negative relation to the object, is unable to supersede it' (§175/126). Since it is unable, finally, to do away with what is other, desire comes to regard otherness *as such* as irreducible, even if individual others can still be negated. Life has a degree of independence for desire, but desire now sees otherness as *irreducibly* independent. It is true that what is other is rendered irreducible *by* desire and its endless renewal of itself; but this does not make it any less irreducible *for* desire.

This experience requires desire to turn into a new shape of self-consciousness: for it must now gain its sense of self, not through negating the other, but through relating to an other that it knows to be genuinely independent. The new shape into which it mutates will still be *self*-consciousness, as we have come to know it. It will still seek an unalloyed sense of self, seek to be 'absolutely *for itself*' (§175/126). Consciousness of oneself will thus still require the *negation* of the other. The new shape will, however, seek to be conscious of itself alone in relation to an other that it holds to be *irreducible*. Yet this is surely contradictory. How can the self be conscious of itself *alone* in the presence of an irreducible other? This contradictory demand can be met, Hegel argues, if self-consciousness relates to another that independently *negates itself* but, in so doing, retains its independence by remaining in being: 'on account of the independence of the object', we are told, self-consciousness 'can achieve satisfaction only when the object itself effects the negation within itself' (§175/126).

The only object that can negate itself in this way and still preserve its independence, Hegel maintains, is *consciousness*. Life 'negates itself', since it *dies* through simply being alive; but in so doing 'it ceases with its distinctive difference to be what it is'. When it dies, the living organism loses the independence it has *as life* and so does not remain 'independent in this negativity of itself' (§176/127). Consciousness, by contrast, can negate or disavow every feature of itself and nonetheless *remain* aware of itself as an irreducible, independent self. Consciousness can do this by denying that it is defined by its age, sex or natural abilities – or even, like Descartes in the first *Meditation*, that it is tied to a body – and becoming conscious of itself as a pure, abstract I, or what Hegel calls the 'genus as such' (*Gattung als solche*) (§175/126). By negating itself in this way, consciousness becomes abstractly *self*-conscious. Accordingly, Hegel concludes, '*self-consciousness achieves its satisfaction only in another self-consciousness*'.[27]

Self-consciousness, therefore, is required by the experience of desire to relate to another self. Note that this relation is made necessary, ultimately, by the fact that self-consciousness is inseparable from *consciousness* of what is other. Self-consciousness does not need another self to praise it or comfort it. It needs another self because only in this way can it learn the lesson of desire and relate solely to *itself* while relating to what is truly *other*. As Hegel puts it, 'only in this way does the unity of itself in its otherness become explicit for it' (§177/127).

The logically necessary result of the experience of desire is thus the *doubling* of self-consciousness (§176/126). There are, however, two problems with the way I have described the development of self-consciousness so far.

The first problem is this: is it enough for the other self-consciousness to be aware of itself as a pure I, to be 'for itself a genus' (§176/127)? Does that enable the first self-consciousness to satisfy itself? I am not sure that it does: for all it allows the first self to see in the other is *another* self-consciousness, *another* I. It does not allow it to see only *itself* in the other, to see itself *rather than* the other. Yet that is what is required here: self-consciousness, Hegel writes, is 'absolutely *for itself*' (§175/126). It would appear, therefore, that, in order to achieve a proper consciousness of *itself*, self-consciousness must confront another self that negates itself in a more radical way than we have described so far. The other self must negate itself in such a way that it sets itself aside and lets the first relate to itself alone.

The second problem is that the account I have given makes it hard to explain why Hegel begins section A of chapter four with the claim that self-consciousness exists 'only in being *recognized* [*als ein Anerkanntes*]' (§178/127). For it is unclear why the fact that the second self negates itself, so that it is 'for itself a genus', should make it necessary for it to *recognize* the first self. The introduction of the concept of recognition at this point is thus left unexplained. Given the importance of recognition for the rest of the *Phenomenology*, this is a serious problem.

We can avoid these two problems, however, if we look again at what it means for the second self-consciousness to 'negate itself', in particular if we look briefly at the account of such self-negation given by Hans-Georg Gadamer. He writes that the first self-consciousness can see itself in the other, only 'if this other is independent and grants that it does not exist in its own right, but rather that, in disregard of itself, it "is for another"'.[28] On this reading, the second self-consciousness not only conceives of itself as a pure I; it also presents itself to the first self as that which is *nothing for itself*, as that which is there not for its own sake but solely for the sake of the first self. This attributes a much stronger sense of self-negation to the second self-consciousness. This second self negates itself by reducing itself to nothing but a reflection of the first.[29]

It has to be said that Hegel's text does not provide clear evidence that this interpretation is right. However, this reading does make good sense of what Hegel says. It is now easy to understand how the first self-consciousness is 'absolutely for itself' in relation to the second: for the first self does not just confront *another* self that is 'for itself a genus', but it relates to a self that presents itself, independently, as no more than a mirror *for the first*. The first self in this relation needs to 'acknowledge [*kennen*] nothing other than itself',[30] therefore, because the second self 'disregards itself' in favour of the first and merely reflects the latter back to itself.

This stronger interpretation of self-negation also explains why Hegel describes the relation of the second self to the first as one of 'recognition'. The act whereby the second self negates itself – by turning itself into nothing but a reflection of the first self – just *is* the act whereby the second self recognizes the first. I recognize another, therefore, simply *by* turning myself into a mirror for that other. In my view, unless the second self's self-negation is understood in this way, the concept of recognition is left without explanation. A cornerstone of Hegel's *Phenomenology* would thus be introduced without any proper warrant.

Note that this derivation of recognition is purely phenomenological; it is not motivated by any moral, political or religious imperative. Recognition is made necessary by the fact that self-consciousness is confronted by a contradiction: it must relate to *itself alone* in relating to what is irreducibly *other*, and it can do so only by relating to an object that *negates itself* in the way we have described. Recognition is made necessary, therefore, by the fact that, in the *Phenomenology*, *self-consciousness does not come first*, but emerges from and is inseparably connected to consciousness. This gives Hegel's account an enormous advantage, for it presupposes nothing but the experience of consciousness itself. It rests on no moral or political imperatives that might be disputed by natural consciousness. The emergence of recognition, however, is not the end of Hegel's story. We now have to see why recognition cannot just be one-way recognition of the first by the second self, but must become two-way, *mutual* recognition in which each self recognizes the other.

Mutual recognition

Self-consciousness might be thought to be simple awareness of oneself. The self-consciousness that is made necessary by the experience of consciousness is, however, more complex than this.

First, it is indeed consciousness of itself as a pure I: it is, and knows itself to be, the 'motionless tautology of: I am I' (§167/121). Second, it must be desire, the movement of affirming oneself through negating inanimate and animate objects (perhaps by breaking something or eating food). Third, it must stand, and know itself to stand, in relation to another self-consciousness.

In this necessary doubling of self-consciousness, Hegel writes, *we* can see the presence of '*spirit*' (*Geist*) – 'the unity of different, independent self-consciousnesses', or '*I* that is *We*, and *We* that is *I*' (§177/127). Self-consciousness itself, however, does not yet embrace this concept of spirit, for it is still only interested in itself. It confronts what it regards as another independent self, but all it sees in that other self is *itself*. The other serves no other purpose in my eyes, therefore, than to recognize *my* independence as a self. Hegel now argues, however, that an ambiguity in the stance of such self-absorbed self-consciousness requires it to recognize the *genuine* independence of the other self in turn. So why is self-consciousness's situation ambiguous?

Self-consciousness is faced by *another* self-consciousness by which it finds itself recognized. It has thus, as Hegel puts it, 'come *out of itself*' (§179/128), since it is not just enclosed within itself, but sees its identity located, as it were, 'over there'. Yet precisely because it finds its own identity *over there* in the eyes of the other, self-consciousness immediately feels that it has 'lost itself' to that other. Equally, however, since it sees in the other nothing but its own self, self-consciousness fails to see the other as genuinely *other*. Self-consciousness's situation is ambiguous, therefore, because the way in which it sees itself in the other deprives it of a clear consciousness of *either* itself *or* the other.

Self-consciousness removes this ambiguity by proceeding 'to supersede [*aufheben*] the *other* independent being in order thereby to become certain of *itself* as the essential being' (§180/128). It does so by reclaiming itself from the other, relocating its identity within *itself* (as it were, 'over here'), and thereby overcoming its previous sense of being what it is only in and through the *other*. This removal of ambiguity is, however, itself ambiguous: for in making this move, self-consciousness deprives itself of the consciousness of itself that it has just enjoyed and 'proceeds to supersede its *own* self'. It does so because it abandons the idea that its identity is to be found reflected in the eyes of the other and is thus something objective.

Yet all is not lost: for, as Hegel points out, this withdrawal of self-consciousness from the other back into itself is ambiguous in a further, more positive sense. In withdrawing into itself, consciousness does, indeed, recover the certainty that it owns its own self: in Hegel's words, 'it receives back its own self' and again 'becomes equal to itself' (§181/128). At the same time, it thereby allows the other self to be genuinely *other* than it: for it no longer sees the other merely as a mirror reflecting it, but 'gives the other self-consciousness back again to itself' and 'lets the other again go free' (*entläßt also das Andere wieder frei*) (§181/128).[31] By withdrawing into itself, therefore, self-consciousness liberates the other from subordination to it and in that very move *recognizes* the other's independence. Furthermore, though Hegel does not make this point explicitly in §181, by letting the other go free, self-consciousness affords itself the opportunity to be *recognized* by an other that it recognizes in turn as genuinely other.

Initially, self-consciousness did not 'see the other as an essential being', because it saw in that other nothing but *itself* (§179/128). Yet it did not enjoy a clear sense of itself either, since it found itself 'over there' in the eyes of the *other* (that it failed to see properly *as* an other). This ambiguity in self-consciousness's situation has now led it to a new situation in which it has a clear sense of its own identity *and* recognizes the independence and otherness of the other. Consequently, it now unites *self-consciousness* and *consciousness* in a way that it has not done so far: for it is conscious of itself in relation to an other that it knows to be genuinely other. Self-consciousness achieves this unity by giving up what it previously sought, namely consciousness of *itself alone*. Self-consciousness gives up this aim by recognizing the full independence of the other, and so finding itself recognized by an other that it recognizes in turn. The perfect unity of self-consciousness and consciousness – finding oneself in and through another – is thus achieved only in a relation of *mutual* recognition between two independent and free self-consciousnesses. In this sense, mutual recognition is the *truth* that is made necessary by the inherent logic of self-consciousness itself.

Note that mutual recognition requires the *cooperation* of two free and independent selves. Neither self can create a relation of mutual recognition, and so achieve true self-consciousness, through its own agency alone: 'action by one side only would be useless because what is to happen can only be brought about by both'

(§182/129). Furthermore, both selves have to acknowledge this fact. The two selves have thus not just to recognize one another freely, but they also have to '*recognize* themselves as *mutually recognizing* one another' (§184/129).

Hegel points out that such mutual recognition echoes the play of forces we encountered above. Like the forces involved in that interplay, neither self-consciousness is purely and simply what it is, but each is 'an absolute transition into the opposite' (§184/129). Each is independent of the other and is recognized by the other as such; but each is equally *dependent* on the other for that very recognition. Hegel does not, however, draw attention to an important difference between mutual recognition and the play of forces. In the play of forces, neither force is genuinely independent, since neither acts spontaneously; each expresses itself only insofar as it is *solicited* to do so by the other (§137/97). In mutual recognition, by contrast, the two selves are genuinely independent, since each recognizes the other *of its own accord*. This difference between mutual recognition and the play of forces suggests that self-consciousness cannot be understood as the work of *forces*, since forces lack, and are unable to establish, the freedom and independence that belong to self-consciousness.

Mutual recognition, as it emerges in chapter four of the *Phenomenology*, remains rather formal and empty: each self recognizes the other as no more than an independent self. Later in *Phenomenology*, such mutual recognition will take a more concrete form in the reconciliation between the hypocrite and the judge (see §670/441). In chapter four, however, Hegel does not develop the idea of mutual recognition any further. Indeed, he turns to examine the life and death struggle in which mutual recognition is clearly absent. The reason for this is that he has come to the end of the process of rendering explicit what is implicit in self-consciousness. This process has led to the insight, on the part of the phenomenologist and self-consciousness itself, that self-consciousness involves *two* selves in a relation of *recognition*. What we now have to do, Hegel maintains, is examine how this 'doubling' of self-consciousness 'appears to self-consciousness' itself, that is, how self-consciousness itself *experiences* this doubling (§185/129).

In line with the preceding chapters, Hegel begins his analysis of this experience by considering doubled self-consciousness in its most immediate and undeveloped form. Immediate self-consciousness reverts to the standpoint of desire and seeks to be conscious of *itself alone*. At the same time, it seeks *recognition* from the other of its independence and 'being-for-self'. Since it is interested only in *itself*, however, it does not accord any recognition to the other. The relation between the two selves is thus not one of mutual recognition, but one in which the two 'are opposed to one another, one being only *recognized*, the other only *recognizing*' (§185/129). Note that what introduces this 'inequality' or asymmetry into the relation between selves is the fact that each has an utterly primitive conception of its own freedom and identity: each is focused only on its *own* freedom and denies that the other enjoys a similar freedom. As Hegel will show, the first experience that is generated by this utterly abstract conception of the self is the *life and death struggle*.

Study questions

1 Why does self-consciousness take the form of desire?
2 Why does self-consciousness take the form of mutual recognition?

The life and death struggle and master–slave relation

The life and death struggle

Each self-consciousness in the life and death struggle considers itself to be free and independent, to be a pure I. Each considers the other, however, to lack such freedom and independence. Accordingly, although each sees the other as another self-consciousness, it also holds the other to be more like a thing than a proper self. It thus takes the other to be immersed in and determined by the realm of perceivable things and, above all, life. 'They are for one another like ordinary objects' – individuals 'submerged in the *being* of *life*' (§186/130).

In direct contrast to the way it sees the other, each self takes its own freedom to consist in *not* being determined by things and, crucially, *not* being attached to life (including one's own body). Indeed, each understands its freedom to involve 'the exclusion from itself of everything else' (§186/129). Each thinks of itself, therefore, as *utterly* free, as having no attachments *at all*, as being 'pure being-for-self' (§186/130). In this sense, like desire, each takes its selfhood to consist in being itself *alone*.

The two selves, however, are not content merely to regard themselves in this way, but each wishes to be recognized by the other as utterly free. Each endeavours to *prove* its freedom to the other by killing the other and risking its own life in so doing. Each seeks the death of the other, because it regards the other as restricting its freedom, and because 'it values the other no more than itself' (§187/131). Each risks its own life in the process in order to show its lack of concern for its own life. In this way, Hegel argues, the two selves become embroiled in a 'life and death struggle' to prove their freedom to one another. In so doing each also, coincidentally, affords the *other* an opportunity to show that he is free, too, and not attached to life after all: 'they prove [*bewähren*] themselves and each other through a life-and-death struggle' (§187/130).

Note that this struggle is not a struggle to stay alive. It is a struggle by two selves to show just how little life matters to them. It results from the utterly abstract – indeed primitive – conception of selfhood and freedom that is entertained by each self. Like some members of inner city gangs, each self seeks to confirm its own sense of selfhood or 'being-for-self' by trying to kill the other with no care for its own life. Hegel's analysis thus shows how a primitive, abstract and self-absorbed conception of *identity* leads to the inflicting of the most severe violence on others. This will not be the last time in the *Phenomenology* that an abstract conception of selfhood brings, or tries to bring, *death* in its wake: we will see the same happen in the sphere of absolute freedom (see p. 164, below).

There is, however, an obvious problem with this life and death struggle. Each self wants to prove its freedom to the other and wants the other to recognize that freedom: I want you to bear witness to my disregard for both your life and mine. But, of course, if I succeed in killing you, I lose the very recognition I seek. 'This trial by death,' Hegel writes, thus 'does away with the truth which was supposed to issue from it', for with death consciousness 'remains without the required significance of recognition' (§188/131). Now in history many such struggles do, indeed, end in the death of one or both of the protagonists. The *logical* lesson that self-consciousness learns from the life and death struggle, however, is that 'life is as essential to it as pure self-consciousness' (§189/132), for only when both parties remain alive can one *recognize* the other as a pure self. Accordingly, self-consciousness, or rather the phenomenologist, now moves on a new relationship between selves, in which this lesson has been taken to heart.

This new relationship does not replace the previous one altogether, but allows the goal sought in it – namely, recognition of one's pure freedom and detachment – to be achieved. One of the selves thus continues to regard itself as free from attachment to things and to life, as pure 'being-for-self'. Yet it now no longer seeks to prove its freedom by killing its rival, but it allows its rival to live so that the latter can recognize it as free. The other self also gives up seeking the death of its counterpart. It does so, however, because it no longer regards itself as a pure, detached self, but now acknowledges its *attachment* to life. In so doing this self also acknowledges its subordination to its counterpart, and so considers itself to be the bondsman or *slave* (*Knecht*) of the latter. Accordingly, it recognizes its counterpart as its lord or *master* (*Herr*). In this way, Hegel argues, the life and death struggle leads logically, if not always as a matter of fact, to the master–slave relation.

The master–slave relation

The relation between master and slave that Hegel examines is not embedded in a world: it does not coincide, for example, with the institution of slavery in ancient Greece or Rome. Hegel has in mind a simple relation between two individuals, one of which – the master – is regarded by both as free from attachment to life and things, and the other – the slave – is regarded by both as bound to and dependent upon life and things. Due to his sense of untrammeled freedom the master enjoys a sense of superiority and power over both the slave and the things to which the slave feels himself bound. The master expresses this sense of power in two different ways: by holding the slave in subjection, and by consuming things around him.

The master revels in the consumption of things because he understands his freedom to consist in the ability to *negate* things utterly. In his own mind (and in the mind of the slave) the master's identity and selfhood reside in 'the sheer negation of the thing, or the enjoyment of it' (§190/133). Hegel distinguishes such enjoyment

(*Genuss*) from simple desire. Desire affirms its sense of self by destroying an other; but, as we saw earlier, it also comes face to face with the independence of what is other (§§174–5/125–6). The master avoids such an encounter by interposing the slave between himself and things, leaving the slave to engage with their independence. The master is thus able to consume things with no sense at all that they offer any resistance to him. As Hegel puts it, he 'takes to himself only the dependent aspect of the thing and has the pure enjoyment of it' (§190/133). The master is able to indulge himself in this way because, unlike simple desire, he encounters only what has been *prepared* by the slave for his consumption. Furthermore, through such preparatory work the slave accords the master the *recognition* that he is, indeed, the slave's lord and master (§191/133).

The slave has a more ambiguous sense of selfhood. On the one hand, what makes him a slave is his feeling of dependence on, and subordination to, life and things (and, of course, the master). He does not, therefore, view things as there simply to be negated and consumed, but sees them as having an independence that resists his efforts to negate them. On the other hand, the slave is not merely a thing himself, but is conscious of being a self. As in the case of the master, this sense of selfhood expresses itself in the *negation* of things. Unlike the master, however, the slave, in his negating of a thing, 'cannot go to the length of being altogether done with it to the point of annihilation' (§190/133), precisely because he takes things to be independent and so to *resist* him. The slave can thus negate things only to a limited extent. Such limited negation does not destroy the thing, but *changes* it and gives it a new form. The name that Hegel gives to this activity of limited, transformative negation is *work* or *labour* (*Arbeit*). Whereas the master's role is to consume things, therefore, the slave's role is to work on things in order to prepare them for the master's enjoyment.

In the master–slave relation, enjoyment and work are thus divided between the two individuals concerned in a manner that inevitably makes one think of Marx's account of capitalist society. Hegel's account differs from that of Marx, however, in at least one important respect. Marx provides an analysis of the way in which objective, *historical* processes of production lead to the division between capitalists and proletarians. Hegel, by contrast, sets out the ways in which the master and slave *conceive* of themselves and their freedom (or lack of it). The master may be deluded about his capacity for unrestrained enjoyment, but that capacity belongs to his self-understanding, and that is what interests Hegel in the *Phenomenology*. Similarly, work – or the limited negation of independent, resistant things – belongs to the self-image of the slave.

Accordingly, the *dialectic* that Hegel describes in the *Phenomenology* also differs from that described by Marx. Marx demonstrates (to his satisfaction at least) that the capitalist system of production and exchange leads, or should lead, to the material transformation of society. The tension that emerges in capitalism makes a revolutionary restructuring of society necessary: production is to be taken out of private hands and into public ownership, and the exploitation of workers by private capitalist producers is thereby to be abolished.[32] In the *Phenomenology*, by contrast, Hegel is interested solely in tracing the changes in *self-understanding* that the master and the slave undergo. This, by the way, does not show Hegel to be an idealist, removed from the realities of social deprivation under capitalism. He examines precisely those realities in his *Outlines of the Philosophy of Right* (1820).[33] The purpose of the *Phenomenology*, however, is to explore the dialectic inherent in consciousness and self-consciousness, and what interests Hegel in the case of both the master and the slave is the way in which their self-understanding is undermined by their own experience.

The dialectic besetting the master is easily grasped. The master sees in the slave 'the *truth* of his certainty of himself' (§192/133). That is to say, he sees his own freedom and power – his 'truth' – embodied in the slave's subservience. At the same time, however, the slave's subservience and dependence also make the master aware of his own dependence on the slave: 'his truth is in reality the unessential consciousness and its unessential action' (§192/134). Mastery takes itself to be unlimited, unfettered, wholly independent freedom. Yet it is *mediated* by the work of the slave, who prepares things for the master's consumption, and by the recognition that the slave accords to the master. Furthermore, mastery depends for its very existence *as mastery* on the subservience of the slave: for one cannot exercise power and dominance, if there is no one there to dominate. The very presence of the slave is thus a constant reminder to the master of the dependent character of mastery itself. As the master becomes more conscious of this dependence, his sense of unambiguous mastery is undermined and his understanding of himself thereby transformed.

'Just as lordship [or mastery] showed that its essential nature is the reverse of what it wants to be', Hegel writes, 'so too servitude in its consummation will really turn into the opposite of what it immediately is' (§193/134). The dialectic that transforms the slave's conception of himself is, however, more complicated than that suffered by the master. *Pace* Jean Hyppolite, the slave is *not* 'revealed to be the master of the master', but is, rather, 'transformed into a truly independent consciousness' (§193/134), albeit within the limits of servitude.[34]

The first thing to consider is the slave's *fear of death*. The master enjoys – initially, at least – a sense of unlimited freedom and power. This involves taking oneself not to be defined or limited in any way by nature or life. I am free, on this understanding, because I am *not* this, *not* that, indeed *not* anything particular at all. I am just me, purely for myself. Such freedom consists, therefore, in *being* oneself but being *nothing* in particular, being pure 'negativity'. This freedom – this sense of not being defined as this or that, and thus of *being nothing* – expresses itself in the case of the master in the unrestricted negating of things and in the enjoyment found in reducing them to nothing.

The sense of being pure negativity, in Hegel's view, is not all that true freedom involves (as we can see from his *Philosophy of Right*). Nonetheless, it has emerged in the *Phenomenology* – together with life – as an essential aspect of self-consciousness. It appears, however, to be lacking in the slave, since the slave understands himself to be dependent on, and so defined by, life and things. Yet Hegel points out that this sense of 'being-oneself-in-being-nothing-in-particular' does belong to the slave after all: for, as Kojève puts it, the slave 'caught a glimpse of himself as nothingness' in the *fear of death*.[35]

The protagonists in the life and death struggle were initially *fearless* in the face of death: they both sought to demonstrate their freedom by risking death in the attempt to kill the other. The master–slave relation emerged, however, when one of the protagonists abandoned this attempt to demonstrate his freedom and conceded that life matters to him after all. As the attitude of this individual towards life changes, so too does his attitude towards death: death becomes the object of fear, because it signifies the utter annihilation of all that now matters to the individual. What is terrifying about death, however, is not the thought of oneself as an inert object – as a cold body on a slab – but imagining oneself *being nothing*. The fear of death, in other words, is not just the fear of *death*, but the fear of actually *being* dead – the fear of *being*, but having all that one is 'inwardly dissolved', and so being *nothing* (§194/134).³⁶ It is in this sense that the slave catches sight of his own 'nothingness' in the fear of death.

Contrary to what initially appears to be the case, therefore, the slave shares in the sense of 'being nothing' that characterizes the master: servitude 'does in fact contain within itself this truth of pure negativity and being-for-self' (§194/134). In the slave, however, this sense of nothingness remains 'inward and mute' (§196/136), buried in the lingering fear that besets the slave, and does not express itself in the masterly desire to consume things. It grounds, rather, the slave's *service* to the lord. Yet this is only half of the slave's story: for the latter comes to see his *work* or *labour* as the explicit expression of his inner nothingness or 'negativity'. It is this new understanding of labour, in conjunction with the fear of death, that transforms the slave dialectically into 'a truly independent consciousness' (§193/134), albeit within the condition of continuing subservience to the master.

Hegel points out that, in the experience of the slave, labour turns out to have a *double-edged* character. On the one hand, as we know, work is something the slave is forced to do, both by the master and by the fact that the slave understands things to resist and limit his efforts to negate them. On the other hand, however, slavish consciousness also 'comes to itself' through work (§195/135).³⁷ That is to say, the slave comes to realize that work is his *own* activity, and the manifestation of his *own* freedom, even if it is required of him by another. Moreover, the slave sees that, in transforming a thing through work, he puts something of his own *into* that thing and gives it a new *form*. He sees that he embodies his freedom in the thing itself. This is a dimension of freedom that the master cannot enjoy. After consuming something, all that is left for the master to contemplate is the empty space in front of him (or perhaps the crumbs on the plate). The slave, by contrast, comes to see his freedom and identity embodied in an independent thing, even if only for a moment before it is consumed by the master. The slave is thus not left staring at nothing, but can look at the transformed object and say '*I* did that; that is *my* handiwork'; as Hegel puts it, 'consciousness, *qua* worker, comes to see *itself* in the independent being' (§195/135). Through the very work the slave is forced to do, therefore, he comes to see his freedom objectified in a way that is denied to the master.

Furthermore – and this is crucial – what the slave sees embodied in the product of his labour is not only his particular ability to create this particular thing, but also the self he feels himself to be in his *fear of death*. The slave sees the thing he has created as embodying himself, the self that has expressed itself in the activity of labour. Deep down, however, he feels himself to be, not only a particular self, defined by the givens of life, but also *pure* 'being-for-self'. He thus sees the latter embodied in the thing he has produced: 'in fashioning the thing, the bondsman's own negativity, his being-for-self, becomes an object for him' (§196/135). The thing thereby becomes for him the objective expression of who and what he *truly* is; and he comes to see *explicitly* 'that being-for-self belongs to *him*' and not just to the master. For the slave, therefore, the new shape he has given to the thing through his labour does not belong solely to *that thing*: 'for it is precisely this shape that is his pure being-for-self, which in this externality is seen by him to be the truth' (§196/135–6).

In his fear of death, the slave catches sight of his own nothingness and acquires a sense – that is itself 'inward and mute' – of being a pure self. Through his labour, however, the slave gains a fully explicit consciousness of being a pure self, because he sees his own pure selfhood embodied objectively in the product of his labour. In this way, through the combination of labour and the fear of death, the slave comes to realize that, within his servitude, he is essentially *free*. He thereby acquires a 'mind of his own' (*eigner Sinn*) through the very activity – labour – which he is forced to engage in by the master and in which he thus 'seemed to have only an alienated existence [*fremder Sinn*]' (§196/136). This consciousness of being a pure self of one's own does not, of course, release the slave from his subservience to the master, but it is consciousness of *freedom* that is gained by the slave despite – or, indeed, because of – his condition of servitude.

To conclude his account of the master–slave relation, Hegel emphasizes that labour alone would not give the slave the sense of freedom that he enjoys, but that the fear of death is also an indispensable condition of such freedom. Labour by itself is the activity of transforming *particular* things in the world: turning this piece of wood into a chair or these ingredients into bread. The freedom the slave exhibits in labour taken by itself is thus still a limited freedom: it consists in the particular ability to give new shape to these particular objects. As such, it bears witness to the fact that the slave's consciousness is still mired in the world of given particularities (or, as Hegel puts it, that 'determinate being still *in principle* attaches to it') (§196/136).

If the slave's freedom were to lie exclusively in his ability to labour, therefore, his sense of self would be defined solely by the particular skills he displays in such labour, and he would have no consciousness of being a *pure* self. These particular skills would be everything to him and he would insist on being able to exercise them. The 'mind of his own' that he acquires through his labour would thus become a stubborn 'self-will': his *eigner Sinn* would become *Eigensinn*. Furthermore, he would show himself to be wholly dependent on – and slave to – those particular skills. In this sense, his freedom would be 'a freedom that is still enmeshed in servitude': he would evince a 'skill which is master [*mächtig*] over *some* things' only (§196/136).

As we have seen, however, the slave's freedom does not lie exclusively in his labour, for such labour is itself grounded in the fear of death. His freedom is thus not tied definitively to the exercise of certain *particular* skills after all, because his labour is itself not merely the exercise of particular skills, but also the expression of the nothingness or 'pure negativity' that the slave in his fear feels himself to be. In other words, the slave's labour does not merely testify to his particular mastery 'over some things', but expresses his fundamental freedom from things *as such*, his fundamental 'no-thing-ness' or 'negativity *per se*'. His labour thus affords him a sense of his *general* freedom to negate and transform things, that is, of his 'universal formative activity' (*allgemeines Bilden*) or mastery 'over the universal power and the whole of objective being' (§196/136). The slave's labour is, indeed, always the exercise of a particular skill; but he is aware that such labour is the *particular* expression of his essential, freedom *from* particularity, or his pure being-for-self. Since the slave knows himself to be, in essence, free *from* particularity, he does not feel the need to cling stubbornly to any one particular skill or set of skills. On the contrary, he knows that he can express his freedom in all manner of particular skills. He understands himself, therefore, to be a multidimensional being who can (in principle, at least) engage in all kinds of labour, albeit under the condition of continuing subservience to the master.

Hegel's account of mastery and servitude is deservedly famous and influential. It shows with penetrating insight that both mastery and servitude are inherently dialectical: the master is less free than he initially thinks because he is dependent on servitude for his very mastery, and the slave is more free than he initially thinks because he finds freedom in *labour* that is grounded in the *fear of death*. It would be wrong to say that Hegel's account of the master–slave relation spawned Marxism and Existentialism by itself, but by drawing attention to the liberating role of both labour and the awareness of death in the experience of the slave, it clearly prefigures some of their most distinctive insights.

Study questions

1. Why does the life and death struggle arise?
2. What role does the fear of death play in the self-consciousness of the slave?

Stoicism, scepticism and the unhappy consciousness

Stoicism

The relation between the master and the slave is asymmetrical. The master, *in contrast* to the slave, is unable to give positive, objective expression to his freedom through labour and so enjoys nothing but his own mastery. The slave, on the other hand, is conscious, *like* the master, of being a pure self-consciousness, a pure I, and so incorporates the core of the master's self-understanding into his own (albeit in the form of the fear of death). For this reason, Hegel maintains, the slave, but not the master, is 'a truly independent consciousness' (§193/134). Indeed, the slave embodies in its *true* form the freedom and independence to which the master himself (mistakenly) lays claim. The master and slave do not, therefore, simply coexist side-by-side, but there is a logical progression from the former to the latter. We phenomenologists thus now move to a new shape of self-consciousness that takes up and renders explicit what is implicit in the experience of the slave.

The slave, we recall, sees himself and his own freedom embodied in the new form he has given to the thing. This thing, however, is not itself something self-conscious: it is simply a *thing* that has been transformed by the slave's labour. The slave encounters self-consciousness in the master. Hegel notes, therefore, that, for the slave, the two processes of seeing *himself* in the object and seeing the object as a *self-consciousness* 'fall apart'. Yet the slave is, of course, himself a self-consciousness. Implicitly, therefore, if not explicitly, in seeing *himself* in the object he is seeing his own *self-consciousness* in it. Hegel thus writes that the 'form' of the thing and the 'being-for-self', or self-consciousness, of the slave are '*for us*, or *in themselves [an sich]*, the same' (§197/137). We phenomenologists now move, therefore, to a new shape of self-consciousness for which they are explicitly the same. Since this new shape sees its own self-consciousness explicitly in the *thing* to which it relates, it does not need to see it embodied in another self. It is thus no longer one of two selves, like the master and the slave, but stands in relation only to things.

It is important to stress that the object to which self-consciousness now relates is a *thing*, and so is not itself self-conscious. Yet how does this new self see its own self-consciousness explicitly in a thing that lacks such self-consciousness? It does so by recognizing the thing to have the very same *form* or *substance* as itself. The slave – whom we have now left behind – stands in relation to an object that is independent of him and, through his labour, gives that object a new form. This form belongs to the independent object, *not* to the slave, although it objectifies for the slave his *own* freedom. The new self, by contrast, sees in the object a form or substance that belongs to self-consciousness *itself* as much as to the object. As Hegel puts it, the 'thinghood which received its form in being fashioned is no other substance than consciousness' (§197/137). In this way, self-consciousness now sees *itself* in the object in a much more explicit way than the slave did: for it sees in the object not just the result of its own activity, but its very own substance. The shape of self-consciousness that discerns this sheer *identity* between itself and a non-self-conscious thing is *thought* (*Denken*). The slave's consciousness does not itself become thought, but thought renders explicit what is implicit in the slave's freedom.

Such thought, by the way, is not yet *philosophical* thought, or 'absolute knowing', as Hegel will understand it in the *Science of Logic*. The task of the *Phenomenology* – to lead natural consciousness to the standpoint of philosophical thought – has thus not yet been completed. The reason why, as we shall see, is that the thought to which the experience of the slave leads is still mired in the perspective of *self*-consciousness. At start of chapter four of the *Phenomenology*, Hegel writes that with self-consciousness we have entered 'the native realm of truth' (§167/120). By the end of the book, however, it will have become clear that, although absolute knowing incorporates self-consciousness, it is by no means reducible to it (see pp. 186–7, below). In what follows, therefore, readers should bear in mind that what Hegel is discussing is not yet absolute knowing, but thought as it first appears in the *Phenomenology*, or 'thinking consciousness as such' (§197/138).

Such thought understands the object to be structured by *concepts* (*Begriffe*); the latter constitute, for thought, what objects are *in themselves*. At the same time, however, thought knows that *it* is structured by concepts, too. Concepts thus constitute 'a distinct *being-in-itself* [*Ansichsein*]', which, for consciousness, 'is not anything distinct from itself': they are the form or substance that things and selves share (§197/137). When consciousness *represents* something, Hegel writes, it regards that thing as *other* than it. When it understands something through concepts, by contrast, consciousness takes the thing to have the same form as its own thought. Thought is thus aware, as representation (*Vorstellung*) is not, of an identity between itself and its object.

In thought, therefore, *self*-consciousness coincides completely with consciousness of the *object*. As Hegel puts it, to think is to 'relate oneself to objective being in such a way that its significance is the *being-for-self* of the consciousness for which it is [an object]' (§197/137). The self and the object do not, however, have equal weight in this relationship, because the move from the standpoint of the slave to that of thought involves a heightening of *self*-consciousness in particular. To put the point very simply: whereas the slave sees itself in the *Other*, thought sees its *Self* in the other. Thought, at this point, is conscious of an identity between itself and its object, only because it recognizes *itself* more explicitly in the object than the slave did. Herein, indeed, lies the distinctive freedom of such thought: 'in thinking, I *am free*, because I am not in an other, but remain simply and solely in communion with myself, and the object, which is for me the essential being, is in undivided unity my being-for-myself; and my activity in conceptual thinking is a movement within myself' (§197/137).

The thought we encounter at this point is thus a further form of *self*-consciousness. As such, it remains governed by the principle that has governed self-consciousness throughout chapter four of the *Phenomenology*, namely, that 'consciousness is to itself the truth' (§166/120). The protagonists in the life and death struggle asserted their own truth by seeking to destroy one another; the master asserted his truth by consuming and enjoying things, and the slave did so by transforming things through work. Thought asserts its own truth by looking to *itself* and its own concepts to find the true form of the object. On the one hand, thought allows the object to be what it is much more than the master and the slave did, since it does not *negate* the object by consuming it or working on it but simply understands it. On the other hand, thought understands the object by looking to, and into, *itself*. Thought remains a form of self-consciousness, therefore, because it finds the truth – the true nature of both itself and the object – *within itself*.

In so doing, however, thought continues to *negate* the object after all: for by turning towards *itself* to find the truth, it turns *away from* the object. The object on which desire and work operate is 'the manifold self-differentiating expanse of life' with all the particular things it incorporates. In order to find the true nature of such life, Hegel writes, consciousness now '*withdraws* from the bustle of existence' into '*the simple essentiality of thought*' (§199/138). That is to say, it *abstracts* from the rich complexity of life and retreats into thought's 'pure universality'. In the process it shows itself to be '*indifferent* to natural existence' (§200/139). Such indifference, which Hegel associates with ancient stoic thought in particular, constitutes an inner freedom that one can enjoy whether one is 'on the throne or in chains', whether one is 'master' or 'slave', that is, whether one is the Roman Emperor Marcus Aurelius or the one-time slave, Epictetus (§199/138). Such freedom comes at a price, however, for the thought into which the stoic withdraws by abstracting from the particularities of life is itself thoroughly *abstract*.

Due to this abstractness, Hegel maintains, stoic thought has no intrinsic content of its own but is itself quite empty and indeterminate. Whatever content it has, therefore, must be derived from the object – the 'living world' – whose truth it seeks to understand. Stoic thought thus acquires content by grasping the *world* as a 'system of thought'; the 'content' it acquires thereby comprises the 'determinate' concepts it forms of the *things* it encounters in the world. Such determinacy does not have its source in thought itself but is '*given* to it' *by* the world: it is 'the alien element' (*das Fremde*) that thought has within it (§200/139).

Since this is the only content abstract thought has, stoicism is 'perplexed', Hegel tells us, if it is asked to provide a 'criterion of truth' from within *thought* itself – a conception of truth and goodness against which to measure things (and actions) in the world. Indeed, all stoicism is able to say in response to such a request is that 'the True and the Good shall consist in reasonableness [*Vernünftigkeit*]' or 'wisdom and virtue'. Such words are 'no doubt uplifting', Hegel writes, but they tell us nothing; and 'since they cannot in fact produce any expansion of the content, they soon become tedious' (§200/139–40). Stoicism looks to *thought* to determine the nature of truth and goodness, but, in Hegel's view, it leaves us with nothing but abstract, uninformative generalities. Whether this is fair to historical stoicism, I leave to others to judge. Hegel's phenomenological claim, however, is that such tedious generalities are necessarily produced by thought that withdraws into itself, and so *abstracts* from the complexity of things, in order to find the truth about such things.

Unlike the master and the slave, the stoic does not carry out any practical negation of things: he does not consume or transform them. He does, however, negate things in *thought*, by abstracting from them and withdrawing into his own thought in the manner described above. Yet stoic negation only goes so far. For the stoic himself, truth is to be disclosed by, and from within, thought; but the actual content of thought lies in the *determinate* concepts that capture the *givens* of nature. The stoic thus carries out only an 'incomplete negation' of things (§201/140): for, by withdrawing into thought to discover their truth, he allows their complex particularity and determinacy to remain *outside* thought, on the one hand, as a matter of indifference, and, on the other hand, as that which determines the content of thought itself. Implicit in the stoic standpoint, however, is the 'absolute negation' of things.

Stoic thought sees *itself* in the object to which it relates. Yet it is in fact at odds with itself, since it does *not* see itself in everything about the object. Specifically, it does not see itself in the complex particularity of things by which it finds itself determined and which is 'the *alien* element' within it. To see itself in *everything* about the object – and so to be fully and explicitly the *self*-consciousness that it is – stoic thought would have to allow nothing determinate to stand outside it at all. It would thus have to negate things absolutely. Since it does not do so, however, such absolute negation remains merely implicit in it. Sceptical thought, by contrast, does negate things absolutely, and does so in the name of thoroughgoing *self*-consciousness. Scepticism thus renders explicit what is implicit in the standpoint of stoicism.

Scepticism

Scepticism undermines everything in the object – all 'the many and varied forms of life' (§202/140) – to which stoicism showed itself to be indifferent and which it thus allowed to go free. Nothing in life is left alone by the sceptic, but everything is cast from being into non-being. In this sense, the sceptic appears to return to the standpoint of the master, who also claims for himself the unlimited capacity to negate things. Unlike the master, however, the sceptic does not actually destroy things by consuming them, but he undermines them *in thought*. He does so by regarding them as having no reality or independence outside thought. 'In scepticism, now, the wholly unessential and non-independent character of this "other" becomes explicit *for consciousness*' (§202/140). Through this self-conscious negation of life and things, Hegel writes, sceptical thought 'procures for its own self the certainty of its freedom' (§204/141). Indeed, compared to stoic thought, it is 'the actual experience of what the freedom of thought is' (§202/140).

By declaring things in the world to be unreal, the sceptic also undermines the veracity of his *own* constantly changing perceptions (§204/141). At the same time, he reinforces his consciousness of himself as pure thought – thought that retains its identity in face of the flux of life it exposes as illusory. Sceptical self-consciousness, we are told, knows itself to be 'the unchanging [*unwandelbar*] and *genuine certainty of itself*' (§205/142).

Like the master, therefore, the sceptic knows itself to be a pure I with the freedom to negate all the things before it. Unlike the master, however, the sceptic's sense of his own freedom to negate is so all-encompassing that it even directs itself at this very consciousness of being a pure, unchanging I. Sceptical thought thus exposes its own purity as an illusion, too, and points out that it is in fact inextricably entangled in changing perceptions that it knows to be illusory. As Hegel puts it, the sceptic admits to being 'a consciousness which is *empirical*, which takes its guidance from what has no reality for it' (§205/142).

Yet precisely in declaring its own perceiving to be unreal, sceptical thought again becomes aware of its pure, unchanging freedom to negate: it 'converts itself again into a consciousness that is universal and self-identical'. And yet, Hegel continues, 'from this self-identity, or within its own self, it falls back again into the former contingency and confusion', for it reminds itself of its entanglement with illusory perception. Through the exercise of his freedom of thought, therefore, the sceptic does not achieve a simple consciousness of himself as pure thought, as a pure unchanging I; rather, he has 'the doubly contradictory consciousness of unchangeableness and sameness, and of utter contingency and non-identity with himself' (§205/142–3).

Note that the sceptic does not *suffer* from this constant shifting of his self-understanding from one alternative to the other; he revels in it, because it is precisely in contradicting what he has just declared himself to be that he enjoys his freedom. Indeed, the sceptic deliberately negates first his changing perceptions, and then his unchanging self-identity, in order to preserve his sense of unlimited freedom: 'point out likeness or identity to it, and it will point out unlikeness or non-identity; and when it is now confronted with what it has just asserted, it turns round and points out likeness or identity'. As Hegel notes, in a striking image that highlights the fundamental immaturity of this sceptical standpoint:

> Its talk is in fact like the squabbling of self-willed young boys [*eigensinniger Jungen*], one of whom says A if the other says B, and in turn says B if the other says A, and who by contradicting *themselves* buy for themselves the pleasure of continually contradicting *one another*. (§205/143)

Sense-certainty and perception prove to be at the mercy of the dialectic, inherent in their own experience, that turns their object into its opposite. They lose their object, therefore, despite their best efforts to hold on to it. By contrast, dialectic does not just *happen* to the sceptic, but is deliberately set in motion by the sceptic himself. The '*absolute dialectical unrest*', or 'perpetually self-engendered disorder', that sceptical thought proves to be is one that such thought *itself* 'maintains and creates' (§205/142). In this respect, the scepticism we encounter at this point in the *Phenomenology* is very different from the 'scepticism that is directed at the whole range of phenomenal consciousness' by the discipline of phenomenology itself. Phenomenology is 'thoroughgoing scepticism', because 'it brings about a state of despair about all the so-called natural ideas, thoughts and opinions' (which are held by Hegel to block the way to speculative philosophy) (§78/61). The phenomenologist does not, however, impose a scepticism of his *own* on to natural consciousness; he simply traces the process by which such consciousness undermines *itself* through its experience. The sceptic, who emerges in chapter four of the *Phenomenology*, negates everything, including himself, in order to demonstrate the unlimited freedom of his *own* self-consciousness. The phenomenologist, by contrast, *gives up* such freedom and immerses it in the content at hand, 'letting it move spontaneously of its own nature' (§58/44).[38] Hegel now argues that sceptical self-consciousness is itself subject to phenomenological scepticism, since it leads logically beyond itself to a new shape of self-consciousness.

The sceptic unites, and knows himself to unite, two opposing qualities in *one* self: he sees himself as both changeable and unchangeable, and so his consciousness 'experiences itself as internally contradictory' (§206/143). Yet, since he shifts from one to the other (undermining each in turn), he does not make it fully explicit that these opposing qualities are, indeed, moments of *one* self. To do so, the sceptic would have to hold them *together* in one and the same consciousness. We now move, therefore, to a new shape of self-consciousness that explicitly 'brings together the two thoughts which scepticism holds apart': the unhappy consciousness.

The unhappy consciousness: from the pure to the incarnate unchangeable

The unhappy consciousness knows that it is *at once* 'self-liberating, unchangeable and self-identical' *and* changeable, 'self-bewildering and self-perverting' (§206/143). Moreover, it knows that these two sets of qualities are both *opposed* to one another and – since they belong together in one self – *inseparable* from one another. The unhappy consciousness thus is, and takes itself to be, more explicitly self-contradictory than the sceptic, since it attributes opposing qualities to itself at the same time, rather than one after the other. Indeed, it unites two opposing *self-consciousnesses* in one self and in this way restores the 'duplication' (*Verdopplung*) of self-consciousness with which the experience of the latter began (§206/143). In the life-and-death struggle and the master–slave relation two self-consciousnesses confronted one another; stoicism, by contrast, is 'the simple freedom of itself' alone. In the unhappy consciousness, there are once again two selves, but these are now lodged within one consciousness. They are the *two* selves that the one '*unhappy, inwardly divided* consciousness' knows itself to be (§207/144).

Insofar as the unhappy consciousness takes itself to be *one* self, it takes itself to be the '*immediate unity*' of the two selves within it (§208/144). Consciousness of this unity is what distinguishes the unhappy consciousness from the sceptic, and such unity is regarded by the unhappy consciousness itself as constituting its true character or 'essence'. The unhappy consciousness is, however, also aware that it is divided within itself into two opposing selves and thus not yet *explicitly* the unity it takes itself in essence to be (see §207/144). It thus knows itself *in fact* to fall short of what in essence it is.

Now one of the selves into which it is divided – the 'simple, unchangeable' one – exhibits the very unity that it takes to be its essence. The unhappy consciousness thus regards this unchangeable self as its essential self – its true self, in which it is free and at one with itself. It regards the other self – the one that is changeable and internally differentiated – as its inessential, merely contingent self. Yet precisely because the unhappy consciousness knows itself to be explicitly *divided*, and so to fall short of its essence, 'it identifies itself with the changeable consciousness, and takes itself to be the unessential being' (§208/144). The character of the *relation* between its two constituent selves leads it to identify itself directly with *one* of them, namely the one that exhibits internal self-division and variability. It thus takes itself to be a changeable, divided self that is separated by its changeableness and self-division from its own true essence, which lies in unity and self-identity.

Since the unhappy consciousness takes *itself* to be changeable, 'the Unchangeable is, for it, an alien being [*ein Fremdes*]' (§208/144). It is *another* self-consciousness – unchangeable and self-identical – from which I remain cut off by my immersion in the vicissitudes of life. I am, as it were, *over here*, whereas the Unchangeable is *over there*. Yet, as we have seen, the unhappy consciousness takes itself to be in essence unchangeable, and so is aware that this other self-consciousness from which it is separated 'is its own essence, although in such a way that for itself again it is *itself* not this essence' (§208/144). The unhappy consciousness is thus *alienated* from its own essence, its own true self, which it sees in another self beyond it.

Since the unhappy consciousness sees its self-identical, unchangeable self as its *true* self, it cannot 'be indifferent towards the Unchangeable'. Rather it seeks to overcome its alienation and become one with its true self by 'freeing itself from the unessential, i.e. from itself' (§208/144). This interest in overcoming its alienation is integral to the very alienation that consciousness feels: for it is alienated not from something quite other than it, but from its *own* true self, which it, as *self*-consciousness, necessarily wants to recover. The problem, Hegel points out, is that in raising itself out of its entanglement in life to union with the Unchangeable, the unhappy consciousness remains aware that this act of elevation is its own work, the work of a finite, *changeable* consciousness. This does not mean that it fails to raise itself to union with the Unchangeable, but that precisely *in* so raising itself it remains conscious *of* its changeability and individuality. In this sense, Hegel writes, its 'victory' over its changeable self is itself a 'defeat' (§209/145).

This has a significant effect on the way the Unchangeable comes to be experienced by the unhappy consciousness: for, as the Unchangeable enters consciousness, it becomes fused with the changeable individuality of which consciousness remains aware. They merge into *one* object of consciousness. As Hegel puts it, 'consciousness experiences just this emergence of individuality *in* the Unchangeable, and of the Unchangeable *in* individuality'; the two prove to be quite inseparable. Furthermore, consciousness becomes aware not just of individuality in general, but 'of its *own* individuality', in the Unchangeable (§210/145). As it raises itself to union with the Unchangeable and the latter enters consciousness, consciousness sees itself and the Unchangeable become one.

Yet, Hegel notes, consciousness also remains aware of the *difference* between itself and the Unchangeable. As well as seeing its own changeable individuality incorporated into the Unchangeable, it also remains conscious that it is *not* itself the Unchangeable, that it is separated from the latter precisely by being a changeable, individual self. The experience that the unhappy consciousness undergoes in raising itself to union with the Unchangeable thus makes it aware of both its unity with *and* difference from the latter. For consciousness, therefore, changeable individuality and the Unchangeable stand in a threefold relation to one another.

First, consciousness remains painfully aware of the division between itself and the Unchangeable. It is thus 'thrown back to the beginning of the struggle' to overcome this division. Indeed, it will remain caught up in this struggle until a new shape of consciousness emerges (namely, reason). As Hegel puts it, this struggle and the division it presupposes are 'throughout the element in which the whole relationship subsists' (§210/145). Second, however, the Unchangeable itself – in its very separation from the unhappy consciousness – is now understood to assume the form of changeable individuality. It is seen as an *incarnate* Unchangeable, taking sensuous shape in space and time. Third, consciousness discerns in this moment of incarnation its very own self, its *own* living humanity, now incorporated into the Unchangeable. The unhappy consciousness not only sees its true self and essence in the Unchangeable, but it also 'finds *itself* as this' – changeable – 'individual in the Unchangeable' (§210/145). It thus stands in relation to an Unchangeable, from which it feels itself profoundly divided, but in which it also sees that division *overcome*.

Hegel points out that the Unchangeable is 'brought closer' to the unhappy consciousness by the fact that it is now understood to be incarnate in space and time (§212/146). It is no longer simply 'the alien being who passes judgement on the particular individual' (§210/145), but is now seen to share in our finite, changeable life. It thus kindles the hope in us that we, in our finitude and changeability, might be able to overcome our alienation completely and become one with the Unchangeable after all. Yet, Hegel goes on to note, such hope must remain 'without fulfilment and present fruition'. This is because the incarnation in space and time that brings the Unchangeable down to earth and so closer to us, also allows it to be *distant* from us in space and time. Our hope of union with the Unchangeable is frustrated because we find 'that in the world of time it has vanished' and 'that in space it . . . remains utterly remote' (§212/147): the Unchangeable, we see, was incarnated *then*, but not now, and *there*, but not here. As changeable, finite individuals, therefore, we feel separated not only from the incarnate *Unchangeable*, but also from its very *incarnation*.

Consciousness thus remains unhappy. Nonetheless, progress has been made, for consciousness now relates, not to a pure, formless Unchangeable, but to one that is 'shaped' (*gestaltet*) and incarnate and, in that sense, like us. The true object of consciousness is thus no longer simply the Unchangeable in opposition to the changeable individual, but 'the *oneness* [*Einssein*] of the particular individual with the Unchangeable', albeit as something that still lies *beyond* my changeable consciousness and life (§213/147).

The unhappy consciousness: devotion, gratitude and asceticism

The opening paragraphs of the section on the unhappy consciousness work out what the proper object of the unhappy consciousness is: namely, the shaped, incarnate, rather than formless, Unchangeable. Hegel now examines the experience that consciousness makes of this object and its own relation to it.

The unhappy consciousness is, first, pure *consciousness*, or simple knowing, for which the incarnate Unchangeable is its *object*. Consciousness is painfully aware of being separated from the Unchangeable, but it seeks to become one with the latter, since it knows it to be its own alienated essence. As we saw in the section on stoicism, consciousness of the unity or identity of oneself and one's object is *thought* (§197/137). To begin with, the unhappy consciousness is not yet conscious of such an identity between itself and the Unchangeable, but it tries to *raise* itself to union with the latter. In so doing it is thus the 'movement *towards* thinking' (§217/148). In German this is expressed as follows: consciousness 'geht . . . *an* das Denken hin'. As such, Hegel writes, consciousness is '*Andacht*' or *devotion*. The unhappy consciousness, therefore, must be a devotional consciousness, where devotion is understood as the movement in which we try to achieve communion with the Unchangeable.

Since devotional consciousness takes itself to be on the way to, rather than to have achieved, communion with its object, it falls short of being an explicitly *thinking* consciousness, such as we saw in stoicism. Furthermore, it is acutely aware of *itself* and its *difference* from the Unchangeable with which it seeks communion.

The form of mindedness that falls short of thought, and in which we remain immediately caught up in ourselves, is named by Hegel 'feeling' (*Fühlen*). Devotion is thus the movement in which we try to raise ourselves *in feeling* to union with the Unchangeable. The unhappy consciousness is, indeed, a form of thought, since it knows the Unchangeable to be its own essence and so knows itself, in principle at least, to be one with its object. Yet it is not yet thought proper and has not yet got as far as *concepts*, in which the unity of subject and object is explicit for consciousness. Its thought is still immersed in feeling and so, as Hegel puts it, is a 'musical thinking', thinking as (devotion accompanied by) 'the chaotic jingling of bells, or a mist of warm incense' (§217/148). Consciousness at this stage is thus an unhappy religious consciousness.

Since the unhappy consciousness is devotional, it can at most come to *feel* itself to be one with the Unchangeable. 'Feeling', however, is consciousness in which we remain caught up in ourselves: we feel *ourselves* to be in a certain mood or condition. Any *feeling* of communion with the Unchangeable will thus leave us immersed in our *own* individual, changeable consciousness, which we know to be separate from the Unchangeable itself. No real communion with the Unchangeable can be achieved through feeling, therefore: for, 'instead of laying hold of the essence', consciousness 'only *feels* it and has fallen back into itself'. Accordingly, the Unchangeable remains, for consciousness, 'the unattainable *beyond* which, in being laid hold of, flees, or rather has already flown' (§217/149).

The first experience of the unhappy consciousness thus simply reinforces its sense of *itself*, for it is returned to itself at the very point at which it feels itself to be one with the Unchangeable. It has thus become more explicitly *self-conscious* than it is at first. The unhappy consciousness is, of course, self-consciousness from the outset, since it always takes its principal object to be itself. At first, however, it is *consciousness* of the Unchangeable as the *object* in which it sees its true self, and it seeks only to become conscious of its communion with that object. In now becoming more explicitly *self-*conscious, it becomes aware – like the master and the slave – of its power to *negate* things. Its relation to the incarnate Unchangeable is thus no longer simply that of consciousness seeking communion, but one in which it knows itself to be a *desiring, labouring* self-consciousness.[39]

Unlike the master and the slave, however, this second form of the unhappy consciousness confronts what Hegel calls 'an *actuality broken in two*' (§219/150). On the one hand, it sees before it things to be consumed or worked on, things to be negated; on the other hand, it takes those very things to be 'the shape of the Unchangeable' and so to constitute 'a sanctified world'. Consciousness takes the Unchangeable to give itself individual expression, to be an incarnate Unchangeable; yet it also takes the Unchangeable to manifest its *universality* in so doing. It thus sees 'all actuality' – the whole world around it – as the 'individuality' of the Unchangeable.

In consuming and working on things, consciousness gains satisfaction or 'enjoyment' (*Genuss*) from exercising its own activity and so reinforces its sense of itself. Yet its satisfaction with itself is limited: for it knows that it can consume and transform things only because the Unchangeable, which manifests itself in those things, has allowed it to do so. Consciousness does, indeed, enjoy itself, but it knows that 'this comes about through the Unchangeable's itself having *surrendered* its embodied form, and having *relinquished* it for the enjoyment of consciousness' (§220/151). Consciousness knows, therefore, that it can negate things *thanks only* to the generosity of the Unchangeable.

Consciousness also feels indebted to the Unchangeable for an aspect of itself. It sees the actual changing (or destroying) of things as its *own* individual activity, as opposed to that of the Unchangeable; this is what it is thanks to *itself*, or, as Hegel puts it, what it is 'for itself'. Yet consciousness also knows that it is not just what it is *for itself*, but also what it is '*in itself*' (*an sich*). This encompasses those features of itself for which it does not hold itself responsible, but which, for it, stem from its being a changeable, empirical object *in the world*. Since the world as a whole, for consciousness, is the expression of the Unchangeable, so also must be that aspect of consciousness itself that it owes to the world. This aspect of consciousness, Hegel writes, 'belongs to the Unchangeable beyond', *not* to consciousness itself, 'and consists of abilities and powers, a gift from an alien source [*eine fremde Gabe*], which the Unchangeable makes over to consciousness to make use of' (§220/151).

The unhappy consciousness takes itself to be active in relation to the 'passive actuality' – the world – that confronts it. It also knows, however, that both sides in this relation have 'withdrawn into the Unchangeable' (§221/151) – that the latter is the true power at work within both the desiring, labouring subject and the world. Since consciousness still thinks of itself as distinct from the Unchangeable, it cannot but regard the power at work within it as 'the beyond of itself'. Yet the unhappy consciousness also regards the Unchangeable as its own essence and seeks to be united with it. Consciousness now achieves such unity, however, by doing the opposite of what it did previously. Devotional consciousness thought that it could raise itself directly to the Unchangeable, while being and remaining what it is: an individual, changeable consciousness. By contrast, desiring, labouring consciousness achieves communion with the Unchangeable by negating itself in a certain way.

For such consciousness, the Unchangeable exercises its power by first negating *itself*, for it makes it possible for us to achieve satisfaction by denying itself the things in which it manifests itself, and offering them to us so that we can consume and work on them. As Hegel writes, 'the unchangeable consciousness *renounces* and *surrenders* its embodied form' (§222/151–2). In so doing the Unchangeable hands the things of the world over to us as a *gift*, as well as bestowing on us our own abilities and powers. Consciousness acknowledges this gift *as* a gift by giving thanks for it. In giving thanks, therefore, consciousness accepts that it is indebted to the Unchangeable. Hegel notes, however, that consciousness thereby *denies itself* the satisfaction of being independently active – of being something of its *own* – for it 'assigns the essence of its action not to itself but to the beyond' (§222/152). In this sense, consciousness negates itself, just has the Unchangeable does. At this point, therefore, consciousness becomes aware that, in giving thanks, it has, at last, become one with the Unchangeable, for they have both shown themselves to be the same activity of '*giving up*' (*Aufgeben*) something of themselves. The first experience of the unhappy self shows that changeable consciousness cannot achieve real communion with unchangeable consciousness, if each remains purely and simply what it is; but its second experience now shows that such communion can be achieved if each *negates itself* and so becomes, albeit from a different starting point, the same process of self-negation.

This communion immediately falls apart, however, for consciousness knows that in several respects it has not negated itself and so remains distinct from the Unchangeable. It has, after all, gained individual self-satisfaction from its consumption and its labour – albeit thanks to the Unchangeable – and in that respect has not denied itself anything but rather confirmed its sense of self. More troublingly, consciousness realizes that even its act of thanking, through which it becomes one with the Unchangeable, is not quite the act of sheer self-surrender that it first seems to be: for 'its *giving of thanks*' is '*its own* act which counterbalances the act of the other extreme, and meets the self-sacrificing beneficence with a *like* action' (§222/152). This is not to deny that such thanking is, indeed, an act of sincere self-surrender, of genuinely accepting one's indebtedness to another. The point is that, even in sincerely surrendering itself, consciousness does *not* surrender itself because *it* initiates and carries out that act of self-surrender. It does not give itself over wholly to the Unchangeable, but, as Hegel puts it, it meets the self-surrender of the Unchangeable with a '*like* action' *of its own*. The result of this second experience, therefore, is that 'consciousness feels itself therein as this particular individual, and does not let itself be deceived by its own seeming renunciation, for the truth of the matter is that it has not renounced itself' (§222/152).

Consciousness thus now finds its own individuality to be *absolutely irreducible*, for it sees the latter even in its act of giving up being something of its own. It thus sees its individuality as cutting it off *absolutely* from its unchangeable essence. The first two forms of unhappy consciousness thought they could become one with the Unchangeable through devotion and gratitude. Consciousness now sees, however, that whatever it tries to do *itself* to bring itself closer to its essence merely reinforces its sense of itself as an individual cut off from that essence.

The third form of the unhappy consciousness thus turns against itself altogether and declares itself to be the 'enemy'. It is, therefore, not just unhappy at being separated from its essence, but truly wretched, because it is convinced that *everything* about it keeps it separated. It thus no longer takes satisfaction in its own consumption and work, because its very enjoyment engenders in it 'a feeling of its wretchedness'. Nor can it perform 'naturally and without embarrassment' the 'animal functions' that belong to being alive; indeed, it sees in these functions above all the enemy 'in his characteristic shape'. They thus become 'the object of serious endeavour' or obsession, and the more consciousness focuses on them, the more it feels 'defiled' by them. Consciousness thus broods over itself and its immersion in what it sees as the filth of life, and is 'as wretched, as it is impoverished' (§225/153–4).

Yet consciousness remains aware that its essence is to be found in the Unchangeable. Indeed, this awareness grounds, or *mediates*, consciousness's hatred of its own individuality: for it hates and wishes it could eliminate the latter, only because it keeps it apart from the Unchangeable. The moment of mediation becomes explicit for consciousness itself in the figure of the 'minister' (*Diener*) (§§227–8/154). The introduction of the minister at this point in the argument might look arbitrary, but it is in fact made necessary by the structure of this third form of unhappy consciousness. On the one hand, consciousness takes itself to be cut off by its own individuality from the Unchangeable. Unlike the first two forms of unhappy consciousness, therefore, it does not think it can bring itself, through its own activity, into contact with the Unchangeable. On the other hand, consciousness knows the Unchangeable to be its *own* essence and so is conscious of the need to become one with the Unchangeable. Since, however, it cannot bring *itself* into contact with the latter, it must allow itself to be brought into contact with it by *another*, by a mediator. This mediator must belong to the world of change and life in order to be able to come into contact with the individual, but it must also communicate the 'will' of the Unchangeable to the individual through the counsel it gives the latter. Like the Kantian 'schema', therefore, the mediator must be a 'third thing' that connects the changeable and unchangeable consciousnesses by combining both within itself.[40] Moreover, since it combines these two opposed consciousnesses, the mediator must itself be another consciousness. The unhappy consciousness must, therefore, relate to the Unchangeable *via a minister*, because it recognizes the Unchangeable as its very own essence, and yet thinks that everything about *itself* keeps it apart from the Unchangeable itself.

Since the structure of the unhappy consciousness itself makes the introduction of the minister necessary, the content of the latter's counsel reflects the viewpoint of such consciousness. For consciousness, its own individual will is utterly opposed to the Unchangeable; conforming to the will of the Unchangeable would thus require the elimination of the individual's own will. In the name of the Unchangeable, therefore, the minister tells the individual to extinguish his will altogether and give himself over completely to the will of the Unchangeable. Since the individual sees the Unchangeable as his own essence, he does what the minister tells him without further ado.

In so doing, consciousness succeeds in relinquishing, and freeing itself from, its own will, as the previous form of unhappy consciousness did not: for now it does not respond to the generosity of the Unchangeable with an action *of its own*, but allows its own will to be completely supplanted by that of the Unchangeable (in the person of the minister). In Hegel's words, consciousness 'casts upon the mediator or minister its own freedom of decision, and herewith the responsibility for its own action', and its action thereby ceases to be 'its own' (§228/154). Furthermore, consciousness relinquishes its 'self-conscious *independence*' by 'thinking and speaking what is meaningless to it' (namely, Latin); it denies itself satisfaction through work by giving up many of the possessions it acquires thereby; and it denies itself the enjoyment that both work and life bring by fasting and mortifying itself. In these ways, consciousness renounces its sense of *self* by genuinely sacrificing the fruits of its labour and submitting itself wholly to the will of the Unchangeable. Consciousness thus gives itself over to a life of *asceticism* governed by what are known as the 'evangelical counsels' of poverty, chastity and obedience; and at this point in the *Phenomenology* it becomes apparent that the unhappy consciousness is realized most perfectly in Mediaeval Christianity.

It is important to remember here that Hegel is doing phenomenology, not – like Nietzsche – genealogy. He is interested, therefore, in what self-consciousness takes itself to be doing, not in what *we* might think is going on. Nietzsche boldly proclaims that from *his* perspective (or perspectives), the 'ascetic ideal' springs from a sick and 'degenerating life'[41]; but Hegel makes no such judgement. What interests him is the way in which self-consciousness understands itself. He points out that the grateful self-consciousness sees *for itself* that it does not really relinquish its independence when it gives thanks for its gifts, but that the ascetic self relinquishes its independence *in its own eyes* because it sees itself as governed completely by the will of another (albeit one in which it sees its own essence).

In relinquishing his independence in this way, Hegel argues, the ascetic ceases to regard himself any longer as a free self-consciousness, but reduces himself, in his own eyes, to a mere living being or 'thing' (*Ding*), determined by the will of the Unchangeable. In seeking to become one with his true, unchangeable self, therefore, the ascetic turns his changeable, individual self into the very opposite of a self, into a merely 'objective existence' (§229/155). At the same time, however, precisely by giving up his own will, the ascetic allows the will of the Unchangeable to enter his consciousness and *become his own will*. At the very extreme of his wretchedness, therefore, the gap between the individual and the Unchangeable finally disappears, and the unhappy self at last obtains 'relief from its *misery*' (§230/155).

More precisely, the self obtains relief *in principle* (*an sich*), or in *our* eyes. In its own eyes, it remains unhappy, because it still takes itself to be separate from the Unchangeable that now inhabits it. Consciousness lets the will of the Unchangeable become its own will, but it still sees that unchangeable will as the will of *another* working within it. As Hegel puts it, 'for consciousness, its will does indeed become universal, essential [*an sich seiend*] will, but consciousness itself does not take itself to be this essential will' (§230/156). The minister assures consciousness that 'blessed enjoyment' is to be found in its misery by allowing the Unchangeable into its heart; but, for consciousness, such enjoyment comes only from *beyond* itself, and it continues to see *itself* as the source of misery. Consciousness is not yet happy, therefore, because it is not yet happy with itself.

Yet this is not the whole story, for the experience of consciousness *itself* makes it aware of its *unity* with the Unchangeable. Consciousness relinquishes its freedom and independence, turns itself into a thing and gives itself over to the will of the Unchangeable. The Unchangeable in turn enters, and takes over, the changeable consciousness of the individual. Individual consciousness is not, however, simply eliminated thereby, but *remains* as that which is different from, but wholly determined by, the Unchangeable. Insofar as consciousness focuses on the lingering difference between itself and the Unchangeable, it thinks of itself as taken over by *another* and so remains unhappy with *itself*: for 'the universal which thereby comes to be for it, is not regarded as its *own doing*' (§230/156). Yet insofar as it thinks of itself as wholly determined by, and *filled with*, the Unchangeable, it sees a profound *unity* between itself and the latter. In this respect, there is no longer a reason for it to feel unhappy with itself, for it knows that, *in its very individuality*, it is one with the Unchangeable. As Hegel puts it, consciousness 'finds that its own action and being, as being that of this *individual* consciousness, are being and action *in themselves [an sich]*' (§230/156). This consciousness of unity remains in tension with, and subordinate to, unhappiness in the unhappy consciousness itself; but it is taken up and affirmed explicitly by the next shape of consciousness that Hegel examines, namely *reason (Vernunft)*.

Reason is a new shape of consciousness, quite different from the unhappy consciousness, but it is made necessary by the experience of the latter. It thus incorporates the results of that experience. On the one hand, therefore, reason is a form of consciousness enjoyed by an *individual, changeable* self. Furthermore, it belongs to an individual self that has turned itself into mere 'being' (*Sein*) (§231/157), that sees itself as a mere empirical thing, or living being, in the world. On the other hand, reason is the *immutable, universal* consciousness that is found *in* changeable, empirical individuals. It thus is, and knows itself to be, the *unity* of the changeable and the unchangeable, the individual and the universal (§231/157).

Reason sees this same unity in its *object*: for its object is also unchangeable being that takes individual form. Since such unchangeable being is universal, reason sees it *everywhere* – in the whole world, not just in our own individual selves. Reason thus sees *itself* – the unity that *it* is – in the *actual world* that surrounds it. This latter idea is captured in Hegel's claim that 'reason is the certainty of consciousness that it is all reality' (§233/158). This striking claim makes it look as though reason reduces the world to a mere projection of itself, but that is not Hegel's point. Reason accepts that there is a world out there that is the *object* of consciousness, but it takes that world to be the same incarnate universality – the same *embodied reason* – as *itself*. Reason is thus a form of *self-consciousness*; but it differs in a significant way from the other shapes of self-consciousness that we have considered.

Reason fulfils the aim of the unhappy consciousness to become one with unchangeable being. It is thus explicitly the *thinking* consciousness – consciousness of the unity of subject and object – that the unhappy consciousness tries to become. Unlike stoic consciousness, however, reason does not *withdraw* from the empirical world into the abstract, lifeless thought of what there is; rather, reason is empirically *embodied* thought that sees itself *in* the empirical world around it. Stoic consciousness withdrew from life into itself, because, like the other shapes of self-consciousness, it asserted itself and its own freedom by *negating* the object in front of it.

The protagonists in the life and death struggle sought to negate the object completely by eliminating all dependence on life and things from their self-consciousness; in so doing they endeavoured to become pure *self*-consciousness, or being-for-self, albeit in relation to the other self who was to accord them recognition. Unlike these struggling selves (and the master and the sceptic), the slave and the stoic both acknowledged the independence and irreducibility of the object; but they, too, asserted their freedom by partially negating the object (through labour or thought). Finally, the unhappy consciousness sought to become one with the Unchangeable by freeing itself from its own changeable individuality, and so saw its own actuality, just as the other shapes saw the world, as 'the negative of its essence' (§232/157). The common thread that runs through all the shapes of self-consciousness, therefore, is that each tries 'to save itself and maintain itself for itself at the expense of the *world*, or of its own actuality', that is, by *negating* the world or its own actuality. Each seeks thereby to a greater or lesser degree, to be a free *self*, not a mere living *thing*. The development of self-consciousness shows, however, that this search to be a free, more or less pure, self leads logically, if not always historically, to *unhappiness* with oneself: for my contingent worldly existence – my very life – eventually comes to be seen as the enemy that keeps me apart from my true, immutable self. Such unhappiness is implicitly overcome only when self-consciousness renounces its own freedom and selfhood, turns itself into the very *thing* it does not want to be, and at the same time lets the Unchangeable – which it takes to be beyond it – *into its life*.

When self-consciousness does this, it is on the verge of reason. Prior to this point self-consciousness thinks that being a free *self* is essentially *at odds* with being a thing or being mere life. Reason no longer holds this to be true, but sees itself *in* perceivable things and *in* living beings. Reason is thus no longer a shape of *self*-consciousness in the strict sense, but opens a new chapter of the *Phenomenology*, in which self-consciousness and sensuous, perceptual consciousness are reconciled with one another. Reason is no longer self-consciousness *tout court*, because it stands in a *positive*, not just a *negative* relation, to the object: it deepens its sense of self (initially, at least), not by negating and transforming the things around it, but by dwelling with them and exploring them in detail. As Hegel puts it, reason is interested in the 'continuing existence' (*Bestehen*), rather than the 'disappearance' (*Verschwinden*), of the world, because it sees in the world 'its own *truth* and *presence*': 'it is certain of experiencing only itself therein' (§232/158).[42]

Study questions

1 What is the principal difference between stoicism and scepticism?
2 Why is the unhappy consciousness led by its experience to become ascetic?

Reason

Up to this point I have set out Hegel's phenomenological argument in some detail. For reasons of space, however, I will have to omit many details from the following accounts of reason, spirit, religion and absolute knowing. My aim, however, is still to make the *logic* that structures the experience of consciousness as clear as possible.

Observing reason

Reason is certain that 'that it is all reality', that it is to be found *everywhere* – in empirical things, as well as in consciousness. Reason takes the world around it to be real and to have continuing, independent existence. Yet Hegel describes its relation to the world as 'idealism', since it sees *itself* – sees reason – in that world (§233/158).

In the *Phenomenology*, Hegel always starts by examining a shape of consciousness in its immediacy. Reason is initially understood, therefore, as the *immediate* unity of individuality and universality. It is individual, changeable self-consciousness that is itself immediately *unchanging and universal*. Such a self thus is, and knows itself to be, the '*simple unity* of self-consciousness' (§235/160), or what Hegel calls, following Kant, the pure 'unity of apperception' (§238/163).[43] As such, it is, and knows itself to be, a pure *I* without any further differentiation.

So understood, reason is quite empty, formal and abstract. Yet it also sees itself in the world around it and so is conscious of being 'the *simple* unity of self-consciousness and being' (§235/160). Hegel names this unity the 'category' (*Kategorie*). Formerly, we are told – that is, in the Aristotelian tradition – a category was held to be an 'essential form' (*Wesenheit*) of being in contrast to consciousness. In the 'one-sided, spurious idealism' of Kant, on the other hand – in Hegel's view, at least – a category is a form of consciousness alone. For reason, however, the category is the thought 'that self-consciousness and being are *the same* essence' (§235/160).

Since reason is initially quite abstract, it is simply the bare consciousness that it can see *itself* in the world. That is to say, it is conscious only that 'everything is *its own*', that it is at home in the world (§238/162). This empty sense of 'mineness' is given content by the *world* that reason encounters – the world of empirical things and living beings. Reason seeks to discover *what* it is, therefore, by *observing* the empirical world around it, and it must do so because it is utterly abstract in itself.

Reason first looks for itself in the sensuous, perceivable things that surround it, but it does not just passively *perceive* things. It regards the world as 'its own' and so 'makes its own observations and experiments [*Erfahrung*]', in order to discover what is rational *in* things. In so doing, it seeks to go beyond their transient perceivable properties and discern the immutable universality, or stable *self-identity*, in the changeable, observable world. In this way, as Hegel puts it, reason 'seeks to possess in thinghood the consciousness only of itself' (§240/164). Reason thus has an *interest* in finding *itself* in things that is absent from sense-certainty, perception and understanding: for, in contrast to reason, the attention of those three forms of consciousness is directed solely towards their *objects*.

'Observing reason' is, however, similar to consciousness, insofar as it seeks to find reason in its *object*, not just within itself. It is thus initially outward-looking and takes the form of what Hegel calls the 'observation of nature'.

Observation of nature

Observing reason encounters things with various determinate properties and looks for what is universal, or 'identical with itself', in them (§§244–5/166). It first seeks such identity by getting to know each thing *as a whole*, and it tries to do this by *describing* all the properties of the thing. The task of description, however, is endless, since there are always further aspects of things, and further things, to be described. Description thus proves unable to bring to mind something whole and self-identical.

What Hegel calls the 'instinct' of reason now causes the latter to turn away from comprehensive description and pick out properties, or 'characteristics' (*Merkmale*), that it regards as *essential* to a thing's identity. Reason deems these to be essential, because they are the features through which things give themselves their own identity, such as the claws and teeth by means of which 'each animal itself *separates* itself from others' (§246/167–8). Reason thus brings to mind a universal that, in its eyes, belongs to things themselves.

As properties of finite, changeable things, however, such characteristics are themselves subject to change: animals, for example, can lose their teeth or claws. Reason is thus forced by its experience to regard these properties, no longer as simple, stable determinacies, but as 'vanishing *moments*' (§248/169). As reason, however, it still looks for what is universal and self-identical, and so seeks the simple self-identity or unity that is evident even in the 'confusion' (§247/168–9) of changing properties. As we saw above, understanding regards forces as 'vanishing' moments, too, but finds in *law* the '*simple element in the play of force itself*' (§§141, 148/99, 104). Likewise, reason now looks for the law that governs the restless changing of properties (§248/169).

Unlike understanding, however, reason thinks of law, not as something purely *intelligible*, but as something that can itself be *observed* in perceivable things (§249/170). It thus carries out experiments in order to observe 'what happens in such and such circumstances' and thereby to discover the laws governing the things concerned (§251/172). The problem is that any laws that are discovered in this way are 'tied to a specific being' – to the specific things on which the experiments are carried out – and so lack the *universality* proper to law. Further experiments, however, yield laws that relate more *general* natural phenomena to one another, such as acid and base or 'positive and negative electricity'. Such phenomena, which Hegel calls 'matters' (*Materien*), are not specific *things* themselves, but they are general phenomena *in* sensuous, empirical things between which laws can be observed to hold (§251/172–3). Each is thus sensuous being in the form of a *universal* or, as Hegel puts it, 'a non-sensuous sensuous being' (*ein unsinnliches Sinnliches*) (§252/173). In the course of his account of observing reason, Hegel makes oblique reference to several contemporary scientists, including Linnaeus and Benjamin Franklin.[44] The development he traces – from description to observable law – is, however, made necessary logically by reason itself, namely by reason's interest in discovering through *observation* what is *universal* in the empirical world.

Hegel now argues that the consciousness of *law*, to which reason has been led by its experiments, makes a transition necessary to a new shape of observing reason. Since reason thinks that law can be *observed* in the world, it does not conceive of law as something explicitly universal and intelligible. It thus has, as its explicit object, the *sensuous* universals, or 'matters', connected by law, not law *as such*. Implicit in reason's idea of law, however, is the thought of a universal 'which is freed from sensuous being' and thus 'a *simple* concept' (§253/173). Hegel now moves to another shape of reason, whose object, while still immersed in the observable, empirical world, exhibits *free* universality, simplicity and self-identity *explicitly*. Such an object, Hegel maintains, is the *organism*, or living being. Inorganic things are unities, insofar as each is *one* thing; but their essential character resides in the properties that distinguish them from *other* things. Organisms, by contrast, are independent, self-relating beings, and so exhibit the *self-identity* of reason more explicitly than mere things.

As we saw above, self-consciousness also relates to living beings, but it consumes them or regards them as things to be worked on. Reason, by contrast, seeks to discover the *laws* that govern organisms.[45] The first laws reason finds govern the relation of organisms to inorganic 'general elements', such as air, water, earth and climate (§255/174), and state, for example, that 'animals in northern latitudes have thick, hairy pelts' (a principle formulated by Hegel's contemporary, the biologist G. R. Treviranus).[46] These laws, however, are not genuine *laws*, since they do not establish any clear, universal connection between organisms and their environment, but suffer all manner of exceptions.

Since reason observes no clear connection between organisms and their environment *in* nature itself, it formulates the thought of a wholly *external* connection between them. This is the thought of an 'external, *teleological* relation' (§256/175), in which the environment *purposefully* prepares the ground for organic life.[47] Such a connection is 'external', in reason's eyes, because it is not evident in observable nature itself: one can observe cattle and sheep grazing, but no observation can show that nature purposefully provides grass, *so that* these animals can graze.

For the phenomenologist, however, the organism, as reason conceives it, is a 'real purpose' *in itself*, since it pursues the *aim*, inherent in its being, of preserving itself and staying alive (§256/175). The organism, as reason conceives it, must try to preserve itself, for this is how it seeks to maintain the self-identity that makes it, in the eyes of reason, a rationally structured being. Reason itself observes that organisms try to preserve themselves, but it does not think of their activity explicitly as *purposive*, because it thinks of purpose as external to them (§259/177–8). Yet reason is not completely blind to the distinction between the inner aim of the organism and the actual fulfilment of that aim. It does not, however, conceive of these two moments in these terms, but pictures them simply as the 'inner' and 'outer' aspects of the organism. Since reason takes its object to be both self-identical and observable, it regards the inner and outer aspects of the organism as 'two *fixed* moments in the form of *immediate being*' (§262/179), as two separate, observable phenomena. At the same time, it understands the organism to be one, self-relating unity. The inner and the outer are thus for it two observably different forms of *one* unified organism; and, since the outer is essentially the *same* thing as the inner, the former, in reason's eyes, does nothing but give outward *expression* to the latter (§263/179).

Now law, we recall, is itself the *unity* of, or constant relation between, different moments (see p. 68, above). Reason thus holds the relation between the inner and outer aspects of the organism to be governed by *law*. This is the law that is inherent *in* the organism – the one that governs, not the organism's relation to the inorganic sphere, but its own relation to *itself*. It states that, in the organism, '*the outer is the expression of the inner*' (§262/179).

The inner aspect of the organism, Hegel explains, comprises three moments: *sensibility*, or the organism's capacity for self-feeling; *irritability*, or its capacity to react to other organisms and things; and *reproduction*, or its capacity to preserve its own life (through eating and drinking) and the life of the species (through producing offspring) (§266/180). The outer aspect of the organism comprises the different biological systems in which these moments are embodied or 'given shape' (*gestaltet*). These are the nervous system (for sensibility), the muscular system (for irritability) and what Hegel calls the 'innards' (*Eingeweide*) (for reproduction), which include both the digestive and reproductive systems (§267/181). The laws 'peculiar to organisms' thus govern the different ways in which the three inner moments find outward shape in different organisms (§268/181).

Hegel points out, however, that, since the inner and the outer, for reason, are both separate, observable phenomena, the inner must exhibit its '*own immediate* externality' quite apart from the outward shape in which the inner is expressed (§274/185). Accordingly, reason considers the three inner moments of the organism to be separate from and external to *one another*. Furthermore, it seeks the *law* that governs the relations between them (§270/182). Yet precisely because reason sees these moments as quite *external* to one another, the laws it formulates are based only on external, *quantitative* comparison. They thus state, for example, that the magnitudes of sensibility and irritability stand in an inverse ratio to one another, so that as one increases, the other decreases (a law formulated by C. F. Kielmeyer in the 1790s) (§271/183).[48] Such a law, however, does not reveal anything specific about sensibility or irritability itself, but is the product of an 'empty play of formulating laws' that 'can be practised everywhere and with everything' (§272/184). It is thus not in fact a law that is inherent in the organism.

In contrast to perception and understanding, observing reason has a more nuanced conception of the organism. Perception treats the organism, like everything else, as a thing with properties and says simply that an animal *has* strong muscles. Understanding goes further and says that the animal 'possesses great *muscular force* [*Muskelkraft*]' (§282/189). Reason, however, reveals the 'force' specific to muscles to be *irritability* (or the capacity to respond to a stimulus). Yet the purely quantitative law that reason formulates to connect irritability and sensibility fails to capture anything *specific* about either, so the advantage reason has over perception and understanding is lost. Indeed, by treating these two moments as *external* to one another, reason falls back into the perspective of 'sensuous perception' (§282/190).

A similar problem besets the laws taken by reason to govern the relation between the inner moments of the organism and their outward expression. As we saw above, self-consciousness recognizes that life is a process in which different moments are constantly becoming *one* (see §169/122–3). Reason accepts that the organism is a self-relating, self-preserving unity, but it also believes that the inner moments of the organism can be observed in their separation from one another (§275/185). Furthermore, it believes that these separate inner moments are expressed in *separate* biological systems. By breaking up the organism into separate, observable systems, however, reason loses sight of the organism's *unity*, and so no longer sees it as a *living* being. The organism is thus reduced by reason to a cadaver – the dead object of anatomy (§276/186).

Reason tries to find law in the *observable* world, and it initially discovers law in inorganic nature: for example, in the connection between acid and base (§251/172). It is, however, in the organism that reason finds itself – its unity and self-identity – most explicitly embodied in nature. Reason thus seeks law in what it observes the organism to be. Its search proves, however, to be fruitless: for a law that connects separate, *observable* aspects of the organism destroys the organism itself (§§277–8/187). Yet this experience does not lead reason to abandon altogether the idea that there is law in what is observable: for it finds such law in what it can observe of *self-consciousness*, that is, of *itself* (§298/201).

The observation of self-consciousness

As we saw above, reason is individual self-consciousness that is immediately *immutable* and *universal*. As such, it is a '*simple unity*' that is empty, formal and abstract (§235/160). The first laws that reason finds within itself are thus those that belong to self-consciousness, or thought, in this empty form. These are the laws of formal logic that require thought to be purely *self-identical*: the laws of identity, non-contradiction and the excluded middle (§299/201). Reason, however, is not just abstract, but also knows itself to be 'all reality'. Accordingly, it must understand the laws of thought to govern that reality, too. For reason, therefore, things themselves must be self-identical and non-contradictory, if they are to be objects of reason.

The laws of inorganic and organic nature are found by reason *in* the observable world: they exist *in* the things and organisms that embody them. The laws of thought, by contrast, exist *for* thought in the *form* of thought itself. Yet reason is still observing reason and so *observes* these laws to be separate from one another, each with an identity of its own (§300/202). This separateness, however, contradicts the *unity* that reason understands self-consciousness and thought to have (just as the separate aspects of the organism contradict its unity).

The unity of self-consciousness is restored in '*active consciousness*' (*tuendes Bewußtsein*) (§301/203). Such self-consciousness does not take itself to be a simple, immediate unity, but preserves its unity in the *activity* of negating what confronts it. Yet since it is reason, active consciousness also sees itself and its own 'actuality' *in* what confronts it. Specifically, it sees in the social world around it the actual, *objective* 'habits, customs, and way of thinking' that guide and inform its own *subjective* activity (§302/203).

Such self-consciousness is the object of a new form of observing reason that Hegel calls 'observational psychology' (§303/203). Self-consciousness is observed by psychology to stand in a twofold relation to the habits and customs that surround it. On the one hand, since it sees its own actuality in those habits and customs, self-consciousness endeavours to make itself conform to them more and more explicitly. On the other hand, since it knows itself to be 'spontaneously active in face of them', it endeavours to make them conform to *it* (and so sets out to negate and change them in some way) (§302/203). What interests psychology in both cases are the 'capacities, inclinations and passions' that it *finds* – through observation – in active consciousness and that, from its perspective at least, govern the latter's activity (§303/203).

Observing reason also tries to find the *law* that governs the relation between self-consciousness and the social world around it (and to determine the 'influence' the latter has on the self) (§306/204–5).[49] This perspective of observing reason is, however, at odds with its object. Reason takes self-consciousness and its world to be two *separate* elements that are *found* to stand in a law-governed relation to one another. Self-consciousness, by contrast, understands the world, not just to be separate from it, but to contain the habits and customs that inform its own activity. Furthermore, it takes itself *actively* to determine its whole relation to that world. From its own point of view, 'the individual either *allows* free play to the stream of the actual world flowing in upon it' – by actively seeking to conform to that world – 'or else breaks it off and transforms it' – and so actively seeks to make the world conform to it (§307/206). For the individual self, therefore, there are not *two* elements that are simply *found* to stand in a law-governed relation, but *one* 'circle' (*Kreis*) of its *own activity* (§308/206).

Yet self-consciousness also knows that an aspect of its *own* activity is not due to itself alone, but is rooted in the habits and customs by which it does, indeed, *find* itself surrounded. It thus takes itself and its own activity to be a unity of 'being that is *found* or *given* [*vorhanden*]' and 'being that it has *made*' (§308/206). The next object of observing reason is self-consciousness that takes itself to be such a unity within *itself* and its own individuality *alone*, independently of the world around it.

Such self-consciousness sees its own body as its '*original* aspect', the aspect for which it is not itself responsible and which it simply *finds* itself to have. Yet the individual also takes himself to be 'what he has *done*' and so turns his body into something 'he has himself *produced*'. He does not regard his body merely as a given, therefore, but sees it rather as a *sign* (*Zeichen*) through which *he* 'makes known what he really is' (§310/207). This individual, who, in his own eyes, is both something given and actual *and* free activity – the unity of *being* and *doing* – is what reason now observes.

Reason takes the individual to be the unity of being and doing both *within* his self-consciousness and in the *outer* form of his body. His inner self unites being and doing, since it has a 'determinate original character' or 'innate peculiarity' (§§311, 316/208, 211), which defines what he *is*, and yet it is also essentially *activity*. Similarly, his body gives visible shape and *being* to his inner self; yet, in so doing, the relevant bodily organ also makes the *activity* of that inner self visible: the self's 'action *qua* action, or the inner as such' is embodied, for example, in 'the speaking mouth' or 'the working hand' (§312/208).

For reason, therefore, the '*organ* of activity' – the mouth or hand – is 'just as much a *being* [*Sein*] as there is *activity* [*Tun*] in it' (§316/210), and in this way it gives direct outward expression to the active inner self of the individual. Yet reason also sees that, in the process of expressing the inner self, such an organ *ceases* to express that self: for once the self's action has been completed and is no longer an ongoing action *of* the self, 'the spoken word' or 'accomplished act' in which it is expressed no longer belongs *to* the self, but can be 'twisted' by others into something quite different from what the individual himself had in mind (§312/208).

Reason finds a more enduring expression of the inner self in those aspects of oral or manual expression that remain constant in different expressive acts. These include the 'sound and range of the voice' or the character of one's handwriting, which continue to reveal who *we* are within, even if our words are given meanings we do not intend (§316/211). In the eyes of reason, therefore, our inner self, which is essentially activity, is best expressed not in bodily *action* as such, but in those features of bodily action that endure and retain their identity across different actions – those features that *are* what they *are*, whatever our bodies may *do*.

Reason also sees the inner self expressed in 'the movement and form of the face and figure in general, which take no part in action' (§317/211). What is expressed in this way, reason holds, is not the self's activity itself, but rather its 'own control and observation' of its activity, its own inward *reflection* on its activity. In our facial expression and bodily posture, therefore, the conversation the individual is having with himself *about* his actions is outwardly visible to others; so we can 'see from a man's face whether he is *in earnest* about what he is saying or doing' (§318/211–12).

In one of the many personal comments that pepper this section of the *Phenomenology*, Hegel points out that facial expression, as something external, can differ from, as much as express, what is within the self: for the self, he writes, the face can also be a 'mask which it can lay aside' (§318/212). Observing reason, however, thinks that it can always read what is within the self in the outer expression of the face. This conviction underlies the judgements we make every day, at first sight, about the character of others; and it also underlies the (in Hegel's view) pseudo-science of *physiognomy*, popularized by J. C. Lavater in the 1770s.

The physiognomist, in Hegel's account, thinks he can observe in facial expressions the innermost inwardness of the self: not just what the self does, but what it *intends* and what it is *capable* of. Indeed, he thinks he can establish *laws* connecting inner character and facial expression. The only thing he can actually observe, however, is the face, which he connects to an unobservable, *'presumed'* (gemeint) inner self (§320/214). Physiognomy is not a real science, therefore, but 'the voicing of *one's own opinion* [*Meinung*]' about what one presumes to be the case (§321/214); and logically, if not in history, it must become aware of this itself.

Physiognomy, as Hegel presents it, studies the facial features of speaking and acting human beings – the *enduring* features of bodily 'expression that is itself a *movement*' (§323/216). The final shape of observing reason takes this focus on what endures – on what *is* – to its logical conclusion and examines the body insofar as it is a 'wholly *immobile* reality' or 'mere thing' (§323/216). Since reason now regards the body in this way, it no longer takes it to express the activity of the inner self directly; instead, it seeks the law-governed, *causal* relation between the inner and the outer. For the inner self to act on, and have an observable effect on, the body, however, it must itself take bodily form (§325/217). For reason, the immediate, bodily expression of self-consciousness is the living brain, and the 'mere thing', in which the brain produces its effects, is the skull (§§327–8/218–19). Observing reason thus takes the form of *phrenology* – developed by Hegel's contemporary, D. F. J. Gall – according to which the brain is held to shape the skull in various ways, and the character of the inner self, which finds expression in the shape of the brain, can thus be read in the visible bumps and hollows on the head (§336/225).

Hegel considers phrenology to be 'foolish' (*albern*) (§346/232). Reason is forced to adopt this 'foolish' view, however, by its own insistence on *observation*: for the latter leads logically to the conclusion that the inner self can be known by *observing* a perceivable thing, namely the skull-bone (§331/222). There is, however, a contradiction in phrenology that will take us beyond observation to a new form of reason. Phrenology holds that there are *laws* governing the relation between brain and skull; this is how we are able to conclude that *these* bumps and hollows are caused by *this* kind of brain and inner character. Yet the inner self and the skull are, *for reason itself*, separate realities, whose connection is sometimes seen to conflict with phrenology's laws. To preserve those laws, the phrenologist asserts that this observed bump *should* indicate this character, even if it is observed *not* to do so in this case (§337/226). By arguing in this way, however, the phrenologist admits that, here at least, the inner self cannot be observed in the skull after all. Implicit in this admission, Hegel says, is the broader thought that no mere observable *thing* can show what self-consciousness *actually* is – that simple '*being* as such is not the truth of spirit' (§339/227). The next shape of reason affirms this thought explicitly and so ceases to be merely *observing* reason.

Study questions

1 Why does observing reason reduce the organism to the dead object of anatomy?
2 Why does observing reason lead logically to phrenology?

Active, self-conscious reason

The new shape of reason is explicitly aware that self-consciousness cannot be reduced to a mere thing, because it is *activity*, indeed (as we have seen above) the activity of *negating* things. Such reason realizes, therefore, that it is self-conscious, not when it observes itself, but when it negates and changes what is other than it – when it is the 'negativity of the other' (§359/239). Reason thus now turns its back on observation and takes on the 'negative' character of self-consciousness that it left behind when it first emerged. Yet it remains reason and so also looks for itself *in* what is other than it. The changes it brings about in the other must thus enable it to see itself in that other. If it is to see in the other its own *self-consciousness*, however, that other cannot be a mere thing, but must be a self-consciousness itself. Reason, therefore, must now be self-consciousness that stands in relation to another self – 'spirit, which in the doubling of its self-consciousness and the independence of both, has the certainty of its unity with itself' (§347/233).

In its initial immediacy, this new shape of 'active' – practical – reason is conscious above all of being an *individual* self-consciousness (§348/234). As such, it is interested in its own individual actuality: its own feelings, life and sense of self. Its initial aim, therefore, is to 'become aware of itself as an individual' – as *this* particular individual – 'in the other self-consciousness' to which it relates (§360/240). Reason fulfils this aim by 'negating' the other self, and in this respect its action is 'an action of *desire*' (§362/240). Yet, precisely because it wants to see itself *in* the other, it does not – like pure desire – seek to destroy the other, but simply takes away the latter's independence and turns it into an *extension of itself*: it 'make[s] this other into itself' (§360/240). The individual thereby gains, not just the fleeting enjoyment of consuming something, but the infinite *pleasure (Lust)* of feeling nothing but himself, his own life and his own sensations, in the other – the pleasure of knowing *himself* to be 'all reality'. The all-embracing character of this pleasure makes it an experience of *reason*, rather than mere self-consciousness.[50]

Yet the individual's pleasure is itself short-lived, for the self does *not* just see *itself* in the other but actually encounters 'the *unity* of itself and the *other* self-consciousness' (§362/241). Moreover, with the loss of its pleasure, its whole sense of itself is destroyed. A more mature self would allow the other – a friend or lover – to be part of itself. The self we are considering, however, locates its pleasure and sense of self in feeling itself to be *everything*, in feeling nothing but *itself* in the other; becoming aware of the presence of the other thus destroys the individual's sense of self altogether.

When the pleasure-seeking individual no longer feels himself to be everything, he feels that he is nothing, that he has lost all that he is. He feels himself crushed, therefore, not merely by *another self*, but by something that is the sheer *negation* of himself: 'the nothingness of individuality' (§363/242). This something is everything the individual is not: universal, abstract, and lifeless, rather than individual, concrete and alive. The individual feels 'smashed', therefore, by 'the negative, uncomprehended *power of universality*' or sheer '*abstract necessity*' (§365/243). In its search for all-encompassing pleasure, the self 'took hold of life', but 'really laid hold of death', and it feels only the cold necessity of this loss (§364/243).

Such necessity is produced by the self's own search for pleasure and so actually belongs to the self, even though the latter takes that necessity to be utterly '*alien* to it'. In being conscious of this necessity, the self is thus implicitly aware of '*its own* essence' (§366/244). The next shape of reason recognizes explicitly that there is necessity and universality *within itself*. This shape still takes itself to be an individual self-consciousness, but it now knows itself to have the universal – in the form of *law* – immediately present within it. Such law is the individual's very *own* law: the '*law* of the *heart*' (§367/244).

Confronting this individual is a reality that preserves the contradiction between the universal and the individual that emerged in the experience of pleasure-seeking reason. This reality is governed by law that is at odds with the hearts of individuals, one in which individuals are oppressed by a 'cruel necessity' (§369/245). The individual, guided by the law of his heart, now acts to remove this contradiction in reality. In so doing, he seeks the double pleasure (*Lust*) of seeing his *own* law become reality and of promoting the 'welfare of humanity' by freeing others from the law that currently oppresses them (§370/245). By implementing his own law, therefore, the individual aims to create a reality in which others may see the law of *their* own hearts embodied, too. Such an individual thus assumes that the law of his heart is in fact the universal law of all hearts and that his pleasure can be a universal pleasure.

In being realized, however, the law ceases to be the law of *this* individual's heart and becomes a genuinely *universal* law valid for all individuals equally. Contrary to his expectations, therefore, the individual no longer sees the law specifically as his *own* (§372/246). Even if it retains the content the individual originally gave to it, once it has been realized the law is no longer the law of *his* heart, but *universal* law as such and so a law with whose form he now feels himself to be at odds.

There is a further problem: the individual wants to make his own law a reality, partly so that others may be freed from the law that oppresses them and come to see the law of *their* own hearts realized in the world around them. From the perspective of those others, however, the law that I implement is the law of *my* particular heart, not theirs (§373/247). So they turn against the law that I have established, just as I turned against the law under which they were living before.

The individual's heart is thus now at odds both with the form of the law it has set up and with the hearts of the other individuals it sought to liberate, and so feels 'alienated' (*entfremdet*) from the reality it has created (§374/247). The individual does not, however, blame himself for this, but takes that reality to be 'deranged' (*verrückt*) by all the other individuals who are seeking to implement the laws of their own hearts (§§376–7/249). In his eyes, his aim is frustrated by a Hobbesian war of all against all, in which 'each claims validity for his own individuality' and there is really only the semblance of universality (§379/251). The individual's heart thus no longer throbs with concern for the welfare for others, but now gives in to 'the ravings of an insane self-conceit' (§377/249): for he thinks that his own heart *alone* harbours a law that is truly universal, and he rages against the 'way of the world' (*Weltlauf*) – which is governed by individual self-interest – for preventing him from implementing it properly (§379/251).

Implicit in this insanity is the thought that *individuality* as such is the source of perversion. The next shape of reason takes up this thought explicitly and concludes that the law within us can be actualized without perversion only if individuality is *sacrificed*. This shape is that of *virtue*. For virtue, what is essential is what is universal – the *law* that it sees as 'the intrinsically true and good' – and the virtuous person must give up his own individual interests, indeed must sacrifice his 'entire personality', in the service of this universal (§381/252). Confronting virtue is the 'way of the world', which, as we have seen, is governed *by* individual self-interest. As a form of 'active' reason, virtue takes it upon itself to bring good into the world by cleansing it of such individual self-interest.

As a form of reason, however, virtue also sees itself, or rather the good within itself, *in* the world it confronts. Yet that world is clearly under the sway of individual self-interest and so not yet *actually* good. Virtue, therefore, believes the good to be the 'inner essence' or 'in itself' (*Ansich*) of the world – the essence that the world *would* manifest, were it not perverted by individuals (§381/252). Yet if the good already belongs to the world, albeit only implicitly, it does not need to be brought *into* the world from the outside by virtue. Virtue claims, therefore, that, by suppressing individual self-interest within itself and fighting it in the world, it really does no more than 'make room' for the good inherent in the world to come into existence on its own.

Since the virtuous person seeks to suppress his own individuality, he must fight the way of the world with weapons that are not specific to him but universal. These are the general 'gifts, capacities, powers' he finds within himself. Yet because he takes these to be *universal*, the virtuous person finds them not only within himself but also in the world. He thinks, however, that such capacities and powers are '*misused*' there, whereas he puts them to '*good use*' (§385/254). Hegel now shows that virtue is not as superior to the world as it thinks it is.

The problem is that the virtuous person wants to help the world become good by completely suppressing individuality, including his own. Yet he is also conscious that any activity through which he puts the capacities and powers within him to 'good use' is his *own* activity as an *individual*. If he is truly to suppress his individuality, therefore, he must suppress even his own virtuous activity and deny that *he* is doing anything *at all* in the service of the good. The 'knight of virtue' must thus regard his own struggle on behalf of the good as a 'sham' that he cannot and may not take seriously. The corollary of this is that he must take 'his true strength' to lie in the fact that the good he advocates 'brings itself to fulfilment' *by itself* (§386/255). If I am a truly self-effacing virtuous person, I believe that the good realizes *itself* and doesn't need me to help it into come into being.

The logical consequence of this, however, is that virtue must accept that there is good in the world *already*. This in turn implies that individual self-interest – which is the 'way of the world' – does not prevent the good from emerging after all, but is itself a vehicle of the good; and *that* means that the virtuous person's *own* activity as an individual can be the vehicle of the good, too. If this is the case, however, virtue may not suppress anything about itself or attack anything in the world *just in case it serves the good*: 'there can be neither a sacrifice of what is one's own, nor a violation of what is alien' (§386/255). The logic of virtue's position thus renders it utterly *impotent* in face of the world: as Hegel puts it, virtue utters 'empty, ineffectual words' which 'edify, but raise no edifice' (§390/257). The way of the world necessarily triumphs over virtue, therefore, because the latter's 'pompous talk' about the good is unable to bring about any change in the world at all.

Virtue's own experience of its impotence leads it to abandon the idea that the good requires 'the sacrifice of individuality' and to see individuality itself as that which *actualizes* the good, as 'the reality of the universal' (§391/258). In so doing, virtue also learns that the *world* is better than it (and the world itself) thinks it is: for it learns that the individual self-interest that governs the world is not at odds with law and the good after all, but actually promotes the good (which is not to deny that some selfishness can be downright destructive).

The next shape of reason takes up the idea that individuality *itself* actualizes what is universal and it makes it the principle of its activity. Such reason thus no longer acts on *something else* in order to see itself or its inner law become a reality in that other, but it actualizes the universal in and through its *own* individual activity alone. It does not seek to change the world around it, therefore, but actualizes the universal in the simple '*setting-forth* or *expression*' of itself (§394/260).

Study questions

1 What is contradictory about seeking to implement the law of one's heart?
2 Why does the 'knight of virtue' prove to be impotent in face of the 'way of the world'?

Individuality that is actual in and through itself

This new shape, Hegel writes, is the thorough 'fusion' (*Durchdringung*) of the individual and what is universal (§394/259). It is also the fusion of individuality and actuality, and is this in two senses. The individual *is* himself something actual, and he brings about something actual through his *activity*; he is thus a complex fusion of 'being' and 'doing' (or 'action') (§401/264).

First, therefore, the individual finds himself *to be* a certain way and so has an 'original determinate nature' (§398/261). The self studied by physiognomy was also found to have a 'determinate original character' (§311/208), but what interested reason in that case was how that nature found *observable* expression in the body (specifically, in the face). Now the self is no longer an object of observation, but the freestanding self-conscious *activity* of self-expression. Its original, given nature is thus its very activity itself insofar as the latter is not yet explicit activity, but a state of *being*: the self's inborn *ability* to act, its 'capacity, talent, character, and so on' (§401/263). Capacities are something universal – a 'universal element' (§398/262) found in all selves – but in this individual they are found in a particular constellation, which distinguishes him from other individuals.

Second, the *activity* of the individual aims at realizing his distinctive capacities. Such activity issues in a *work* (*Werk*) that expresses who and what the individual is (§402/265). Indeed, Hegel notes, it is precisely through such a work that the individual becomes *fully* aware of what his capacities actually are (§401/264). Through his actual activity, therefore, the individual creates an actual work in which his actual capacities find expression. These capacities are universal human capacities, present in this individual in a particular way. The individual's activity is thus the process of actualizing both his own individuality *and* what is universal, and so is the thorough fusion of individuality, universality and actuality.

Since there is nothing in the work that is not his *own* work, the self-expressing individual fulfils the aim of seeing *himself* in his object more completely than any shape of reason so far. Accordingly, in contemplating his work the individual '*can experience only joy [Freude] in himself*' (§404/266). We have clearly come a long way from the unhappiness in which pure self-consciousness culminated. Yet the experience of this individual proves to be more problematic than he first thinks it will be.

The problem is that, in creating a work, I put it out into the world and confront *other* individuals with it. They see in my work the expression of my particular individuality; but, of course, they want to contemplate a reality that expresses *their* individuality. They thus see in my work 'an alien reality, which they must replace by their own in order to obtain through *their* action the consciousness of *their* unity with reality'. I, in turn, become aware of a disparity between myself and my work: for I know myself to be the free, unconstrained activity of self-expression, but what I come to see in my work is 'something transient' that is supplanted and obscured from view by 'the counter-action of *other* forces and interests' (§405/268). I become aware, therefore, that the work that I have freely created in order to express myself inevitably succumbs to 'the self-regarding jealousies of the Spiritual Animal Kingdom'.[51] Yet this does not put an end to my joy: for, despite the sorry fate of my works, I remain convinced that I *succeed* – and always succeed – in expressing myself through my activity.

This conviction, however, requires me to alter my understanding of my activity: for, if I think that my activity is always successful, I cannot equate it with the ultimately unsuccessful activity of creating specific works. I must take it to be fulfilling a more universal aim. Such an aim is universal because it *remains* my aim, *whatever I do* (§409/270). In my eyes, therefore, my 'true work' as an individual must consist in actualizing this universal, rather than in creating specific works. Hegel names this universal 'the main thing' (*die Sache selbst*) or, as Quentin Lauer translates it, 'what really matters' (§409/270).[52] I never fail to fulfil my aim, because I know that, in all my activity, I am always doing *what really matters* (§412/272).

A work gives expression to the *particular* universals – the particular capacities and talents – in an individual. By contrast, 'what really matters' is something genuinely *universal*. This new object of consciousness does not, however, have a distinctive content of its own. It is universal because it is a *form* that any activity can take on or, as Hegel puts it, a 'predicate' that consciousness can attach to anything it does (§411/271). Consciousness claims that it is doing 'what really matters', whatever it does, and in this way it preserves the idea that it is *always* actualizing its inner universal and expressing itself. It is thus always able to find joy and satisfaction in its activity, even if the latter produces no actual works at all (§413/272).

Consciousness honestly thinks it always does 'what really matters', but it doesn't notice that there is an ambiguity in its new object. On the one hand, 'what really matters' is whatever *my* activity is directed towards, whatever *I* take to matter. In my eyes, therefore, *I* am the one who does what matters, and the latter requires *my* activity to make it a reality. On the other hand, 'what matters' is something genuinely *universal*: the 'free, *simple, abstract* "matter in hand" [that] has the value of essential being' (§411/271). In doing what matters, therefore, I take myself to be doing what really does matter *in itself*, what demands to be done for its own sake. Both these ideas are equally important to consciousness and the latter switches from one to the other without realizing it (§415/273). The ambiguity in its commitment becomes apparent, however, when consciousness encounters other individuals.

When an individual declares that he is doing 'what really matters', the others initially take him to mean that he is doing what matters in itself and that he simply wants *it* to be done, no matter by whom. They claim, therefore, that they have already done what matters, or they furnish their assistance in bringing it about, on the assumption that this will please the first individual. They soon discover, however, that he is not pleased, because he actually wants to do what matters *himself*, and when they see that this is what really matters to him, they feel deceived (§417/274). Yet, of course, they, too, want to be *the ones* who do what matters and so are no more interested in simply seeing the latter *be done* than the first individual. They are thus equally guilty of deception.

It becomes apparent to all, therefore, that what really matters to each self is 'its *own* action and effort, the play of its *own* powers' (§417/275). Accordingly, each individual now thinks that the others will pursue on their own what matters to them and leave him to do by himself what matters to him. Yet they are once again deceived. For each wants to do, not just what matters to *him*, but what matters universally, what matters to everyone. Each wants to be involved, therefore, wherever people are doing what might matter to all. Accordingly, each self interferes in the activity of others, or at least gives it 'the stamp of its approval and praise' (§417/275). An individual who opens up a subject-matter thus 'soon learns that others hurry along like flies to freshly-poured-out milk, and want to busy *themselves* with it' (§418/275).

In this experience, however, consciousness learns that both aspects of its object are essential: 'what matters' both matters to the individual himself *and* is understood by him to be something universal. Every individual does what *he* thinks matters, but he also thinks that, ultimately, it matters to *everyone*. Each acknowledges implicitly, if not explicitly, therefore, that 'what matters' is a matter *for* everyone, not just for him – that 'what matters' requires 'the action of *each* and *everyone*' (§418/276). The next shape of reason acknowledges this explicitly.

For this new shape, therefore, 'what matters' is fully and explicitly *universal*. This means, on the one hand, that it matters universally to all without qualification. As such, it has 'the value of the *absolute*': it is what is absolutely 'authoritative' for individuals (§420/277). On the other hand, it is the object of the *combined* action of *all*. In contrast to the previous shape of reason, individuals now no longer compete with one another, but join together, to do what matters. In this way, they form the *community* that Hegel calls 'ethical consciousness'. Since these individuals remain different from one another, however, they introduce the principle of difference into their community and into the universal itself. The latter thus divides itself into the different *laws* of the community. These laws are immediately understood by everyone to be what matters and to be authoritative. As Hegel puts it, '*sound reason* knows immediately what is *right* and *good*' and 'the law is valid for it immediately' (§422/278). Such reason thus does not need to create laws for the community, but it does need to render them explicit by proclaiming them for all to hear. When it does so – in the shape of the individual – it becomes 'law-giving' (*gesetzgebend*) reason.

There is, however, a problem with the laws that reason proclaims. On the one hand, they are universal and unconditional in form: 'everyone ought to speak the truth' or 'love thy neighbour as thyself'. On the other hand, they apply to individuals with different natures and in different situations. They derive their content, therefore, from the different individuals that act in accordance with them: what I say when I speak the truth depends on what *I* know, and how I show my love for my neighbours depends on *my* particular situation. The laws thus turn out to have the *form* of universality, but no universal *content* (see §426/281).

The next shape of reason makes the pure form of universality alone the explicit object of its interest. Accordingly, it no longer proclaims laws that are meant to have their own universal content (but fail to do so). Instead, it uses the pure form of universality as a standard or 'criterion' to *test* given 'contents' – principles entertained by individuals – to see whether they are capable of being laws (§428/281). Like law-giving reason, law-testing reason understands being universal to mean being self-identical and non-self-contradictory (see §419/277). Like Kant (on Hegel's interpretation), therefore, reason examines whether or not a principle remains free of contradiction when it takes on the form of a universal law, and it deems only those that do so to be valid laws.[53]

This is reason in its *purest form*. Such pure reason discovers, however, that all manner of principles can take on the form of a law without contradiction, including ones that contradict one another. The principles that everyone should own property *and* that no-one should own property both pass reason's test and so count as valid laws (§430/282).[54] Reason's experience shows, therefore, that 'the criterion of law which reason possesses within itself fits every case equally well, and is thus in fact no criterion at all' (§431/284). That is to say, the pure form of universality proves not to be the *authority* that it is supposed to be, for nothing fails its test and it is thus unable to keep the realm of law itself free from contradiction.

The last two shapes of reason both take themselves to be conscious of a universal that is 'authoritative in and for itself' (§420/277). The laws proclaimed by reason lack genuine universality, however, since their content is contingent on the knowledge and situation of individuals. And, as we have just seen, the pure form of universality employed by pure reason to test laws lacks genuine power and authority. The failure of these two shapes, however, does not lead reason to give up the very idea of a universal that is truly authoritative. On the contrary, it leads reason to the thought of a universal that is the object of *neither* law-giving *nor* law-testing reason: it leads consciousness to 'return into the universal' (§435/285) in which the last two modes of reason have been 'superseded'. But this is as far as reason can go: for implicit in this thought is the idea of a universal that is no longer the object of reason at all. To see what such a universal must be, we have briefly to reflect on what is common to the shapes of reason we have encountered.

Throughout the development of reason the *individual* has been understood to actualize the universal. First, observing reason looks for law in the realm of individual empirical things. Second, the self-conscious individual seeks to make the law of its 'heart' a reality in the world. Third, the individual understands himself to actualize what is universal in and through his *own* activity (in the 'spiritual animal kingdom'). Experience eventually leads reason to understand the universal to be something authoritative *in its own right* or 'in and for itself' – to have 'the value of the *absolute*' (§420/277). Yet the individual still takes *himself* to be the one who gives actuality to that universal: *he* takes it upon himself to proclaim to the community the laws that govern it. Indeed, even in *pure* reason, when the individual takes as its principle the pure form of universality, *he* judges whether laws contain a contradiction (§435/285). Furthermore, in both cases the content of the laws concerned is determined by individuals (see §§424, 434/279, 285).

A universal that is no longer the object of reason is thus one that is not first actualized *by* the individual. Such a universal is genuinely actual and authoritative because it *actualizes itself*, albeit in and through individuals. The shape of consciousness that has this universal as its object is *spirit* (*Geist*).

Spirit takes the universal – the law – to exist and have validity 'in and for itself' (§436/285). The law is thus held to have its own intrinsic content and not to derive its content from the individuals who act in accordance with it. Indeed, the law is held to be *prior* to the individual and so, for example – as in Sophocles' *Antigone* – to be 'the *unwritten* and *infallible* law of the gods' (§437/286). Yet spirit does not regard the law as an alien authority to which it must simply submit itself; it sees in the law the ground of its own identity and so, like reason, sees itself in the law. Indeed, it knows itself to be nothing but law, or 'ethical substance', that has become *conscious of itself* (§436/286). In the realm of spirit, therefore, individuals understand the law to acquire its *own* 'actuality', 'existence', 'self' and 'will' in *their* self-consciousness (§437/287). They understand that law becomes actual and effective in the world as 'the *pure will of all*' (§436/285).

Study questions

1 What is the ambiguity in reason's idea of 'what really matters'?
2 What is the difference between law-giving and law-testing reason?

Spirit

Spirit is 'essence that is *in* and *for itself*' (§438/288). It is law that is valid in itself, and this law is also 'for itself' – or conscious of itself – in individuals. Spirit thus constitutes a community or 'world' of individuals, bound together by law. The law itself, or '*ethical substance*', is 'the *ground* and *starting-point* for the action of all', and it in turn becomes something actual in and through the different individuals who make it the '*purpose* and *goal*' of their activity (§439/288–9). The law-governed community is thus not an inert unity, but is '*actual* and *alive*' in the individuals that belong to it. It is '*ethical actuality*' (§439/288–9).[55]

As consciousness turns into this community, Hegel's phenomenology finally becomes the phenomenology of *spirit*. All further shapes of spirit remain shapes of consciousness in the broad sense, insofar as they fall short of the identity of subject and object that characterizes speculative thought. Yet they are no longer shapes of consciousness in the narrow sense (or of self-consciousness or reason), but 'shapes of a world' (§441/290). All previous shapes are in turn now to be understood as *moments* of spirit, with no independent existence of their own.

True spirit

Ethical life

Spirit is the unity of individuality and universality, of self-consciousness and ethical substance (or law). Unlike the formal universal of law-testing reason, it is also a concrete universal that gives itself its own content by differentiating itself. It differentiates itself into the two moments that comprise it: a law of individuality and a law of universality, each of which governs a different 'mass' or sphere of the community (§§445–6/291–2). Each law, however, is a distinctive expression of the *whole* spirit and so combines within itself the principles of both individuality and universality.

The first law expresses the fact that law in the realm of spirit becomes conscious of itself in individuals. Hegel calls this law of self-conscious spirit 'the human law' (§448/293). It is something *universal* insofar as it is known by all and informs the customs of all; it is given *individual* embodiment in the citizens and the ruler of the community (such as Creon, the mythical ruler of ancient Thebes in Sophocles' *Antigone*). One might think that this human law corresponds to the law of individuality, mentioned above, since it governs the lives of individuals. The common purpose of these individuals, however, is to live together in a law-governed *community* or *state*. The latter, Hegel writes, is 'what is truly universal' (§451/294), the whole in which everyone lives. The human law is thus in fact the law of *universality*.

Over against this human law is a law that expresses the fact that law in the realm of spirit exists and is authoritative in its own right, is absolutely valid in itself. This law is thus named by Hegel '*the divine law*' (§449/293). The latter constitutes the ultimate ground of the state – 'the general possibility of ethical life as such' (§450/293) – yet it also underlies a community that is different from but falls within the state, namely the family. The law that binds the state together achieves a clear *consciousness* of itself in the citizens. By contrast, the law that binds the family together is held to be an *immediately existing* substance. The ties between family members are thus themselves immediate: they are based on what people *are*, rather than what they are *conscious* of being. That is, family ties are grounded in what people find themselves to be, thanks to *nature* – in the natural differences between man and woman, parent and child, and brother and sister (§450/293–4).

Yet the family is not determined by nature alone, but is an ethical, spiritual relation between self-conscious human beings. Furthermore, like the state, it is a community with a common purpose. That purpose, however, is the opposite of that of the state. Whereas the state aims at maintaining 'what is truly universal' – namely *itself*, the state as a whole – the family is concerned with 'the individual as such', specifically the individual family member (§451/294). The law governing the family, therefore, is the law of *individuality*.

Yet, at the same time, as a form of spirit, the family and its members are also concerned with what is universal. These two concerns come together, Hegel claims, when the family directs its ethical action towards 'the *whole* individual' or 'the individual *qua* universal' (§§451/295). This, however, leads to a surprising conclusion, for the 'whole individual' is the individual who has completed his whole life – the individual, who is no longer living, but *dead*.

Death is a purely natural state, a state of 'pure being' (§452/295). The ethical action of the family consists in turning that natural state into one that is willed and affirmed by consciousness. The family does not, therefore, leave its dead member to decay naturally, but actively 'marries' him to the earth by burying him and pouring libations for him (§452/296–7). The family also cares for and educates its living members, but the principal duty imposed on it by divine law is the duty to bury its dead. This duty is made necessary by the *logic* of the family in this initial shape of spirit: for only the dead family member is an individual who has completed his life and so become 'universal'.

The family, as we have noted, is both a natural and an ethical union of individuals. Insofar as it is an ethical union, its members recognize one another as free and equal, just as in the state citizens recognize one another as equal before the law. One relation within the family, however, exhibits this ethical character more purely than any other. The relation between husband and wife is one of 'mutual recognition', but it is not wholly free, since it is partly determined by the natural bond between the sexes; parents and children, on the other hand, do not recognize one another as equals

(§456/298–9). Brother and sister, however, regard one another as 'free individualities', without being sexually attracted to one another (§457/299–300). This is because they are already united by blood and so are not moved by nature to *become* one flesh. Brother and sister, though naturally different, thus enjoy a purely ethical relation to one another.

Now, in this its initial shape, spirit is 'the *immediate* unity of substance' – or law – 'with self-consciousness' (§459/301). As a consequence, spirit finds each of the two laws to be immediately connected with one of the two natural sexes: the human law with the man, and the divine law with the woman. Accordingly, the brother leaves the family to participate in the state, whereas the sister becomes 'the guardian of the divine law' (§459/301). Hegel claims, therefore, that the divine obligation to tend to the dead family member falls to the *sister*, who must bury her unburied brother. Such sisterly concern for the dead brother is, in Hegel's view, inherent in the family at this stage in the *Phenomenology*. At the same time, of course, it matches the concern shown by Antigone for her dead brother Polyneices in Sophocles' *Antigone*.

The family and state acknowledge different laws, but they are not intrinsically at odds with one another. Indeed, they form a single world – 'the ethical realm' – that is 'unsullied by any internal dissension' (§463/303). They are set against one another, however, by the *individuals* who act in their name (§464/304). These individuals recognize the laws, in whose name they act, as intrinsically and immediately authoritative (and so do not need first to examine whether they can count as laws). Moreover, as noted above, their connection to those laws is itself understood to be immediate and so determined by *nature*: the man takes himself to be governed by the human law, the woman by the divine law (§465/305). These laws are set *against* one another because the man and the woman also take their allegiance to their respective laws to be immediate and *exclusive* (§466/305–6). Each acts, therefore, to make his or her own law the *whole* law and so seeks to subject the other's law to his or her own. Creon, for example, asserts the law of the state against that of the family, and so denies Antigone the right to bury her dead brother, whereas Antigone asserts her right, based in divine law, against that of the state.

By asserting his or her own right, therefore, each individual violates the right and law of the other and incurs *guilt* (*Schuld*)

(§468/308). Each takes the other, however, to *lack* right and authority and so to exercise unjustified 'violence' or to be stubborn and disobedient (§466/306).⁵⁶ Yet each encounters in the other a law that he or she *should* respect, since it forms the other side of the spiritual whole to which both belong. Logically, therefore, each individual 'must acknowledge' (*anerkennen*) his or her guilt (as Creon does and Hegel *thinks* Antigone does) (§470/310).⁵⁷ Through such acknowledgement, each individual accepts that the *whole* law is valid and that one-sided allegiance to one law only must come to an *end*. Yet each individual is naturally, and thus irrevocably, attached to one law. Each accepts, therefore, that he or she must come to an end, too. That is to say, each accepts his or her downfall or death – a *negation* that is experienced as the work of an 'all-powerful and just *fate*' (§472/311).

Before we move on, three points need to be made. First, in his account of ethical life, Hegel makes explicit reference to Sophocles' *Antigone* and implicit reference to Aeschylus' *Seven against Thebes* and Sophocles' *Oedipus the King*.⁵⁸ His purpose, however, is not to examine those plays themselves, but to disclose the *logic* inherent in immediate ethical life and the experience it must undergo. He refers to these plays only to illustrate aspects of such ethical life. Second, Hegel gives an account here of the ethical world that *suffers* tragedy, but not of the artistic spirit that *creates* tragic dramas. His phenomenological account of the latter is contained in chapter seven of the *Phenomenology* on religion, and his philosophical account is contained in his lectures on aesthetics.⁵⁹ Third, Hegel is here not providing a speculative, philosophical account of the family or the state; that is to be found in his *Philosophy of Right*.⁶⁰ He is simply showing how the family and state must be understood at this stage in phenomenology. The world he describes may appear in Sophocles' *Antigone*, but it is not the world that the nature of freedom, as philosophy understands it, requires us to live in.

The world of right

The next shape of spirit renders explicit what is implicit in the experience of the previous shape. The universal is thus now understood to be *one* undifferentiated unity or universal. The individuals, in whom this universal becomes self-conscious, are in turn no longer distinguished from one another, and limited in their vision, by nature, but are conscious of their *equality* as *persons* (§477/316). Just as they are no longer rooted in the immediacy of nature, so, too, persons are no longer rooted in the immediacy of pre-existing, divine law. The universal thus ceases to be a *law*, whose 'substance' and intrinsic authority *precede* self-consciousness, and becomes *right* that has its authority in being recognized *by* self-conscious persons (§478/316). Furthermore, right is recognized *by* persons to be actualized *in* persons, so the latter know themselves to be bearers of inviolable right.

The new world is thus an aggregate of persons, conscious of their intrinsic rights as *individuals*. As such, it lacks an explicit consciousness of ethical unity, and so no longer constitutes a state in the previous sense but is a 'spirit*less* community' (§477/316).[61] Moreover, each person conceives of himself quite *abstractly* as a bare rights-bearing self – as a 'pure one' – and in this respect resembles the stoic. The person, however, is not only a *self-conscious* individual (like the stoic), but also a member of an '*actual world*' of right (§479/317). This world of right – which Hegel associates with the Roman Empire – is, indeed, the world in which stoicism itself has its proper home.

Although the person takes himself to be a pure, abstract, rights-bearing *self*,[62] he also belongs to the realm of spirit, albeit to a spiritless form thereof. Spirit is the unity of self-consciousness and being, of what is *for* itself and what is *in* itself. The person, therefore, must take himself to stand in relation not just to other persons but also to being, to reality. Since, however, the element of universality or law now exists in and for self-consciousness alone as right, the being or reality that the person confronts is utterly *without* law and so is 'set free and unorganized' (§480/317). Accordingly, this reality is governed by sheer lawless contingency and arbitrariness. This reality is what enables the person to actualize his right, for it supplies the manifold things that the person can take into rightful ownership. The space of contingency, by which the person finds himself confronted, thus gives *content* to the otherwise empty *form* of his right. I have the right to own whatever is not the property of another, but a 'power which is arbitrary and capricious', and which lies beyond me and all other persons, determines what can *actually* be owned (§480/318).

In the realm of spirit, however, being or reality is inseparable from self-consciousness. The capricious power that confronts persons thus itself takes the form of another self-consciousness, another person. This person – the 'lord and master of the world' (*Herr der Welt*) – is 'the universal power and absolute actuality' that determines whether and how any other person can actualize his rights (§481/318). This lord, who is embodied in the figure of the Roman emperor, is, however, *contingency* and *arbitrariness* personified. When the lord exercises his power, therefore, the self-conscious person is made to experience his own powerlessness and 'lack of substance' (§482/319). The person is thus caught in a double contradiction: on the one hand, he confronts a reality that is meant to actualize his rights, but he feels disempowered by and 'alienated' (*entfremdet*) from that reality; on the other hand, he is conscious of his own 'validity' and right as a pure self-consciousness, and yet feels deprived of his 'essence' by the lord (§483/320). The next shape of spirit is alienated from its world and from itself – at least to a degree – from the start.

Study questions

1 How do the state and family in 'true spirit' differ from one another?
2 Why does the person feel a sense of alienation?

Self-alienated spirit

Culture

'Self-alienated spirit' has two aspects to it, which reflect the fact that it is made necessary by the previous shape. First, it is '*actual*' (*wirklich*) consciousness. As such, it is conscious of an actual world or reality, which it sees as its own world – as 'its substance' (§490/325) – but which it also takes to exist 'freely' on its own account and in that sense to be *alien* to it (§485/321). Second, spirit is '*pure*' consciousness of its unity with what is true, universal and substantial: the 'unity of the self and essence' (§485/321). Such pure consciousness is a moment *of* actual consciousness. Yet it also sets itself *apart* from actual consciousness and, in this latter respect, takes the twofold form of *faith* and *pure insight*. Hegel first examines self-alienated spirit in its immediacy, namely as actual consciousness of an actually existing world.

The person began as the simple bearer of right, but then became *conscious*, through his experience, of his alienated condition. The new shape of spirit is made necessary by such experience and so is itself more explicitly *self-conscious* than the person is initially. As such, it is more *active* than the person. Unlike the latter, therefore, this new spirit does not merit recognition simply because of what it *is* (§488/324), but it is accorded recognition only after it has actively *acquired* 'education' or 'culture' (*Bildung*) (§489/324). Individuals acquire culture by negating their particular, *natural* selves and bringing themselves into accord with what is universal in the world of culture, namely law and recognized custom. Such individuals see that world as 'a fixed and solid reality' over *against* them and so take their task to be that of conforming to that world (§490/325). In so doing, however, they come to sustain that world themselves, and the 'fixed reality' they confront comes to be partly *their* work.

The world of culture must in turn reflect the fact that it is both the embodiment of what is *universal* and valid *in itself* – namely, law – and the work of *individuals*. Thus, like Antigone's world but unlike the world of right, it differentiates itself into spiritual 'masses' or spheres (*geistige Massen*) (§492/326). In the first sphere, the universal manifests itself as such, as a '*self-identical* spiritual essence', but in the second it is what allows individuals to become conscious of themselves *as* individuals. (A third sphere, in which the universal itself takes the form of an individual self-conscious subject, namely a monarch, emerges later.)

Hegel now notes that the individual relates to the world as both *pure* and *actual* consciousness, and that each consciousness understands the world to divide into different kinds of sphere. Pure consciousness conceives of such spheres in an abstract manner as simple, independent 'spiritual powers'. It conceives of the first sphere – that of *self-identity* – as 'the good', and of the second as 'the bad' (§493/327). For pure consciousness, therefore, the real world is simply divided into what is good and what is bad. Actual consciousness, on the other hand, understands the world to be divided into two concrete, objective realities. It takes the first, in which the universal manifests itself as such, to be the sphere of *state power* and the second to be the sphere of *wealth*. Each is the work of all and is a community or 'universal spiritual being'

(§494/328);⁶³ but state power confronts individuals with what is explicitly *universal*, namely law, whereas wealth allows them to enjoy the fruits of their combined *individual* activity.

The individual also relates to these *actual, concrete* spheres of public life as *pure* self-consciousness that takes itself to stand above, and to be free from, these spheres. Such pure consciousness thus thinks it can choose to favour one or the other, or, indeed, neither (§495/328). Furthermore, it takes itself to be free to relate these two concrete spheres to the values it has identified, that is, to *judge* state power and wealth to be *good* or *bad*. Pure consciousness judges each sphere according to whether or not it finds itself, and so retains its *self-identity*, in it: the sphere in which it does so, and which it thus takes to be the *same* as itself, is deemed good, and the one that differs from it is deemed bad. Accordingly, insofar as it seeks *individual* satisfaction in the world, pure consciousness judges wealth to be good and state power to be bad; but insofar as it looks in the world for the *universal* ground of its being – the law and order that guide it – it judges state power to be good and wealth to be bad (§495/329).

Note that, in both these ways of judging – despite their different evaluations of state power and wealth – pure consciousness sees the world as both the same as *and* different from itself (§499/331). According to consciousness's own standards of 'good' and 'bad', however, it is good to see the world as the *same* as oneself, but bad to see it as different, because the 'good', for consciousness, is precisely that which is *self-identical*. If consciousness is to be consistent, therefore, *this* fact must now become the focus of its attention. It must judge, not just the world, but its *own* relation to that world; and in so doing it must consider, not whether it is interested in its own individuality or the universal, but whether it finds the world to be the *same* as or *different* from itself. *That* distinction will determine whether or not the individual himself is good or bad.

Pure consciousness thus now turns its attention to the *actual consciousness* to which it belongs, which is interested in both its own individuality and what is universal in equal measure, and it passes judgement on two different forms of such consciousness. The actual consciousness that finds its identity confirmed in both spheres of state power and wealth is judged to be good or '*noble*' (*edelmütig*); and the one that finds itself in neither is judged to be bad, 'ignoble' or 'base' (*niederträchtig*) (§500/331). The noble sees in state power his 'own simple *essence*' and so serves the latter out of respect for it. He also finds his individual needs met by wealth and so gives thanks to the latter as his 'benefactor'. The base individual, by contrast, sees in state power nothing but a hateful oppressor, and so obeys the state only with 'secret malice' (§501/332). He finds only fleeting satisfaction in the sphere of wealth, and so despises it, too, (as much as he loves it) because it denies him a share in enduring, universal wealth.

Hegel turns first to the self, whose relation to the world is that of immediate identity: the noble self. Since the noble finds his essence in the state, he renounces his own individual aims for the sake of the latter and becomes its *servant*. His education into the ways of the state thereby gives him a sense of self-worth and validity, and brings recognition from others: he comes to *count* in the eyes of state power (§504/333). Equally, his service enables state power to change from being a mere idea – a 'universal *in thought*' (§504/333) – into being something *actual*: for the state acquires its actual power through the obedience shown it by individuals, through their actual acknowledgement of its law.

The noble thus finds his honour in being the *vassal* of, and advisor to, state power, and the world he helps create proves to be that of *feudalism*. As Hegel notes, however, the only way to prove completely that one has renounced one's own interests for the sake of the state is to *die* in its service. Simply by staying alive, therefore, the noble risks appearing to retain *particular* interests of his own that are at odds with those of the state, the *universal*. This in turn 'makes his counsel about what is best for the general good ambiguous and open to suspicion' – the suspicion, namely, that it stems from *base* motives (§506/334). So how can the noble remove this suspicion? He can do so only if, while remaining alive, he can renounce himself as completely as he would, *if he were dead*. To do this, he must show the world that, *in* his individuality, he is nothing *particular* at all but utterly *universal*.

The noble can show himself to be this fusion of individuality and universality by showing himself to be a pure 'self' or *I* (*Ich*): for 'I is *this* I – but equally the *universal* I' (§508/335). When I say 'I', I identify *myself*, as *this* specific individual; and yet I say nothing specific or particular about myself, but simply give expression to the I that everyone is, that is wholly universal. It is only in *language*, however, that I can show myself to be such an I. My actions and my physiognomy may give expression to my particular intentions or feelings, but language 'alone expresses the *I*, the I itself' (§508/335). Furthermore, my language shows me to be an I, to be something *universal*, not just when I say 'I' explicitly, but whenever I say anything at all and am *heard by others*: for when my speech is heard, I 'infect' others with myself, become one with them and in this way come to be 'universal self-consciousness' (§508/335).

It seems initially as though Hegel introduces language at this point from an external point of view. Yet it becomes clear that language is made necessary by the experience of the noble consciousness itself. In Antigone's world and the world of right, spirit is the immediate *unity* of the individual and the universal: the ethical individual identifies immediately with the state or family, and the person is the immediate embodiment of right. The noble, by contrast, sees the universal – in this case, state power – as a world over against him, from which he stands divided. He also sees this world as *his* world and so works to become *one* with it; yet, as we have just noted, his service to the state fails to bring about the union he seeks, and so the reality of his situation remains marked by division. Since this is the case, his consciousness of his unity with the world must now find expression in a reality that is itself *distinct* from his own divided reality. This other reality forms a 'middle term' (*Mitte*) that connects the individual and his world in a common consciousness. This middle term is *language* – 'the spiritual whole issuing forth between them' (§509/336). Language is thus made necessary by the experience of nobility itself. Indeed, this is the first time in the *Phenomenology* that conscious experience has required language to be its element. Hegel makes reference to language in discussing sense-certainty (and implicitly elsewhere), but only now does consciousness require language in its *own* eyes.

The noble thus turns his consciousness into a common, universal consciousness by speaking to and being heard by others. Yet he must also do more than this, for if he is to preserve his nobility in relation to *state power* in particular, he must speak to the latter in the appropriate way. His speech must show that his *sole* interest lies in the celebration and furtherance of state power itself: the heroism of service must thus become 'the *heroism of flattery*' (§511/337). Such flattery proves that, in the eyes of the noble, state power is *absolute* and *unlimited*. In so doing, it shows that the noble himself owes everything to state power, including his very being as a *self*, as an *I*. If, however, the noble is to hand over 'his very I' to the state, he must take such power in turn to be embodied in a *self* that he can see as the source of his own. The noble, therefore, must flatter not just state power in the abstract, but a *monarch* in whom state power is absolute. We have thus moved from the world of feudalism to that of the Sun King, Louis XIV of France.[64]

The nobles flatter the monarch by uttering his *name* and thereby raising him in public consciousness above every other individual in the state. Conversely, the monarch sees his own absolute power reflected in the fact that the nobles do not merely serve and advise him, but reduce themselves to a '*ornamental setting*' (*Zierat*) around his throne and continually '*tell* him what he *is*' (§511/338). In this way, the *individual* monarch becomes conscious of his absolute, *universal* power. Yet, Hegel notes, this individual enjoys power and independence that is in fact 'self-alienated', since it is nourished by the flattery of the nobles (§512/338). As the nobles realize this, they come to see that state power actually belongs to them. Furthermore, they come to see the state as the site of their *own* individual advantage. That is, they come to see the state, not so much as a power over them, but as a source of *wealth* and satisfaction for them (§512/338). The nobility, through its flattery, thus turns absolute state power into its very opposite.

As individuals are enriched by state power, they constitute their own world of wealth (§514/339). The noble, who achieves individual satisfaction in this world, expresses his gratitude for the benefits it brings him. At the same time, however, he has a keen sense of being at the mercy of the *other* individuals in the world of wealth, of being 'in the power of an alien will' (§516/340). Moreover, he comes to think that, not just the realization of his rights, but his whole well-being as an individual – his very *self* – depends utterly on others. His gratitude for the genuine satisfaction he achieves is thus shot through with a profound sense of powerlessness in face of the world and its contingencies. Indeed, he feels himself to be quite 'torn apart' (*zerrissen*) by that world, feels that his *own* 'I' is actually lost to him and 'belongs to *another*' (§517/340).[65] The noble individual thus becomes *alienated* from, and dissatisfied with, the realm of wealth and the state power that helped produce it, and in this respect his consciousness becomes indistinguishable from an ignoble or *base* consciousness (§519/341).

The individual feels dissatisfied with *losing* his sense of self in the world of wealth, only because he knows that he *has* a self to lose, that he *is* a self in his own right. His enduring sense of *self* finds expression in his feeling of 'outrage' (*Empörung*) at a world that reduces him to a mere *thing*, to a mere 'accident of its caprice' (§§517, 519/341–2).⁶⁶ The outraged self thus feels that it loses *and* retains its identity in its dealings with the world: it feels torn in *two* by the world, but also at *one* with itself in confronting that world in outrage. Moreover, this self is conscious of remaining 'absolutely self-identical *in* its absolute disruption', of being *one* internally *divided* self (§520/343). This means that it is aware both of not being and of being internally divided, and so of *not* being the very thing it *is*. In other words, it is conscious, in its outrage, of being internally inconsistent and *confused*. Yet, Hegel notes, this very confusion is completely *clear* to it (§523/345).

This self is also conscious of the 'confusion' in the world of culture itself, for it is aware that absolute state power is not absolute (but dependent on flattery), that wealth is good and yet bad for the self, and that nobility and baseness are not in fact opposed to one another (§521/343). It declares everything in its world, and everything about itself, to be the opposite of itself in its distinctive *language*, and in so doing becomes the mouthpiece for the self-alienation and 'perversion' (*Verkehrung*) at the heart of culture as a whole (§520/343). The language of the outraged, confused, yet self-aware self is best exemplified, Hegel suggests, by the knowing 'madness' of 'Rameau's nephew' in Diderot's novel of the same name, which Hegel knew from Goethe's translation.⁶⁷

Yet precisely by expressing its *outrage* at the world and its own divided condition, the self passes *judgement* on the latter and places itself above them, thereby becoming *vain* (§526/347–8). Hegel now examines the shape of spirit that places itself more explicitly above and beyond the world's confusion. This shape takes a twofold form.

Faith and pure insight

In setting itself apart from the world, this new shape is *pure*, rather than actual, consciousness, and so is *thought*. Yet in its immediacy it is still conditioned by the reality it transcends. Its thought thus draws on images taken from the actual world and so is representational thought or 'picture-thinking' (*Vorstellung*) (§527/348). At the same time, such spirit takes itself to be conscious of what is true, universal and substantial – of the 'absolute essence' (*absolutes Wesen*) (§529/350) – insofar as the latter is free of the self-alienation that it suffers in the world. Since its element is *Vorstellung*, it *pictures* this universal essence or substance as a 'supersensuous world' lying beyond the actual world of state power and wealth (§529/351). Such spirit, Hegel maintains, is not yet religion proper – which we will encounter later in the *Phenomenology* – but *faith* that *flees* from the world into the beyond (§§527–8/349).

Pure consciousness also takes a different form that grows out of the consciousness of *self* that is present in outrage. Such pure consciousness takes the pure self, or '*pure I*', freed from all confusion, to be its object, and indeed to be what it is itself (§529/351). This pure I is not the particular self that differentiates one individual from another, but 'the universal self' that is found, more or less explicitly, in all individuals. Pure consciousness understands this pure *I*, or self, not the supersensuous world of faith, to be what is truly substantial and essential (§536/354). Furthermore, as this I, it looks *negatively* on the world – like the outraged self – and seeks to give everything in that world the explicit 'form of the self' (§529/350–2). That is to say, it allows no power in the world to stand unchallenged, but aims to make everything explicitly *rational*, just like itself. In its eyes, indeed, the proper task of worldly culture is actually to promote this end. Hegel calls this consciousness '*pure insight*'. It is the insight that everything is essentially, and so must become explicitly, rational (§537/355).

Enlightenment

When pure insight has become widespread in the world of culture, it takes the form of general *enlightenment*. As such, the target of its criticism ceases to be the world itself and becomes *faith*. Faith and pure insight are both forms of pure consciousness. Whereas, however, faith locates the essence – the ultimately *true* – in the supersensuous beyond, insight locates it in the self. Each, therefore, sees the other as its opposite (§§541–2/357).

For insight in the form of general enlightenment, faith itself takes the form of a generalized consciousness. Insight understands the latter to be fooled into its erroneous beliefs by the self-serving deceptions of the priesthood, which conspires in this regard with political despotism (§542/358). Since, however, insight takes itself to be *universal*, it directs its attention to the general mass of the faithful in the conviction that, in spite of the hold the priesthood has over them, they will in fact prove to be 'receptive' to reason (§545/359). Indeed, insight thinks that, once it has been introduced to the faithful, it will spread among them of its own accord, like an infection. In this way, it surmises, the priests and despots will be deprived of the basis of their power (§§543–5/358–9).

Yet insight also sets out *actively* to negate and undermine faith and so enters into a 'violent struggle' with it (§546/360). Insight, however, still takes itself to be universal, and so must regard faith, too, as mode of insight. It attacks the latter, therefore, for being erroneous, *'false* insight' (§§542, 549/357, 362). Insight knows itself to be self-consciousness that sees itself in its object. It thus declares faith to be a form of self-consciousness, too, and so claims that 'the absolute essence' – the God – to which faith relates is actually just 'a product of consciousness itself' (§549/362). Since faith does not recognize this, it is said to be in *error* about itself. Faith, however, is well aware that it finds *itself* in its object, for it feels confirmed by God and places its trust in Him. Furthermore, it is also aware that God becomes the 'spirit of the community' thanks to the activity of the faithful and that this spirit is thus partly the *'product'* of consciousness (though it does not, of course, hold God as such to be our creation). Faith, therefore, does not take itself to be as much in 'error' as insight claims (§549/363).

Insight also claims that the God of the faithful is actually something quite 'alien' to them, foisted on them by the priests, but that faith cannot see this. Faith takes this charge, however, to contradict the previous charge that faith is a form of *self-consciousness*. It also takes it to be at odds with its own *trust* in God. Once again, therefore, faith rejects the criticism made of it by insight (§550/363).

The problem with insight, from faith's perspective, is that it does not enter into and understand *faith's* perspective. All insight can see in faith is a failure of *insight* into the nature of faith itself; but this blinds insight to faith's *own* point of view. This is apparent in further criticisms of faith made by insight.

Insight attacks faith, for example, for subjecting itself to something *other* than itself, but it characterizes that other in terms that faith does not accept. Insight reduces that other to what *it* regards as the opposite of self-consciousness, namely a mere sensuous *thing*. Accordingly, it maintains that the object of faith is in fact just 'a piece of stone' or 'a block of wood' (a statue) or 'a piece of dough' (the host) – things in which a pure self cannot see itself reflected. What faith reveres, however, is not just a sensuous thing, but the God who is represented by that thing (§§552–3/365). Insight also attacks faith for relying on contingent and uncertain historical evidence that is incapable of grounding true insight. Faith, however, does not take itself to depend on such evidence, but has its certainty within *itself*. It bears witness *itself* to the truth in which it has faith (§554/366). In each case, therefore, what insight attacks is not what faith takes itself to be, but what insight takes to be opposed to insight. It only ever attacks its *own* other.

Insight also puts forward its own positive, enlightened view of the world. Insight rejects the God it sees as the fictional product of faith's imagination. Yet this does not lead it to do away altogether with the idea of an 'absolute being'. All that is left to insight, however, once it has stripped from the absolute all that one can superstitiously imagine it to be, is an utterly empty object of reason: the 'vacuum' or 'void' of the Supreme Being (to whom Robespierre would devote a cult in 1794) (§557, 562/369, 372). Over against this empty absolute, insight sees a world of individual, sensuous things – the world of *nature*. Insight then relates the objects of nature to the absolute. On the one hand, insight maintains, the absolute 'makes, fosters and cherishes' the things of the world, which thus have 'intrinsic being' (or are *an sich*). On the other hand, created things are the opposite of the absolute and so are *not* absolute in themselves. In this latter respect, things are available for other things to *use*; insofar as they have intrinsic being, however, they can in turn put other things to use. The principle governing the world of enlightenment, therefore, is that 'everything is *useful*' (§§559–60/370).

This applies to consciousness, as much as to things. Everything is useful *for* consciousness, and conscious individuals are themselves – or should become – useful *to* one another (§560/371). Indeed, as the Enlightenment philosopher Helvétius argued, even *religion* has its utility (§561/371).[68] For faith, however, the reduction of God to an empty absolute and the reduction of the value of religion to utility are both an 'abomination' (§562/372). Furthermore, as we have seen, faith feels that it suffers injustice at the hands of insight, when the latter criticizes it, for insight 'does not recognize that what it condemns in faith is directly its own thought', its *own* other (§565/373). Yet faith also has to acknowledge that, ultimately, insight has 'absolute *right*' (§565/374) on its side. This is because, even in its blinkered one-sidedness, insight points to features that do actually belong to faith *itself*. More specifically, insight 'reminds faith, when one of its modes is present to it, of the others which it also has, but which it always forgets when the other one is present' (§564/373).

Insight claims that the God of faith is merely the fictional product of human imagination (§§566/374). This clearly distorts faith; yet, when the latter insists that God lies beyond consciousness, insight's charge serves to remind the believer that he himself participates *actively*, through his obedience and service, *in* God's work in the world. On the other hand, when faith declares its trust in God, insight reminds it that it has also declared God to lie utterly *beyond* consciousness. Similarly, when insight charges faith with 'revering' pieces of stone and wood, this charge, though unfair in itself, contains an important grain of truth: for by locating the divine *beyond* the here and now, faith sets the things of this world *apart* from God and so does effectively give them an *intrinsic* value of their own (§567/375). Moreover, faith reveres what it *pictures* the divine to be and so imports into what it reveres aspects of the *sensuous* world (such as space and time) (§567/375).

The overall effect of insight's critique is thus to make faith aware that its different views of itself and the absolute are all one-sided and partial. As such, they all reflect faith's *finite* perspective – the perspective it has through belonging to *this* world, to the earth (§572/378). This means, however, that faith's pure, *infinite* consciousness is left completely without content, with an utterly 'empty *beyond*'. Faith, therefore, comes to share the very same consciousness as enlightenment: both now relate to 'an absolute without predicates, an absolute unknown and unknowable'. Yet, whereas insight is satisfied with its empty absolute, faith is not and so turns into a '*sheer yearning*' for something more than such emptiness (§573/378).

Having come to see the absolute as nothing but emptiness, faith 'mourns over the *loss* of its spiritual world' (§573/378). Insight, by contrast, considers the absolute in a more positive way to be its own essential, albeit abstract, *object* – what Hegel calls 'the *pure Thing*' (§574/379). It takes itself to be *finite* consciousness over against this pure, *absolute* 'thing'. As such, however, it finds that it stands in a twofold relation to the absolute. On the one hand, insight takes the latter to be a simple 'predicateless absolute' – the abstract deity of Deism. On the other hand, it starts from its finite, sensuous perception of things and, by stripping away what we see and hear, proceeds to the thought of *pure matter* in the abstract – the absolute object of eighteenth-century French Materialism (§578/381).

Enlightenment has thus now come into conflict with itself, rather than with faith (§575/380): for it has learnt that its object cannot just be *one* undifferentiated absolute, but 'must contain difference within itself' (§579/382), albeit in the form of two internally *undifferentiated* absolutes. The next shape of enlightenment takes its object to be explicitly *differentiated*. As such, however, this object is no longer the empty, abstract absolute of Deism and Materialism, but the world of *manifold* finite things that insight confronts. This is the world in which all things have their own intrinsic being ('being-in-itself'), but in which they are also related to, and at the disposal of, other things (are 'for an other') – the world in which, as we saw above, everything is *useful* to everything else (§580/383).

Insight is now more explicitly *self-conscious* than when conscious of the empty absolute or pure matter: for in the world of utility, it encounters a realm in which everything is there *for it*, indeed there for it, as this finite *individual*, to enjoy. In its own eyes, therefore, it finds complete *satisfaction* in its world (§581/384). Yet insight does not see its selfhood as such in that world, but sees itself only in the availability to it of self-less *objects* (§582/385).[69] In the next shape of spirit, however, consciousness sees itself explicitly in its world, and so takes itself to be absolutely self-relating and *free*.

Absolute freedom

The self now no longer beholds useful things, but gazes only at itself: it is 'the absolute seeing of *itself* doubled' (§583/386). As such, it is no longer a finite, individual self over against the world, but a 'universal subject' that constitutes the very world it confronts. Like insight, this free self knows *itself* to be what is universal, essential and substantial. Unlike insight, however, it does not take itself just to be the *pure* consciousness of reason, but also knows itself to be 'the essence of all actuality' (§583/386). That is to say, it knows its own will to be the will that governs the *world*: the universal or 'general will' (§584/386). Since it is a form of spirit, this universal will actualizes itself in *individuals* (see pp. 144–5, above). It is thus the general will as the Abbé Sieyès (rather than Rousseau) conceived it, namely 'the will of all *individuals* as such' (§584/386).[70] In the world this will creates, every individual does what all do, and the will of all is done by each.

As this universal will 'ascends the throne of the world' (§585/387), it subjects that world to a *revolution*. In the world of culture, individuals belong to different spheres, such as the nobility and the realm of wealth, which give them their *particular* identity and status. In the world of freedom, by contrast, such differences between individuals no longer count, since all are equally dedicated to upholding universal law and doing 'universal work', work for the benefit of all. The different spheres, or 'estates', within the world of culture are thus abolished, and everyone is simply a citizen (§585/387). In absolute freedom, indeed, all differences are removed except that between the individual and the universal law; and even this difference has merely the '*appearance* of an opposition', since the individual understands that law to be completely at one with his own will (§586/387).

Hegel now points out, however, that the universal will is incapable of carrying out any 'positive work' (§588/388). It is absolutely free, yet it is unable to act constructively. The problem is twofold. First, the will could create an enduring, *objective world* of freedom with its own internal differences. The latter would take the form of institutions, such as a legislature (to pass laws), an executive (to implement them), and organizations that reflect different kinds of labour. Individuals would then be assigned to these different institutions. In this way, however, the activity of individuals would be restricted to a particular branch of the whole, and they would no longer work directly for the *whole* itself: they 'would cease to be in truth universal self-consciousness' (§588/389). The universal will cannot create such a world, therefore, without sacrificing the universality of the will as the latter is here understood.

Second, if the will refrains from creating such a world and simply carries out *individual* actions, it runs into a similar difficulty. In the world of freedom, the universal will only becomes an actual will in individuals. An individual action in the name of the universal law must, therefore, be undertaken by an *actual individual*. This means, however, that other individuals are excluded from the action or play only a limited part in it. The action thus ceases to be the action of *all*, of 'an *actual universal* self-consciousness' (§589/389). In this case, once again, the universal will's *positive* work fails to preserve the *universality* of the will.

All that is left to it, therefore, is '*negative action*' (§589/389). The only way the will can preserve its universality is by asserting itself as a universal will *against* whatever opposes it and *negating* the latter. The only thing that could oppose the universal, however, is the individual will. After the revolution, therefore, all the universal will can do is *eliminate* any individuals who are not in tune with the universal will. 'The sole work and deed of universal freedom is therefore *death*' (§590/390). Absolute freedom can tolerate nothing other than itself and so must destroy anything opposed to it in a 'fury of destruction' (§589/389).

Death is imposed on wayward citizens by *individuals* acting – and governing – on behalf of the universal will. These individuals appear to others to constitute a *faction* that pursues its own particular interest, but they regard themselves as the universal will in action, as 'the *actual* universal will' (§591/390). Both parts of this thought are essential to their self-understanding: they take their will to be universal *and* to be actual and effective. Accordingly, what they see ranged against them is a will that is neither universal, *nor actual*. In other words, they see their enemy in 'unactualized [*unwirklich*] pure will', or mere *intention* (§591/390–1). Such unactualized intention is not read off from actual action, but is rather thought or *suspected* to be there. Individuals are thus condemned to death on the mere suspicion of being counter-revolutionaries, and absolute freedom turns out to lead logically to a reign of *terror*, such as that imposed on France in 1793–4 (§592/391).

Absolutely free self-consciousness now finds its reality – death and terror – to be the very opposite of the freedom it took itself to enjoy (§592/391). In this respect, it proves to be the most profoundly *self-alienated* form of spirit. Yet implicit in its experience is the promise of a new form of spirit that is no longer self-alienated but 'certain of itself'. Experience shows consciousness that its universal will brings about the death of the actual individual, that it causes the *immediate actuality* of the individual to disappear. The next shape of spirit shuns death, but takes itself to be a universal will insofar as it is *itself* a 'vanished immediacy' and something *non*-actual (§§594–5/393–4). Such spirit remains that of an actual individual, but this individual acquires a universal will by withdrawing *out* of the world of actuality into pure *thought* and becoming '*pure knowing and willing*'. Furthermore, he sees his pure knowing and willing as what is essential and substantial in its own right. He is thus certain of being *spirit* – the unity of self-consciousness and essence or substance – purely *within himself*. As such, he is an inner, *moral* spirit. This moral spirit confronts a realm of actuality that now lacks the form of self-consciousness altogether and is 'self-less' (§594/393).

Study questions

1 How do the noble and base consciousness differ?
2 Why does absolute freedom lead to death?

Self-certain spirit

The moral world-view

Since moral self-consciousness knows its own pure will to be what is essential, it takes the latter to have absolute authority over it as an individual. Accordingly, it conceives of its pure will as the source of binding *duty* (§599/395). Such consciousness also relates to a *world* that is quite other than it: the realm of nature. In the eyes of morality, however, nature counts for nothing, whereas duty is essential (§600/396). Moral consciousness feels bound, therefore, to assert and fulfil its duty in the realm of *nature itself*. In so doing, it also seeks to carry out its aim as a moral *individual* and so to achieve satisfaction or 'happiness' in the fulfilling of its duty (§602/397).

Yet the moral individual finds external nature to be indifferent to his aim; he thus learns that he is often unable to fulfil his duty in the world. Equally, he knows within his *thought* that duty is essential and that, ultimately, nature can have no power to prevent its fulfilment. He is thus bound by the very idea of duty to think of nature as ultimately being in *harmony* with morality. This is not just wishful thinking; moral consciousness *must* think of the harmony of morality and nature – and thus of morality and happiness – 'as something that necessarily *is*'. That is, it must *postulate* the existence of such harmony in spite of its discouraging experience (§602/397).[71]

Moral consciousness is also led by its experience to further postulates. As an individual, the moral self not only confronts external nature, but also has a sensuous nature of its own in the shape of desires and inclinations (§603/398). It aims to satisfy these inclinations in all its actions; yet it also understands duty to govern its actions. The moral self feels bound, therefore, to fulfil its *duty* in the actions it undertakes to satisfy its *inclinations*. That is to say, it feels bound to promote the *unity* of duty and inclination. Yet our *particular* inclinations are always found to be at odds with our pure, *universal* will. In face of this experience, however, moral consciousness does not abandon the task of reconciling duty and inclination. Rather, it postulates that, despite our current experience, our sensuous nature will eventually be brought into '*conformity with* morality', albeit only after an infinite amount of time (§603/398–9).[72]

Hegel notes, too, that moral consciousness confronts many different situations in the world, which require it to fulfil its duty in many different ways. It thus finds itself subject to many different duties (§605/400). Yet what consciousness heeds in those many duties is the element of *pure duty* alone; there is nothing sacred in their particular *content*. Nonetheless, consciousness understands these different duties and their content to be necessary. Since it finds nothing within its own concept of duty that would sanctify the content of such duties, it postulates '*another* consciousness, which makes them sacred' (§606/401). The latter is not only conscious of pure duty, but also knows all the particular things one must do to conform to duty. It is thus not just another *finite* moral consciousness, but a source of wisdom and holiness *beyond* the finite self: the 'lord and ruler of the world' (§606/401). Moral consciousness, in other words, postulates the existence of God.[73]

The postulates of moral consciousness overlap in many respects with those identified by Kant in the *Critique of Practical Reason* (1788).[74] Note, however, that Hegel is here not examining Kant's moral philosophy in particular, and so is not trying to be 'fair' to Kant. He is analysing the shape of moral spirit that is made necessary *logically* by the experience of absolute freedom. He now exposes the 'pretence' (*Verstellung*) at the heart of morality, (§617/405).[75] Morality, we discover, is not *serious* about anything in its world-view. Three brief examples will suffice to show what Hegel has in mind.

Consider the first postulate. Moral consciousness regards the harmony of morality and nature as a mere *postulate*, because it takes there to be no such harmony in actuality. Yet consciousness understands moral action to be the fulfilment of duty *in the world*. It thus takes such action to bring the actual world – nature itself – into harmony with morality. Through its action, therefore, consciousness shows that it does not seriously hold the harmony of morality and nature to be a mere postulate after all (§618/406). Moral consciousness takes the world to be indifferent to morality, and so can embark on moral action, only if it *postulates* that the world is in fact in harmony with morality. Its very action demonstrates, however, that it only *pretends* to regard such harmony as just a postulate.

A further pretence can be discerned in the second postulate. Consciousness takes universal duty to be at odds with particular inclination. Yet it also aims to fulfil its duty in actions that satisfy inclinations and so to bring about the *unity* of duty and inclination. Indeed, it postulates that this unity must be and will be achieved. It shows that it does not take its own postulate seriously, however, by projecting such unity into an infinitely remote beyond (§622/410). Consciousness is guilty of pretence, therefore, because it declares moral perfection to lie in overcoming the struggle between morality and sensuous inclination, but it is content to continue *indefinitely* in a state of moral imperfection (§§623–4/410).

In confronting different situations in the world, consciousness finds itself subject to many different duties. Yet its own sense of pure duty cannot sanctify the particular content of these duties. Consciousness is led, therefore, to formulate its third postulate: that there exists a God who sanctifies these different duties and so is a 'holy lawgiver' (§626/411). Yet consciousness takes its own sense of pure duty to be absolute and holds to be sacred only what *it* can judge to be so. It is thus 'not really in earnest about letting something be made sacred *by another consciousness* than itself' (§626/412). Consciousness postulates the existence of a holy lawgiver, therefore, whose authority it only pretends to acknowledge.

As consciousness becomes aware of these (and other) examples of pretence in its moral world-view, it accuses itself of *hypocrisy* – of 'assert[ing] that to be true which it holds to be untrue' (§631/414).

Since, however, it takes itself to be a pure moral consciousness it flees such pretence and draws back into itself. Yet to the extent that it remains a *moral* consciousness, it remains mired in pretence and hypocrisy. Indeed, its very claim to have rejected hypocrisy would simply be another instance of it (§631/415).

Conscience

Implicit in this rejection of moral hypocrisy, however, is a new shape of spirit – *conscience* – that gives up the various antitheses that characterize the moral world-view (§637/418). The moral self faces the *task* of fulfilling its duty in an indifferent world. Conscience, by contrast, knows that it actually *fulfils* its duty in all that it does: it is conscious of *being*, rather than just feeling that it *should* be, a moral agent. Indeed, it is certain that everything about it as an individual is in harmony with duty, that there is an immediate identity between the latter and itself (§632/416).

Such certainty is itself '*immediate certainty*' (§637/419), grounded in nothing but itself. Conscience's '*own conviction*' assures it that its actions are always dutiful and, indeed, tells it what duty requires in any specific case (§637/419). Conscience is thus a wholly self-certifying moral consciousness. The previous moral self understands duty to have authority *over* it (even though duty has its source in its own pure will); conscience, by contrast, takes *itself* and its own self-certainty to have ultimate authority and to be 'the absolute truth' (§633/416).

Duty is thus whatever an individual's conscience is convinced it is (§640/421). Yet duty is also held by conscience to be *universally* valid. Conscience must thus understand duty to be what everyone is convinced of. The same is true of dutiful actions. My actions are dutiful, not only because my conscience tells me they are, but because conscience in general recognizes them to be such. General *recognition* is thus what makes my dutiful action a reality (§640/420). Moral consciousness, by contrast, understands the dutiful action to be something objective in the world, rather than something certified by all selves.

Now, unlike the moral self, conscience does not confront an indifferent, independent world, but it does act in specific situations, which, as concrete and real, have 'many aspects' (§643/422). In such situations, conscience has different options and must decide what to do. Yet the bare conviction that its action is always dutiful contains nothing that would enable it to make such a decision. Conscience can do no more, therefore, than base its decision on its immediate, natural inclinations (§643/423). So it does what it is inclined to do in the genuine conviction that it is dutiful. Others would perhaps act differently in this situation, but they recognize the validity of the individual's action because he does what he believes is dutiful. In this way, they make it clear that acting dutifully does not mean doing this, rather than that, but means being convinced of the rightness of your action, *whatever you do* (§644/424).

Yet others cannot see from *what* I do that I am indeed acting from the proper conviction, so I risk being judged immoral or evil (§649/427). To avoid such judgement, I must make my inner conviction evident to others, and I do so in *language* (§652/428). By expressing my conviction in language, I turn it into something that is there – that *exists* – for others. As they then hear my words, my sense of conviction enters 'general self-consciousness' (§651/428) and thereby acquires a certain objectivity. This act of expression is not just one among many that is available to conscience, but is *the* act in which conscience *shows itself* to be dutiful. Conscience does its duty if it is convinced it is doing it; it thus shows itself to be dutiful by showing itself to be convinced; and it can do that only by expressing its conviction in language. The most important thing conscience can do, therefore, is *declare publicly* that it is convinced of the rightness of its actions (§654/430). Hegel notes that there is no point in asking whether such a declaration is true, because conscience is self-certifying (§654/429). Conscience that *says* it is acting out of conviction deserves recognition for doing precisely what conscience is supposed to do.

Since conscience takes itself to be self-certifying, it regards its own inner voice to be absolute, to be a 'divine voice' (§655/430). Indeed, each conscience regards all the others as divine, too. Despite disgreeing about what should be done in a given situation, they all praise one another for acting out of pure conviction. In the spiritual animal kingdom, individuals are in competition with one another; in the realm of conscience, by contrast, everyone acknowledges the equally inviolable authority of all. They 'rejoice' over their 'mutual purity' and delight in their shared 'excellence' (§656/431).

Conscience is a shape of spirit and so recognizes an ultimate authority; but it identifies that authority with *itself* and its own self-certainty. It is, indeed, conscious of what is other than itself: it acts in given situations and expresses itself to other selves. Yet it sees *itself* as what is substantial and divine. Implicit in the standpoint of conscience, Hegel maintains, is a further shape of spirit that withdraws *completely* into itself. In this shape, nothing other than the self has any 'stability', and consciousness is submerged in 'absolute *self-consciousness*' (§657/432).

The beautiful soul, the hypocrite and the hard-hearted judge

This new shape expresses itself in language, but its words do not give it an objective, public existence; rather, they refer the self immediately back to *itself*. They are perceived by the self to be nothing but the *echo* of itself. This self thus remains immersed in itself, unable, and unwilling, to actualize itself in speech or action. This self treasures the 'splendour of its inner being' and the 'purity of its heart' and knows itself to be a 'beautiful soul'. Yet in the 'hollow object' it produces – its echoing words – it also sees a reflection of its inner emptiness. In expressing itself, therefore, it *loses* itself, and so is an *unhappy* beautiful soul that 'vanishes like a shapeless vapour' before its very eyes (§658/432–3).[76]

Absolute self-consciousness, however, also *manifests itself* in action, and, in so doing, becomes a further shape of spirit (§659/433). This self belongs to the world from which the beautiful soul withdraws – the world of conscientious action – and so proclaims to others that it is acting dutifully. Yet it is also 'reflected into *itself*' and as such is conscious of being an individual quite *distinct* from other individuals (§659/433). It also takes itself to be distinct – and thus exempt – from the universal, from duty. Moreover, it takes such duty to have a definite content – to be what *those* individuals, as opposed to *me*, declare our universal duty to be. It thus rejects not only the very idea *that* it needs to act from a sense of duty, but also the '*given specific* duty' that is publicly advocated by others. This self pays lip service to such public duty, because it seeks recognition from others as their equal; yet in its actions it knowingly satisfies its *own* inclinations, just as it pleases.

The individual agent sees nothing wrong with this, because he takes himself and his own interests to be what is essential. In his view, therefore, he is entitled to act according to his '*own* inner law and conscience', rather than what *they* recognize duty to be (§662/435). In the eyes of these others, however, the agent is *evil*, because he indulges his desires with no regard for universal duty. Furthermore, he is a *hypocrite*, because he claims to respect duty when his actions clearly belie his fine words (§660/434).

From the agent's perspective, however, those who accuse him of evil base this judgement on *their* particular conception of 'universal' duty and law. Their very judgement thus makes it legitimate for him to follow *his* own particular law (§663/436). This aspect of moral judgement reinforces the agent's sense of being different from the judge. Two other features of the moral judge, however, make the agent aware of his identity with the latter.

First, the judge condemns the agent for his selfishness, but he does not engage in concrete action himself for fear of appearing selfish in turn. His only 'action', therefore, is to utter *words* – to pass judgement on the agent and to declare his own respect for universal duty. This means that the judge expresses 'fine sentiments' about dutiful action *without acting dutifully*, and so is in fact a hypocrite, *just like the agent*. As the agent comes to recognize the judge's hypocrisy, but also to see that the judge is just like him, he comes face to face with his *own* hypocrisy, from which his sense of entitlement has so far shielded him. The agent thus 'comes to see his own self in this other consciousness' (§664/436).

Second, the judge knows that the agent fails to do what the judge thinks duty requires, but he has no grounds for denying that the agent himself is convinced that his actions are dutiful. As we have seen, conscience is self-certifying, so if the agent declares himself convinced of his goodness, the judge cannot prove otherwise. The assertion that the agent acts from base, selfish motives cannot rest, therefore, on what the agent himself does or says, but must be founded on what the judge is predisposed to believe about agents. The judge suspects that all actions are motivated by selfishness, and 'no action can escape such judgement' – just as 'no man is a hero to his valet', whatever he may do (§665/437).[77] The judge thus proves to have the same base view of action as the agent, namely that it serves selfish ends. Through his 'deedless words' (*tatloses Reden*) in praise of dutiful action, however, he wants to show himself to be finer than he is (§666/438). Once again, therefore, he proves to be a hypocrite in the eyes of the agent.

When the agent declares that he and the judge are just like one another, he *confesses* his own hypocrisy at the same time, for he says to the judge: 'you are a hypocrite – *just like me*' (§666/438).[78] Note that such a confession is not an act of self-abasement on the part of the agent. It is built into the agent's declaration that both he and the judge are *equally* hypocrites. Since the agent recognizes this identity between the two of them, he expects the judge to do the same.

The judge, however, rebuffs the agent's confession with his unyielding 'hard heart': he will not acknowledge that he has anything in common with the agent and insists on his own inner purity. In so doing, he confronts the hypocritical agent with 'the beauty of his own soul' (§667/438–9). Such 'beauty' expresses itself in the continuing 'utterance' of judgement or in 'stiff-necked', judgemental silence. This refusal to give expression in *language* to 'any continuity with the other' is, however, a refusal of one's common humanity. The hard-hearted judge thus shows himself to be 'a consciousness which is forsaken by and which itself denies spirit' (§667/439).

Yet logically – if not always in fact – the judge's hard heart must eventually break (§669/440). In confessing his hypocrisy to the judge, the agent no longer sets himself apart from the latter but declares both of them to share a common or 'universal' consciousness. The judge is himself the advocate of shared values, of what is universal. In the *form* of the agent's confession, therefore, the judge must recognize the interest in the universal that he himself advocates, even if he rejects the claim that he is a hypocrite. By recognizing this *identity* between himself and the agent, however, the judge ceases to set himself *apart* from the latter and gives up his purely judgemental stance. He now recognizes the agent, in his confession, to be good, *just as he is*. With this recognition, Hegel writes, the judge *forgives* the agent (§670/440–1). Such forgiveness is the mirror image of the agent's confession: in both cases, the individual relinquishes his separate identity and becomes one with his adversary. In this respect, both confession and forgiveness are transformative: neither the agent nor the judge remains what he is, but each lets go of himself and comes to be reconciled with the other. In so doing they form a single community of 'mutual recognition which is absolute spirit' (§670/441).

In the sphere of reason, *individuals* are held to actualize, and give content to, what is universal. In the sphere of spirit, the universal is understood to be essential, substantial and authoritative *in its own right*, but also to actualize itself in individuals. This process culminates in the self-righteous hypocrite and judge taking their own selves to be absolute (§671/441). Now, however, these selves have *let go* of themselves, *given up* all self-righteousness and come to see their identity in their union with one another; and only in this respect do they understand what is absolute and divine to be manifest in and among them. At this point we move from spirit to *religion*. We have already encountered deficient forms of religion in, for example, the unhappy consciousness, faith and the moral belief in God (§§672–6/443–4). Only now, though, does religion proper make its appearance in the *Phenomenology*.

Study questions

1 Why is moral spirit guilty of pretence?
2 How does conscience differ from moral spirit?
3 In what sense is the judge a hypocrite himself?

Religion

Conscience understands itself to be absolute: it knows its own inner voice to be 'divine' (§655/430). By contrast, the hypocrite and the judge acknowledge, through their acts of confession and forgiveness, that they are *not* absolute. Yet they also come to see their union as the manifestation and presence *of* the divine. The two sides of this final shape of spirit are rendered explicit in religion. Religious consciousness understands that it is *not* absolute or divine itself, but human consciousness of an absolute that is *other* than it. Yet it also understands the absolute to overcome this very distinction and become *one* with humanity. At least this is true of the more developed forms of religion, as we shall see.

Since religion is the truth of spirit, it is what Hegel calls 'self-knowing spirit' (as opposed to merely 'self-certain' spirit) (§677/444). It is thus not only consciousness of an absolute that is other than it, but also human *self-consciousness*. Accordingly, religious human beings see *themselves* in the absolute to which they relate. Not all religions, however, allow human beings to see themselves in the absolute in the same way or to the same degree, because not all let them see their own *self-consciousness* as such in the absolute. Each religion, Hegel argues, takes the absolute to have a different 'shape' (*Gestalt*) (§684/450). For some religions, the absolute takes the shape of something natural, such as light or animal life; for others, namely Greek religion and Christianity, it takes the shape of a (more or less explicitly) *self-conscious* being. The latter religions, therefore, allow human self-consciousness to see itself more clearly in the absolute than the former, and in that sense they fulfil the purpose of religion more adequately.

Natural religion

In his phenomenology of religion, Hegel does not consider the historical connections between religions. He considers the way in which the experience of one religion points forward *logically* to another by containing implicitly what the next one renders explicit. Note that Hegel makes no mention of certain religions, such as Buddhism, Daoism or Islam. This is not because they are unimportant historically, but because they are not made necessary by the experience of religious spirit that the *Phenomenology* describes.

Hegel first considers the religion of the 'light-being' (*Lichtwesen*), which some scholars identify with Zoroastrianism and some with Judaism.[79] This religion comes first because it is *logically* the simplest and most abstract. Absolute being is understood to have the shape of immediate being, or the being found in *nature*. Yet the absolute is also understood to be 'filled with spirit' (§686/453). Indeed, it is taken to exhibit the *form* of immediate self-consciousness and so to be the *lord* (*Herr*) of the world.

Yet absolute being is not understood to be *explicitly* self-conscious in itself. It is taken to be simple, 'shapeless' *natural* being. The dimension of nature that is most like self-conscious spirit, in being immaterial, is *light*. This initial form of religion thus takes the absolute to be the 'light-being' that rules over all people and things. Such light sends forth 'torrents of light' and 'streams of fire' (§686/453), but, as the lord or power over them, it dissolves them back into *itself*. Implicitly, therefore, if not explicitly, the 'light-being' has the form of a *self* (§688/453). It thus points forward logically to the second form of natural religion, in which absolute being is understood to take the overt shape of a self, albeit one that still lacks explicit *self-consciousness*.

The 'self-ish' shape taken by absolute being in this next religion is that of plant and animal life. This religion – found in ancient India[80] – is thus a *pantheism* in which divinity is encountered not in the shapeless simplicity of light, but in a multiplicity of differently shaped plants and animals. Plants, we are told, enjoy a 'calm' (*ruhig*) existence;[81] animals, by contrast, assert themselves against one another in a 'hostile movement'. The people that espouse the religion of animals thus comprise 'a host of separate, antagonistic national spirits who hate and fight each other to the death' and see their distinctive identities embodied in different, mutually hostile animal shapes (§689/454).

Hegel notes, however, that in the antagonism between these national spirits and their corresponding animal shapes, selfhood or 'being-for-self' proceeds to *negate* itself (§690/454). One self negates *another* in the conflict between the spirits, but each self also negates *itself* in that conflict by exposing itself to destruction. Furthermore, each self negates itself through its own activity, that is, through asserting *itself*.

This self-negation, or self-sublation, of selfhood is rendered fully explicit when the self, through its own activity, turns itself into that which is *not* a self at all, but an object or *thing* (*Ding*). Such activity is ambiguous because it gives expression to the *self* or *spirit* in a thing that *lacks* selfhood. As Hegel puts it, such activity produces 'itself as object' (§691/455). This ambiguous conception of self-expression underlies the third form of natural religion, the religion of the 'taskmaster' (*Werkmeister*), or 'artisan', found in ancient Egypt.

Briefly, the main stages in the phenomenological development of this religion are these. First, religious spirit produces purely abstract, spiritless things – pyramids – which house self-conscious spirit, but only insofar as the latter is *dead* (§692/455). Religious spirit thus does not see its own living self-consciousness reflected in the object it creates.

Second, the thing produced is rendered more 'self-like' by being adorned with plant-like forms (in the case of architecture) or being given the shape of an animal (in the case of sculpture). The artisan, however, still does not give the thing the shape of a self-conscious human being, and so religious spirit still does not see itself explicitly in the object it creates. Such spirit recognizes itself in its object only in the sense that it knows the thing before it to be its *own work*, to be an artefact that it has produced (rather than something natural, such as light) (§693/456).

Since the object of religious consciousness lacks *self*-consciousness, it does not express any inner spirit or selfhood of its own through *language*. Indeed, even when the shape of the object produced is human, it remains a 'soundless shape' that fails to express *itself*, but at best resounds on being touched by the rays of the rising sun, as the famous Memnon Colossi in Western Thebes were once reputed to do (§695/457).

Finally, however, the artisan produces an object that *does* express itself in language, or rather is *imagined* to do so, namely the sphinx. The sphinx is not yet a fully self-conscious human being, but is an enigmatic creature – a mixture of human and animal – whose speech contains 'a profound, but scarcely intelligible wisdom' (§697/458). Nonetheless, in the sphinx, religious self-consciousness 'comes face to face with an inner being that is also self-conscious and self-expressive', albeit one that is still struggling to free itself from the unconscious and the animal. In the sphinx, therefore, 'spirit meets spirit', and so comes to be explicitly conscious of *itself* in being conscious of its object (§698/458).

The sphinx is the imperfect expression of self-conscious spirit. The object of the next religion, however, gives clear expression to self-conscious spirit. Religious spirit ceases thereby to be a mere artisan and becomes an *artist*. This new religion – that of the ancient Greeks – is thus named by Hegel the 'religion of art'.

Study questions

1. What distinguishes religion proper from *faith* in the realm of spirit?
2. Why is Egyptian religion the highest form of natural religion?

The religion of art

In Hegel's account, Greek religious spirit first produces an object or *thing* with the explicit 'shape of the self' (§706/461) and sees divinity in that shape. It creates a statue of a god in *human*, rather than animal, form, and so in the work of art comes face to face with spirit that is clearly *self-conscious*.

Yet the object of such art is not *actually* self-conscious. It is, after all, a mere thing, a piece of stone or bronze, albeit one that is 'pervaded with the light of consciousness' (§707/462). Actual self-consciousness is not to be found in such an object, but in the artist who produces it. To begin with, therefore, the religion of art is characterized by the 'separation of the work' from the 'self-conscious activity' of the artist himself (§708/463). Since the work itself lacks actual self-consciousness, the divinity expressed in that work remains somewhat 'self-less' and *abstract*. It is divinity with the shape of a self, but still immersed in, and defined by, nature to a large degree.[82]

The artist at this first stage of the religion of art knows that he has produced a thing without genuine self-consciousness: he 'learns in his work that he did not produce a being *like himself*' (§709/463). If a work is to be produced that does express self-conscious spirit, therefore, a different element must be found, more suited to such expression than stone or bronze. That element is *language*, in which self-consciousness expresses itself directly and immediately. The god 'who has language for the element of his shape' can thus give direct expression *himself* to the self-consciousness that was previously the preserve of the artist (§710/464).

In the religion of art, and indeed other religions, the *oracle* is the 'first language' of the divine. Such oracular language, however, is taken by religious self-consciousness to be the 'language of an *alien* self-consciousness' and so not to be its own work (§711/465). Yet what is required now is a work of art, produced *by* religious self-consciousness, in which the divine gives itself linguistic expression. The language in which the *divine* expresses itself must thus be *human* language. The new artwork in which the divine finds expression is, therefore, the *hymn* sung by the human votaries of the god concerned (§710/464). In such a hymn, religious self-consciousness knows itself to be 'one' with the divine (§715/467). It is now also able to see – or, rather, hear – itself and its own actuality *in* the very object of its art, because the work it produces is precisely its *own* language infused with divinity.

Yet, since the self-consciousness and language that now characterize divinity actually belong to the religious spirit that sings the hymns, such divinity remains abstract and relatively 'self-less' *in itself*. The divinity expressed in both sculpture and hymn is thus an abstract divinity, what Hegel calls an absolute '*Wesen*' (being or essence), rather than truly self-knowing spirit (see §717/468). Indeed, sculpture and hymn are themselves 'abstract' works of art. Their abstraction *as works of art* lies in the fact that they are one-sided. The sculpture presents the divine in a thing that is distinct from religious self-consciousness, whereas the hymn remains too enclosed within such self-consciousness (§713/466). This abstraction is overcome, at least to a degree, in religious ritual or 'cult' (*Kultus*).

In the cult, the divine is understood to be distinct from, and to lie beyond, religious self-consciousness, and yet also to descend 'from its remoteness' (§714/467) and become one with self-consciousness. In the hymn the self is aware of *being* one with the divine, but now it is aware of the movement in which the divine *becomes* one with the self. In the cult, however, the divine does not become one with the self through its own agency, but through the work of religious self-consciousness itself.

Since the cult involves the *interaction* between the human and the divine, both must take the form of something *actual* (*wirklich*). Religious self-consciousness thus takes the form of actual, worldly consciousness, and 'the divine being presents itself as *actual nature*' (§717/468). Cultic activity, therefore, is directed at natural objects – animals and fruit – that are owned by the community, but are understood to be the signs or the embodiment of divinity. Cultic activity is specifically the '*surrender*' (*Hingabe*) or sacrifice of these possessions by pouring away their blood or letting them 'rise up in smoke' (§718/468).

This sacrifice has a twofold significance. On the one hand, whoever owns the animals and fruit 'renounces' all possession of them and right to the 'enjoyment thereof', and offers them up to the divine being. On the other hand, the sacrifice is also the sacrifice of the *divine* itself: 'the animal sacrificed is the *sign* of a god; the fruits consumed are the *living* Ceres and Bacchus themselves' (or, to give them their Greek names, Demeter and Dionysus). Religious individuals carry out this sacrifice of the divine. Yet the sacrifice is made possible, in the eyes of those performing it, by the fact that the divine being has already 'sacrificed itself *in principle* [*an sich*]'. It has done so by relinquishing its remote, abstract divine identity and turning itself 'into an individual animal and into fruit' in the first place (§718/468). By sacrificing the divine in the form of the animal and the fruit, therefore, religious self-consciousness continues what the divine has already initiated and becomes the agent, *in the here and now*, of divine self-sacrifice.

Sacrifice does not, however, consist simply in the surrender of the animal and fruit, but also involves the consumption and, indeed, enjoyment thereof. The sacrifice, as Hegel puts it, is 'really the preparation of the offering for a meal' (§718/469). This act of consumption is integral to the cult, because it completes the process in which the divine renounces its separate identity and *becomes one* with self-consciousness. In the cult, in other words, the self feels itself become one with the divine by *eating* it. The enjoyment attained in such consumption is thus twofold: the self enjoys *itself* while eating the food, but at the same time it enjoys its 'unity with the [divine] being' (§718/469).

In this cultic activity the abstractness of the divine is overcome, since the latter becomes one with self-consciousness. In another sense, however, that abstractness is *not* overcome, since the divine never manifests any actual self-consciousness of its own (even though it is implicitly spirit (§720/470)). In the cult the divine is taken into a self-consciousness *that does not belong to the divine itself*. Religious self-consciousness also remains to a degree abstract. Cultic activity presupposes that the divine has sacrificed itself 'in principle' by becoming animals and fruit, but religious self-consciousness nonetheless thinks of such activity as its *own* work. It thus comes to enjoy *itself* and its *own* actuality through that activity. In this respect, despite becoming one with the divine, religious self-consciousness still remains abstractly enclosed within the self.

Cultic activity leads logically to the 'mysteries' in which the nature of the divine is 'revealed' (*geoffenbart*) to self-consciousness (§722/471). Such revelation occurs precisely because the divine becomes one with self-consciousness. Prior to his discussion of the mysteries, Hegel notes that the religion of art incorporates cults of both the upper and lower gods (§718/468). He points out, however, that there can be a *mystery* cult only of the lower gods, and he mentions by name Ceres and Bacchus (that is, Demeter and Dionysus), even though they are also to be found among the Twelve Olympians on the Parthenon frieze.[83] Only the lower gods are the subject of mysteries, because only they are revealed specifically through cultic activity. The upper gods – the Olympians, minus

Demeter and Dionysus – already include 'as an essential moment self-consciousness as such' (§724/472), albeit one that is *imagined* rather than fully actual. Accordingly, as Hegel goes on to show, their nature is disclosed most clearly in epic and dramatic poetry, not in cultic activity. The lower gods, by contrast, inhabit the 'dark night of concealment' (§723/472) and so reveal themselves above all in the mystery cult.

In the mysteries, the *'simple* essence' of the lower gods shows itself to be the recurring movement, first out of that 'dark night' up into consciousness, and then of 'again losing itself in the nether darkness'. That is to say, it shows itself to be 'tumultuous life' (§723/472). The religious self-consciousness that becomes one with the divine in the mysteries thus itself takes the form of 'untamed revelry' or 'bacchic enthusiasm' (§§723, 726/472–3).

The religion of art begins with what Nietzsche would call the 'Apollinian' art of sculpture.[84] By progressing through hymn and cultic activity to the mystery cult, this religion has now shown itself to be just as much Dionysian as Apollinian.[85] In the concluding section of his discussion, however, Hegel returns once again to the Apollinian side of the religion of art. This is made necessary by the fact that the Dionysian aspect of this religion remains too enclosed within the 'inwardness' of self-consciousness and fails to do justice to the idea, inherent in Greek sculpture, that the divine is something *objective* (§725/472).

In the final stage of the religion of art, therefore, the divine is given clear, objective shape.[86] At the same time, religious spirit understands that shape to be the work of *human* self-consciousness, specifically of human imagination or representation (*Vorstellung*) (§729/475). The divine is thus *pictured* or *imagined* by self-consciousness as the realm of the upper, or Apollinian, gods. This imagined realm is given actual 'existence' (*Dasein*) by human language, specifically epic, or narrative, language. The singer of the epic is thus 'the individual and actual spirit' by whom the world of imagination is produced and sustained and through whom the divine is brought to life for the community (§729/475). This relation between the divine and the human is also reflected in the content of the epic. The gods are self-conscious beings, but it is human beings – heroes – who actually carry out their divine aims in the world (§730/476).

In tragic drama – which presents the conflicts that arise in immediate ethical life (§736/480)[87] – the unity between the divine and the human is deepened. Already in the epic the divine constitutes the 'pathos' that animates the heroes and moves them to action (§730/476–7). In tragic drama these heroes are now not merely imagined, but are *actual* speakers and agents on stage. They are given actual existence by actors – 'actual human beings, who impersonate the heroes' (§733/479). The actor is thus not merely an external accessory in Greek tragic drama, but he is 'essential to his mask', since it is in the actor that the hero, and ultimately the divine itself, is actualized for religious spirit.

In sculpture the divine is given objective expression, and in the hymn the divine is expressed in human language. In tragic drama the principles of sculpture and the hymn are fused and the divine, as the 'pathos' within the heroes, is given *objective* expression in actual human beings *speaking* on stage. In comedy, the human actor – and through him human self-consciousness as such – then shows that he is in fact the power over, and what Hegel calls the 'fate' of, the gods (§744/485). He does so by playing with, and ultimately dropping, the mask through which he represents the dramatic character and the divine that informs the latter. In comedy, indeed, human self-consciousness becomes conscious of itself as the *only* genuine actuality and the 'absolute power'. It sees that 'whatever assumes the form of essentiality over against it, is instead dissolved in it' and 'is at its mercy' (§747/487–8). In this way, the comic spirit turns the religion of art into the celebration of humanity and so brings that religion *qua* religion to an end.

To sum up: in the religion of art the divine is understood to be self-conscious, rather than something natural; yet it is not held to be *fully* self-conscious *in itself*.[88] It becomes fully self-conscious divinity only in and through the activity of *human beings* – their singing, their cultic activity, their frenzied dancing, their poetic language and their acting on stage. In such activity (prior to comedy) human self-consciousness knows itself to be one with the divine; yet it also knows that it has become one with the divine through its *own* aesthetico-religious activity. Greek religious spirit does not find itself fully incorporated into the *divine*, therefore, because it knows that the latter is itself actualized only through *human* activity.

Study questions

1 What distinguishes the religion of art from natural religion?
2 What role does sacrifice play in the religion of art?

Manifest religion

Manifest religion, or Christianity, renders explicit what is merely implicit in Greek religion, and absolute being is at last understood to be fully self-conscious *itself*: 'being that is essentially *self-consciousness*' (§759/495). *Human* self-consciousness is thus able to see itself incorporated into the absolute in a way that was not possible previously (§759/495). Yet the form in which religion knows the absolute remains that of picture-thinking (*Vorstellung*). The different moments of the absolute thus appear as 'independent sides which are externally connected with each other' (§765/498), and absolute being is understood – at least initially – to be distinct from the actual self-consciousness that it comes to exhibit.

Yet absolute being is known to be self-conscious spirit *in itself*. This means that it must be spirit, and not just simple being or essence (*Wesen*), even *prior* to acquiring actual self-consciousness. For manifest religion, therefore, the absolute, considered purely in itself as 'God the Father', negates the simplicity of its being and comes to be 'for itself'. This moment of being-for-self is other than the absolute itself: it is the *Word* (*das Wort*) uttered by the absolute. Yet the two are not just other than one another, since absolute being 'beholds only its own self in its being-for-self' (§770/501). The absolute in itself is thus the *movement* of becoming-other-than-itself and recognizing itself in the other that it becomes, and 'this immanent movement proclaims the absolute being to be *spirit*' (§771/501). Manifest religion proves to be committed, therefore, to what Christian theologians call the 'immanent Trinity' – the idea that God is Triune *in himself*.[89]

Manifest religion knows, however, that it is not enough to conceive of God in this way. If God is to be spirit, he must 'become an actual self' (§766/499). He becomes actual spirit by first *creating a world* and then becoming *incarnate* in that world in the form of an actual, self-conscious human being, namely Christ (§§774, 780/503, 507–8). Note here the significant difference between manifest religion and the Greek religion of art. In the latter, the divine acquires actual self-consciousness through the aesthetico-religious activity of human beings. In manifest religion, by contrast, God comes to be actual human self-consciousness through himself: God's Word becomes incarnate, not through *our* work, but through the wholly *divine* activity of self-renunciation.

In becoming incarnate, God 'renounces his abstract and non-actual nature': he ceases being divine purely within himself, and enters the actual world of space, time and history (§777/506). God then renounces himself again, insofar as he 'sacrifices his immediate existence', and accepts *death*, in the figure of Christ (§780/508). Hegel stresses that, for manifest religion, the death of Christ is not just the death of an historical individual, but also the *death of God* himself. It is the death of God incarnate, but that death is itself the culmination of the process in which God lets go of, or dies to, his own 'abstract' identity as God the Father (or the purely 'immanent' Trinity). Christ's death, for manifest religion, is thus 'the death of the *abstraction of the divine being*' and is accompanied by the painful feeling 'that *God himself is dead*' (§785/512).

In manifest religion, as in the religion of art, therefore, *sacrifice* is essential to the life of the divine. In Christianity, however, *we* do not sacrifice the divine, but God – both in himself and in the figure of Christ – sacrifices *himself*. The hypocrite and the judge came to manifest the divine by letting go of themselves in their acts of confession and forgiveness. Letting go of, or dying to, oneself is now seen to be constitutive of the divine life itself. In the religion of art, by contrast, it is *we* who carry out any sacrifice: it is in *our* act of killing the animal and eating the fruit that the gods are understood to die. It is true that our sacrifice of the divine presupposes that the latter 'must already have sacrificed itself *in principle*' by turning itself into the animal or fruit in the first place. Nonetheless, 'the sacrifice of the divine substance, insofar as it is an *act* [*Tun*], belongs to the self-conscious aspect', and so is the work of human beings (§718/468). In cultic activity *we* become the agents of divine self-sacrifice.

After dying in the world, Hegel explains, the incarnate God of manifest religion is resurrected 'as spirit', namely, as the *community* of believers (§§779, 781/507, 509). In this way, God, who is spirit in himself, completes the process of becoming actual self-conscious spirit in the world. As Hegel puts it, 'substance' becomes '*actual* and simple and universal self-consciousness' (§785/512–13).[90] (The Triune God thus becomes the 'economic' Trinity, or Father, Son and Holy Spirit *in time and history*.)

For manifest religion, however, this 'spiritual resurrection' of the divine also requires activity on our part. Specifically, we have to 'take hold of' (*ergreifen*) the incarnation and death of God; we have to take God's self-sacrifice to heart and let it inform our lives. As we do so, God becomes our indwelling, guiding spirit. He comes to be, not just the God who died once, but the 'spirit who dwells in his community, dies in it every day, and is daily resurrected' (§784/511).

In manifest religion, therefore, as in the religion of art, the divine and the human enter into a mystical union, and in both cases this involves activity on the part of humanity. In the religion of art, that union arises through the cultic activity of religious believers. The sacrifice at the heart of the cult is *our* work above all; it is through *our* ingestion of the meat or the fruit that we become one with the divine. In manifest religion, by contrast, our activity consists solely in taking hold of an event that we know to have occurred *already*, and not just 'in principle' but in history. This is 'the *event* [*Geschehen*] of the divine being's own externalisation' – God's own 'historical [*geschehene*] incarnation and death' (§784/511). God does not enter into us, therefore, because of a sacrifice that *we* have performed; rather, we appropriate and allow ourselves to be transformed by the sacrifice that God has made – that is, by the self-sacrificing love that God himself is, and that he is, *actually* and *historically*, in Jesus Christ. Furthermore, we do not turn God into our indwelling spirit through *our* own activity. Our taking hold of God's incarnation and death does no more than let God *himself* become spirit in us. God's spiritual resurrection in us requires that we be open to his self-sacrifice; but it is not *our* work, it is not the product of *our* religious activity.

This difference between the two forms of mystical union reflects a broader difference between two different conceptions of the divine. Greek divinity is not yet fully self-conscious spirit *in itself* and so becomes one with humanity, and thereby *acquires* actual self-consciousness, through *our* activity alone (be it cultic sacrifice, Dionysian revelry or poetic creation). The Christian God, by contrast, *is* understood to be fully self-conscious spirit *in himself* and so to become actual spirit in the world *through himself*. He becomes one with humanity through his own self-sacrificing love, a love that we simply have to take hold of. In Christianity, therefore, humanity knows its self-consciousness and actuality to belong to divine being itself in a way that is not possible in Greek religion, despite the apparent 'humanism' of the latter. And insofar as religious faith sees its own *self-consciousness* reflected in and incorporated into the absolute being that is the object of its consciousness, Christianity fulfils the purpose of religion as no other religion does.

In another respect, however, Christian self-consciousness does not see itself in absolute being. This is because it pictures absolute being – God or Holy Spirit – as something *other* than itself, as something 'alien' (*fremd*) (§771/502). Accordingly, Hegel writes, the fact 'that substance has here succeeded in becoming absolute self-consciousness' is 'the action of an *alien* satisfaction' (§787/514). Religious self-consciousness thus does not feel completely reconciled and united with absolute being here and now. Complete reconciliation is understood, rather, to be 'something in the distant *future*', the salvation *to come*.

Religious self-consciousness sees itself in absolute being insofar as the latter is understood to be God or Holy Spirit at work *in and as* humanity; yet it does not see itself in absolute being insofar as God ultimately remains something *other* than humanity. This continuing separation between absolute being and humanity is due, in Hegel's view, to the fact that religion *pictures* (*vorstellt*) absolute being precisely as 'God' and 'Holy Spirit'. Yet the truth beheld by religious self-consciousness is that God overcomes the separation between the divine and the human and becomes *one* with humanity (§759/495). In this way, such truth, which is the 'simple content of the absolute religion' (§759/494), points *beyond* the form of *Vorstellung* that preserves the otherness of God. That is to say, manifest religion points logically beyond itself to absolute knowing, or speculative philosophy, in which the profoundest identity between absolute being and humanity is recognized.[91]

Study questions

1 What is the relation between the divine and the human in manifest religion?
2 What is meant by the term 'spiritual resurrection' (§784/511)?

Absolute knowing

Let us review the development we have been following. *Consciousness* takes itself to stand in relation to something other than it; *self-consciousness* then focuses on itself and its own freedom. *Reason* combines these two perspectives by finding itself *in* the object to which it relates, and so enjoys the certainty 'that it is all reality' (§233/158). At the same time, reason finds what is universal *in* what is individual – first in individual things and organisms, and then in its own individuality. Indeed, it understands the individual to be what *actualizes* the universal. Finally, reason becomes conscious of a universal that is truly universal, and authoritative in its own right – a universal that 'has the value of the *absolute*' (§420/277).

Spirit takes over this universal and understands it to actualize *itself* in and through individuals. This leads to the emergence – in conscience – of the individual who thinks that his voice *is* the voice of the absolute. We then pass – via the hypocrite and judge, who both *renounce* their absoluteness in an act of reconciliation – to *religion*. In manifest religion the divine is itself understood to renounce itself by becoming incarnate and accepting death. It then becomes actual and self-conscious in a community of individuals who take to heart its self-sacrifice. In this way, humanity and the divine become one. For religious consciousness, however, we become one with a God who remains essentially *other* than us. Absolute knowing now renders explicit the truth that is implicit in manifest religion and understands there to be an essential *identity* between human self-consciousness and absolute being.

Absolute knowing does so by replacing 'picture-thinking' (*Vorstellung*) – 'the form of otherness' (§796/521) – with *thought*. As we saw in the discussion of stoicism, thought is the explicit awareness that the object is 'no other substance than consciousness', that subject and object have the very same *form*, namely that of the 'concept' (*Begriff*) (§197/137). Absolute knowing thus no longer pictures the absolute as 'God', but *conceives* of it as being that is conceptually – that is, rationally and logically – structured. Note that such knowing does not take its object to be another self-consciousness. It takes it to be *being* (*Sein*) or *existence* (*Dasein*) as such, but it understands the latter have the same form as itself – the 'self-like' (*selbstisch*) form of the 'concept' (§805/528). As Hegel puts it in the *Logic*, 'being is known to be pure concept in its own self, and the pure concept to be true being'.[92]

The nature of absolute knowing can be thrown into sharper relief by distinguishing it from other shapes of consciousness we have encountered. Unlike the beautiful soul, for example, it is not simply 'absolute *self-consciousness*' (§657/432), but it 'has a *content* which it *differentiates* from itself', namely being, existence or 'substance' (§799/523). It discerns an identity between itself and its object, therefore, not because it sees no difference between them, but because it understands the being from which it *differs* to have the *same* form as it does and so no longer to be essentially *other* than it. Unlike stoicism, on the other hand, absolute knowing does not *withdraw* into a self that is utterly abstract in order to find the truth about being, but understands being to be conceptual and logical in and for itself (see §§199, 804/138, 527). This is not to deny that absolute knowing finds the truth of being within thought; but it does so by thinking through being's *own* intrinsic logical development.

Furthermore, absolute knowing understands itself to be the consciousness that being, or substance, comes to have *of itself*. The individual, who knows 'absolutely', knows himself to be a specific individual: '*I*, that is *this* and no other *I*' (§799/523). He also knows his knowing to be his own activity – 'the *self's* own *act*' (§797/522). Yet he also knows his own activity to be the activity *of* substance itself: he knows that substance knows itself in his knowing. As Hegel puts it, absolute knowing is the 'knowledge of this subject *as* substance and of the substance *as* this knowledge of its act' (§797/522). Unlike religious consciousness, therefore, absolute knowing does not take itself to be one with being that is essentially other than it, but it knows itself to be the very knowing that being has of itself. It knows its *own* activity to be that of being, substance, reason *itself*. This, indeed, is what it means to be *absolute* knowing.[93]

To know absolutely is thus not to take *oneself* to be absolute (like conscience or the beautiful soul), but to understand oneself to be the self-consciousness that absolute being comes to have of itself. Absolute knowing is thus founded on the very willingness to renounce one's *own* absoluteness that founds true religion. This is evident in what one might call the 'method' of absolute knowing. This consists, not in active judgement and inference, but in the 'seeming inactivity [*scheinbare Untätigkeit*] which merely contemplates how what is differentiated spontaneously moves in its own self and returns into its unity' (§804/528). That is to say, absolute knowing requires us to *let go* of ourselves and *let* being unfold itself in thought (see §58/43–4).

This, of course, is the 'method' that is also employed in phenomenology, as we saw above (pp. 11, 17). This is unsurprising, since phenomenology is itself the work of absolute knowing. There is, however, an important difference between phenomenology and absolute knowing proper. The latter is *philosophical* 'science', the first part of which is speculative logic (§37/29). Its task is to disclose the nature of being in thought, and its 'element' is the unity of thought and being.[94] Phenomenology, by contrast, is the study, not of being, but of the experience of consciousness. Furthermore, there is a distinction in phenomenology between consciousness and its object that has been overcome in philosophy.

> Whereas in the phenomenology of spirit each moment is the difference of knowledge and truth, and is the movement in which that difference is cancelled, science on the other hand does not contain this difference and the cancelling of it. On the contrary, since the moment has the form of the concept, it unites the objective form of truth and of the knowing self in an immediate unity. (§805/528-9)

Phenomenology is thus interested in the relation *between* consciousness and its object, whereas philosophy is concerned with 'the pure concept and its onward movement'.

As we have seen in this guide, phenomenology justifies the standpoint of philosophy to natural consciousness by rendering explicit what is implicit in the experience of each shape of consciousness. This process culminates in absolute knowing that understands 'substance' and 'subject' to form a perfect unity and to share the form of the concept. Before philosophy itself can begin, however, a further act of abstraction is required. If the beginning of philosophy is to be truly presuppositionless, then it must set aside even the concepts that have emerged in phenomenology. Instead of starting with the determinate concepts of 'substance', 'subject' and 'concept', therefore, it must start with the bare minimum that absolute knowing can be. This is the idea that pure thought, that has been freed from the 'opposition of consciousness', is the thought of sheer *indeterminate being*.[95]

In the course of the chapter on absolute knowing, Hegel notes that speculative philosophy cannot arise until the time is ripe; that is to say, humanity cannot attain the standpoint of truly absolute knowing until it has experienced the limitations of all the other forms of consciousness in *history* (§§800, 803, 808/523, 526, 530–1). Once history has brought us to absolute knowing, however, one of our tasks is to retrace that development in thought in order to understand the logic that made such knowing necessary. In so doing, thought must put to one side the wisdom it has acquired in history and proceed as if 'it had learned nothing from the experience of the earlier spirits' (§808/530). It must start afresh 'without preconceptions' (*unbefangen*) and allow the series of shapes through which it has passed in history to be 'reborn out of knowledge'. *Phenomenology* is the unprejudiced study of this rebirth. The task of phenomenology, therefore, is not only to justify philosophy to natural consciousness, but also to enable philosophy itself to understand the history to which it is indebted.

Study questions

1 How does absolute knowing differ from religion?
2 How does phenomenology differ from philosophy proper?

CHAPTER FOUR

Reception and influence

Despite its considerable difficulty, Hegel's *Phenomenology* has exercised a profound influence on subsequent generations. In particular, his analyses of the master–slave relation and the unhappy consciousness have proven to be sources of inspiration and ongoing debate in a wide variety of disciplines. Initial reaction to the *Phenomenology*, however, was mixed. The book was published in 1807 with a print-run of only 750 copies and the first edition was still available in 1829.[1] Yet it was described by one contemporary, G. H. Schubert, as 'one of the most widely admired literary phenomena in the area of philosophy'.[2] The philosopher J. F. Fries disliked the book because of its unpalatable language; yet the writer Jean Paul Richter praised it for its 'clarity, style of writing, freedom and strength'.[3]

As I noted above (p. 34), Ludwig Feuerbach criticized Hegel's analysis of sense-certainty in 1839 for merely exposing the limits of language, while pretending to undermine sense-certainty itself. In my view, Feuerbach's criticism is misplaced. Karl Marx, however, judged Feuerbach to be 'the only person to have a serious and critical relationship to the Hegelian dialectic'.[4] Marx's own understanding of the *Phenomenology* – which he saw as 'the true birth place and secret of Hegel's philosophy' – would become the most important factor determining the future impact of Hegel's book.[5]

Surprisingly, none of Marx's surviving texts on Hegel focuses directly on the master–slave relation, even though his concept of labour appears to owe much to Hegel's account of that relation.[6] Marx's text on the *Phenomenology*, entitled 'Critique of Hegel's

Dialectic and General Philosophy' (1844), examines various general themes in Hegel's book that Marx finds best expressed in the chapter on absolute knowing. The 'greatness' of the book, Marx contends, lies in the fact that 'Hegel conceives of the self-creation of man as a process'. More specifically, we are told, Hegel 'grasps the nature of labour' and understands 'man as the result of his own labour'. The problem, however, as Marx sees it, is that 'the only labour Hegel knows and recognizes is abstract, mental labour'.[7] This, Marx continues, is because Hegel conceives of man in a wholly abstract manner as 'spirit' or 'self-consciousness', and forgets about the natural and historical conditions of such self-consciousness.[8]

Marx thus takes Hegel to be a philosophical idealist, whose understanding of humanity is removed from the concrete circumstances in which people live. Hegel does, indeed, provide profound insights into labour and human alienation; but his own account of these phenomena is itself alienated from real historical alienation, because he reduces all alienation to 'the alienation of self-consciousness'.[9] In putting forward this critique, however, Marx completely overlooks the fact that in his most famous work Hegel is doing *phenomenology*, not presenting his own *philosophical* account of humanity. Hegel focuses on self-consciousness in his phenomenology because the whole point of that discipline is to examine the experience of consciousness; but this does not mean that in his philosophy Hegel abstracts humanity from its historical conditions in the way Marx describes.

Marx's interpretation of Hegel strongly influenced the way in which the *Phenomenology* was understood by many subsequent readers, including Georg Lukács, Ernst Bloch, T. W. Adorno and Jürgen Habermas. Other important readings of the *Phenomenology* were given in the first half of the twentieth century by Martin Heidegger, in his 1930–1 lectures, and by Jean Wahl, in his 1929 study of the unhappy consciousness, which greatly interested Jean-Paul Sartre.[10] The only interpretation of the *Phenomenology* whose influence is comparable to that of Marx, however, is the one given by Alexandre Kojève in his Paris lectures. These lectures, which were attended by, among others, Maurice Merleau-Ponty, Jacques Lacan, Emmanuel Levinas and Sartre, were held between 1933 and 1939 and published in 1947.[11] Like Marx, Kojève shows no understanding of the phenomenological character of Hegel's text. In contrast to Marx, however, he focuses explicitly on the master–slave relation and, indeed, bases his whole interpretation of Hegel on it. Kojève understands Hegel to provide an anthropological account of human being, according to which humans are driven by the 'desire for "recognition"'. It is this desire that inevitably leads to the unequal relation between master and slave that, in Kojève's view, governs the whole of human history.[12]

Both Kojève and Marx produced interpretations of Hegel's *Phenomenology* that have proven to be immensely fruitful for later generations. Yet, despite containing valuable insights, those interpretations hardly do justice to what Hegel understood phenomenology to be. By contrast, Jean Hyppolite, who deliberately avoided Kojève's lectures, produced a detailed commentary on the *Phenomenology* in 1946 that is still one of the best guides to the subtleties of Hegel's text. Through his teaching, even more than his published work, Hyppolite influenced thinkers, such as Michel Foucault, Gilles Deleuze and Jacques Derrida, all of whom studied with him.[13]

In the English-speaking world in recent years, there has been a great flowering of interest in the *Phenomenology*, and many rich and insightful studies of that work have been published by, among others, H. S. Harris, Quentin Lauer, Terry Pinkard, Robert Pippin, Robert Solomon, Robert Stern, Kenneth Westphal, Merold Westphal and Robert Williams. Probably the most influential of these English-language studies is the one by Pippin, published in 1989. According to Pippin, Hegel puts forward the 'idealist' thesis – inspired by, but also subtly different from, that of Kant – that 'any relation to objects must be understood as a moment *within* the self-conscious activity of a subject'.[14] Phenomenology's task is to defend this thesis. It does not do so directly, however, but defends the thesis indirectly by 'undercutting' the opposite assumption that consciousness stands in relation to a wholly *independent* realm of 'being as it is in itself'.[15]

Pippin's interpretation of the *Phenomenology* has ignited vigorous debate among Hegel scholars and has caught the attention of leading philosophers, such as John McDowell and Robert Brandom. It should be noted, however, that his conception of absolute knowing differs from the one that I have been presenting in this guide. I argued above that, for Hegel, absolute knowing is thought that knows being or substance *in itself* and, indeed, that knows itself to be the consciousness that being has *of* itself (pp. 186–7). In Pippin's view, however, this misses the point of Hegel's 'idealism'. Pippin's Hegel claims, not that thought knows *being* as such, but that thought determines what *counts* as 'being', what such '"being" could *intelligibly* be' for a self-conscious subject.[16] The difference is subtle, but it is significant.

The *Phenomenology* is without doubt a challenging work; but its rich account of the twists and turns of consciousness has impressed and inspired generations of readers. These readers, however, have by no means always agreed with one another. Indeed, the range of approaches to Hegel's text that have been adopted by its readers is very broad. The *Phenomenology* has been read as a work of metaphysics, epistemology, hermeneutics, anthropology, theology, and, of course, phenomenology. In the Guide to Further Reading, students will find a list of secondary texts that reflects some, at least, of these widely differing approaches.

NOTES

Chapter One

1 Hegel (1984), 80, translation amended.
2 The Preface was written later and sent separately; see Hegel (1984), 119.
3 Hegel (1984), 114.
4 See Hegel (1988), 1, 21.
5 Hegel (1999), 29.
6 See, for example, Hegel (1999), 49, 51. In the Preface to the *Phenomenology*, the 'ground and soil of science' is described as '*pure* self-recognition in absolute otherness' (§26/19).
7 Hegel (1999), 60.
8 Hegel (1991), 66 (§28), Hegel (1999), 64, and Hegel (1969), 1: 61.
9 Hegel (1991), 81 (§41 and Addition).
10 Hegel (1991), 81 (§41), and Houlgate (2006), 12–28.
11 Hegel (1991), 124 (§78 and Remark).
12 Hegel (1991), 124 (§78 Remark), Hegel (1970a), 168, and Hegel (1999), 70.
13 Hegel (1999), 82.
14 Kant (1929), 46 (B 7).
15 In the *Encyclopaedia* Hegel maintains that, ultimately, Kant's 'critique consists in the *assertion* that within itself thinking is only *indeterminate unity*' (and thus cut off from being); see Hegel (1991), 100 (§52). Truly critical thinking, by contrast, starts by suspending all such assertions and assumptions.
16 Hegel (1999), 70.

17 See Hegel (1999), 48.
18 Hegel (1999), 49.
19 Hegel (1999), 45.
20 Rosen (1974), 127, 129.
21 Miller translates *Begriff* as 'Notion'.
22 Hegel (1999), 28, and Hegel (1969), 1: 17.
23 By contrast, the analysis of consciousness, presented in the section of Hegel's *Encyclopaedia Philosophy of Spirit* that is entitled 'Phenomenology of Spirit', does presuppose the categories of the *Logic* and is explicitly guided by them, rather than by the experience of consciousness. See Hegel (2007), 142–64 (§§413–39).
24 Miller translates 'in der Eigentümlichkeit dieser Bestimmung' as 'uniquely qualified by that determination'.
25 See, for example, §802/525.
26 Hegel (1999), 69.

Chapter Two

1 Miller reinforces this impression by writing: 'But, in fact, in the alteration of *the* knowledge'.
2 'Allein wie vorhin gezeigt worden, ändert sich ihm dabei der erste Gegenstand' (66). 'Dabei' here refers back to the knowing (*Wissen*) of the object, and is rendered correctly by Miller as 'in being known'.
3 Later in the text Hegel states that the 'passage of the Concept into *consciousness*' requires of self-knowing spirit, or science, the 'release of itself from the form of its self' (§806/529). It is hard to tell, however, whether this is directly relevant here, since Hegel talks there about self-knowing spirit becoming '*sensuous consciousness* – the beginning from which we started', rather than the *phenomenological study* of such consciousness.
4 See also §§262, 364–5, 375/179, 243, 248.
5 Miller misses this by translating 'ist für uns . . . geworden' simply as 'there comes to view'.
6 See, for example, §253/173: 'we have now to see . . . what new shape [*neue Gestalt*] its observational activity assumes'.
7 In that sense, logic can be said to lie '*behind* consciousness'; see Hegel (1988), 552.

8   See also §§185, 405/129, 266.
9   Indeed, in the case of self-consciousness, this working out is largely done by self-consciousness itself; see §175/126: 'experience makes it aware'. The object of desire becomes life, however, 'for us'; see §168/122.

Chapter Three

1   Hegel (1999), 68.
2   See O'Connor (2000), 127: 'the assumption of immediacy, with which the subject desperately deceives itself about itself as mediation'.
3   Stern (2002), 48.
4   See Feuerbach (1983), 113–16.
5   This is implicit in the idea that we must have the now pointed out to us, but also 'enter the same point of time or space' as sense-certainty (§105/74). The implication is that sense-certainty will point out its now to itself, too.
6   See Kant (1929), 132–3 (A 100–2).
7   See Hegel (2007), 173–205 (§§445–67).
8   The same might be said of the relation between consciousness and self-consciousness; see §164/118: 'The *necessary advance* from the previous shapes of consciousness . . . expresses just this, that not only is consciousness of a thing possible only for a self-consciousness, but that self-consciousness alone is the truth of those shapes'.
9   Köhler and Pöggeler (1998), 67.
10 In the *Logic*, by contrast, in which concepts are considered in themselves, without reference to *consciousness*, the concept of a thing with properties does not arise until the middle of the work, in the doctrine of essence; see Hegel (1999), 484–98.
11 The distinction that emerges here is close to that between primary and secondary qualities in early modern epistemology. Miller's translation obscures Hegel's original meaning; see §123, l. 8.
12 Miller writes that they exist 'on their own account'; see §124, l. 5.
13 See, for example, Nietzsche (2003): 'hatred of a world that makes us suffer expresses itself in the imagining of a different world, a *valuable* one: here, the metaphysician's *ressentiment* towards the real is creative'.

14 See Houlgate (2005), 138–44.
15 Hegel does not mention Galileo and Kepler by name, but he clearly has them in mind in §150. For Hegel's account of Kepler's laws in his *Encyclopaedia Philosophy of Nature*, see Houlgate (2005), 147–53.
16 Hegel has Newton's law of universal gravitation in mind at this point (though he does not mention Newton by name). On Hegel's view of Newton, see Houlgate (2005), 153–6.
17 On the parallels between Hegel and Einstein in this regard, and in others, see Houlgate (2005), 130, 156–60.
18 Miller has 'permanence of impermanence'.
19 See Houlgate (1986), 198–213.
20 On dialectic, see Hegel (1991), 128 (§81).
21 'The reason why "explaining" affords so much self-satisfaction is just because in it consciousness is, so to speak, communing directly with itself, enjoying only itself'.
22 See also Hegel (1991), 125 (§80).
23 See Butler (1987).
24 Butler (1987), 9.
25 Pinkard (1994), 50.
26 Aristotle (1951), 60 (1253a18).
27 Insofar as the other is life that has come to be independently self-negating, the other is actually a 'living self-consciousness', not just self-consciousness *tout court* (§176/127).
28 Gadamer (1976), 61.
29 It should be noted that Gadamer does not himself use the term 'reflection' in this context.
30 Gadamer (1976), 62.
31 Miller has: 'the other self-consciousness equally gives it back again to itself'.
32 See, for example, McLellan (2000), 257–8.
33 See Hegel (2008), 219–24 (§§241–9).
34 See Hyppolite (1974), 172.
35 Kojève (1980), 47.
36 'innerlich aufgelöst'. Miller has 'quite unmanned'.
37 Miller has 'becomes conscious of what he truly is'. The German is 'kommt . . . zu sich selbst'.

38 Self-conscious scepticism is also different from the scepticism that precedes speculative logic: for the latter does not seek to flaunt its freedom to engender 'disorder', but aims to set aside arbitrary presuppositions and let thought develop immanently; see Hegel (1991), 124 (§78 Remark).
39 See p. 25, above and p. 196n. 5.
40 See Kant (1929), 181 (B 177).
41 See Nietzsche (1969), 119–20 (*Genealogy* 3, §§12–13).
42 Miller has 'transiency' for *Verschwinden*.
43 See Kant (1929), 152–9 (B 131–42).
44 Hegel (1988), 584–5.
45 Observing reason that sees claws as characteristics of animals does not, therefore, yet see animals explicitly as *organisms* (but rather as things with essential properties).
46 Hegel (1988), 586.
47 See Kant (2000), 239–41 (§63).
48 Hegel (1988), 587.
49 Psychology can also study the relation of self-consciousness to nature, but the relation described here is the one that is made necessary by reason.
50 Hegel makes reference to Goethe's *Faust* in §360/240 by misquoting from memory a speech by Mephistopheles from *Faust*, Part One (1808).
51 Stern (2002), 127.
52 Lauer (1976), 169. Miller has 'the heart of the matter'.
53 See also Hegel (2008), 130–1 (§135 and Remark).
54 Both principles can also be seen as self-contradictory, if taken in the appropriate sense (§431/283).
55 Miller just has 'the *actuality* of that substance' for '*sittliche Wirklichkeit*'.
56 Hegel clearly has in mind here the ways in which Antigone and Creon view one another.
57 Antigone's declaration is actually more ambiguous than Hegel thinks: 'I stand convicted of impiety, the evidence my pious duty done. Should the gods think that this is righteousness, in suffering I'll see my error clear. But if it is others who are wrong, I wish them no greater punishment than mine.' See Grene and Lattimore (1960), 1: 212 (*Antigone*, ll. 924–9).

58 See §469/309 (*Oedipus the King*), and §473/311–12 (*Seven against Thebes*).
59 See Houlgate (1998), 448–82.
60 See Hegel (2008), 162–80, 228–304 (§§158–81, 257–320).
61 Miller has 'soulless'.
62 Hegel uses the term 'self' (*Selbst*) to refer to only certain forms of spirit (see §633/416). I use it in a looser sense, however, to refer to self-consciousness generally.
63 The phrase 'allgemeines geistiges Wesen' is not translated by Miller (see §494, ll. 15–18).
64 See Lauer (1976), 194, 197.
65 Note the difference between the noble spirit at this point and the unhappy consciousness. The former feels that his whole self belongs to another, whereas the latter feels cut off only from his pure, unchangeable self.
66 Miller translates '*Empörung*' as 'rebellion'.
67 Hegel does not mention the novel by name, but draws on, or quotes directly, from Goethe's translation of it in §§489, 522/325, 345. Diderot's novel was written in French between 1761 and 1772 and first published in Goethe's German translation in 1805.
68 See Hegel (1988), 607–8.
69 'Utility is still a predicate of the object, not itself a subject.'
70 See Stewart (1951), 50: 'individual wills are the sole elements of the general will'.
71 See Kant (1996), 227–46 (on the highest good), esp. 235: 'in practical principles a natural and necessary connection between the consciousness of morality and the expectation of a happiness proportionate to it as its result can at least be thought as possible' (*Critique of Practical Reason*, 5: 119).
72 See Kant (1996), 238–9 (on the postulate of immortality) (*Critique of Practical Reason*, 5: 122–3).
73 See Kant (1996), 239–46 (on the postulate of God's existence) (*Critique of Practical Reason*, 5: 124–32).
74 The overlap is, however, not exact, since Kant's three official postulates are those of immortality, the existence of God, and freedom, the last of which does not arise in Hegel's phenomenology of moral spirit. See Kant (1996), 246 (*Critique of Practical Reason*, 5: 132).
75 Miller translates 'Verstellung' as 'dissemblance or duplicity' (and in §617 renders 'Verstellen' as 'shiftiness').

76 Many writers at the time were interested in the concept of the beautiful soul, including Goethe and Jacobi. Hegel might well have in mind here the 'Confessions of a Beautiful Soul' from Goethe's *Wilhelm Meister's Apprenticeship* (1795–6), as well as Jacobi's *Woldemar* (1779). See Hegel (1988), 612.
77 'No man is a hero to his valet' is probably proverbial, but a variant of this saying is also attributed to Madame de Cornuel (?1614–94).
78 These words are mine, not Hegel's.
79 See Jamros (1994), 139, 172–3.
80 See Jamros (1994), 141, 173.
81 Miller has 'passive'.
82 See §707/462: 'the *essential* being of the god is, however, the unity of the universal existence of nature and of self-conscious spirit'.
83 See Price and Kearns (2003), 234, 387.
84 See Nietzsche (1993), 14.
85 See Hyppolite (1974), 551.
86 I have omitted Hegel's intervening discussion of athletic festivals (§§725–6/472–4).
87 Hegel does, however, also make reference at one point to Macbeth and Hamlet (§737/481).
88 See §744/485: the gods are 'as *universal* moments, not a self and are not actual [*kein Selbst und nicht wirklich*]. They are, it is true, endowed with the form of individuality, but this is only in imagination and does not really and truly belong to them'. Miller mistakenly translates 'nicht wirklich' as 'not equal'.
89 Jamros (1994), 62.
90 See Lauer (1976), 248: 'God himself is fully present as Spirit – both "substance" and "subject" – only in the spirit of the "community".'
91 See Stewart (1998), 407.
92 Hegel (1999), 60.
93 In this respect, Hegelian absolute knowing is akin to what Spinoza calls the 'the mind's intellectual love of God', which is 'the very love of God by which God loves himself'. See Curley (1994), 260 (*Ethics*, V P36). See also Hegel (2007), 263 (§564 Remark): 'God is God only in so far as he knows his own self; his self-knowledge is, moreover, a self-consciousness in man and man's knowledge *of* God, which proceeds to man's self-knowledge *in* God.'
94 Hegel (1999), 60.
95 Hegel (1999), 49, 69.

Chapter Four

1. See Jaeschke (2003), 503, and Köhler and Pöggeler (1998), 26.
2. Nicolin (1970), 99.
3. Nicolin (1970), 87.
4. Marx (1971), 159.
5. Marx (1971), 160.
6. Siep (2000), 262.
7. Marx (1971), 164.
8. Marx (1971), 165.
9. Marx (1971), 165.
10. Hyppolite (1974), xix.
11. Hyppolite (1974), xxiii.
12. Kojève (1980), 7, 9.
13. Hyppolite (1974), xvi, xxvi–xxvii.
14. Pippin (1989), 114, my emphasis.
15. Pippin (1989), 98.
16. Pippin (1989), 98, my emphasis.

GUIDE TO FURTHER READING

German editions of Hegel's works

Hegel, G. W. F. (1969), *Wissenschaft der Logik*, ed. E. Moldenhauer and K. M. Michel, 2 vols, *Werke in zwanzig Bänden*, vols 5, 6, Frankfurt am Main: Suhrkamp Verlag.
— (1970a), *Enzyklopädie der philosophischen Wissenschaften im Grundrisse (1830). Erster Teil: Die Wissenschaft der Logik*, ed. E. Moldenhauer and K. M. Michel, *Werke in zwanzig Bänden*, vol. 8, Frankfurt am Main: Suhrkamp Verlag.
— (1970b), *Phänomenologie des Geistes*, ed. E. Moldenhauer and K. M. Michel, *Werke in zwanzig Bänden*, vol. 3, Frankfurt am Main: Suhrkamp Verlag.
— (1988), *Phänomenologie des Geistes*, ed. H.-F. Wessels and H. Clairmont, Hamburg: Felix Meiner Verlag.

Translations of Hegel's works and letters

Hegel, G. W. F. (1967), *The Phenomenology of Mind*, trans. J. B. Baillie, New York: Harper & Row.
— (1977), *Phenomenology of Spirit*, trans. A. V. Miller, Oxford: Oxford University Press.
— (1984), *The Letters*, trans. C. Butler and C. Seiler, Bloomington, IN: Indiana University Press.
— (1991), *The Encyclopaedia Logic* (with the *Zusätze*), trans. T. F. Geraets, W. A. Suchting and H. S. Harris, Indianapolis, IN: Hackett.
— (1999), *Science of Logic*, trans. A. V. Miller, Amherst, NY: Humanity Books.

—(2001), *Spirit. Chapter Six of Hegel's Phenomenology of Spirit*, ed. D. E. Shannon, trans. The Hegel Translation Group, Toronto, Indianapolis, IN: Hackett.
—(2005), *Hegel's Preface to the Phenomenology of Spirit*, trans. and commentary Y. Yovel, Princeton, NJ: Princeton University Press.
—(2007), *Philosophy of Mind*, trans. W. Wallace and A. V. Miller, revised by M. Inwood, Oxford: Clarendon Press.
—(2008), *Outlines of the Philosophy of Right*, trans. T. M. Knox, revised by S. Houlgate, Oxford: Oxford University Press.
Houlgate, S., ed. (1998), *The Hegel Reader*, Oxford: Blackwell.

Secondary literature on Hegel

Brandom, R. B. (2002), *Tales of the Mighty Dead. Historical Essays in the Metaphysics of Intentionality*, Cambridge, MA: Harvard University Press.
Browning, G. K., ed. (1997), *Hegel's Phenomenology of Spirit. A Reappraisal*, Dordrecht: Kluwer.
Butler, J. P. (1987), *Subjects of Desire. Hegelian Reflections in Twentieth-Century France*, New York: Columbia University Press.
Crites, S. (1998), *Dialectic and Gospel in the Development of Hegel's Thinking*, University Park, PA: The Pennsylvania State University Press.
Deligiorgi, K., ed. (2006), *Hegel: New Directions*, Stocksfield: Acumen.
Denker, A. and Vater, M., eds (2003), *Hegel's Phenomenology of Spirit. New Critical Essays*, Amherst, NY: Humanity Books.
Feldman, K. S. (2006), *Binding Words. Conscience and Rhetoric in Hobbes, Hegel, and Heidegger*, Evanston, IL: Northwestern University Press.
Feuerbach, L. (1983), 'Towards a Critique of Hegel's Philosophy' (1839), in *The Young Hegelians. An Anthology*, ed. L. S. Stepelevich, Cambridge: Cambridge University Press, pp. 95–128.
Findlay, J. N. (1958), *Hegel. A Re-examination*, New York: Oxford University Press.
Forster, M. N. (1998), *Hegel's Idea of a Phenomenology of Spirit*, Chicago, IL: University of Chicago Press.
Fulda, H. F. and Henrich, D., eds (1973), *Materialien zu Hegels 'Phänomenologie des Geistes'*, Frankfurt am Main: Suhrkamp Verlag.
Gadamer, H.-G. (1976), *Hegel's Dialectic. Five Hermeneutical Studies*, trans. P. C. Smith, New Haven, CT: Yale University Press.
Harris, Henry S. (1997), *Hegel's Ladder*, 2 vols, Indianapolis, IN: Hackett.
Heidegger, M. (2002), 'Hegel's Concept of Experience', in *Off the Beaten Track*, ed. M. Heidegger, trans. J. Young and K. Haynes, Cambridge: Cambridge University Press, pp. 86–156.

—(1988), *Hegel's Phenomenology of Spirit*, trans. P. Emad and K. Maly, Bloomington, IN: Indiana University Press.
Houlgate, S. (1986), *Hegel, Nietzsche and the Criticism of Metaphysics*, Cambridge: Cambridge University Press.
—(2005), *An Introduction to Hegel. Freedom, Truth and History*, 2nd edition, Oxford: Blackwell.
—(2006), *The Opening of Hegel's Logic. From Being to Infinity*, West Lafayette, IN: Purdue University Press.
—(2009), 'Phenomenology and De Re Interpretation: A Critique of Brandom's Reading of Hegel', *International Journal of Philosophical Studies*, 17, 1: 29–47.
Houlgate, S. and Baur, M., eds (2011), *A Companion to Hegel*, Oxford: Wiley-Blackwell.
Hyppolite, J. (1974), *Genesis and Structure of Hegel's Phenomenology of Spirit*, trans. S. Cherniak and J. Heckman, Evanston, IL: Northwestern University Press.
Jaeschke, W. (2003), *Hegel-Handbuch. Leben – Werk – Schule*, Stuttgart: J. B. Metzler.
Jamros, D. P. (1994), *The Human Shape of God. Religion in Hegel's Phenomenology of Spirit*, New York: Paragon House.
Keenan, D. K., ed. (2004), *Hegel and Contemporary Continental Philosophy*, Albany, NY: SUNY Press.
Köhler, D. and Pöggeler, O., eds (1998), *G.W.F. Hegel. Phänomenologie des Geistes*, Berlin: Akademie Verlag.
Kojève, A. (1980), *Introduction to the Reading of Hegel. Lectures on the Phenomenology of Spirit*, ed. A. Bloom, trans. J. H. Nichols, Jr, Ithaca, NY: Cornell University Press.
Krasnoff, L. (2008), *Hegel's Phenomenology of Spirit. An Introduction*, Cambridge: Cambridge University Press.
Lauer, Q. (1976, revised 1987), *A Reading of Hegel's Phenomenology of Spirit*, New York: Fordham University Press.
Lukács, G. (1975), *The Young Hegel. Studies in the Relations between Dialectics and Economics*, trans. R. Livingstone, London: Merlin Press.
Maker, W. (1994), *Philosophy Without Foundations. Rethinking Hegel*, Albany, NY: SUNY Press.
Marx, K. (1971), 'Economic and Philosophical Manuscripts', in *Karl Marx. Early Texts*, ed. D. McLellan, Oxford: Blackwell, pp. 130–83.
Marx, W. (1975), *Hegel's Phenomenology of Spirit. A Commentary on the Preface and Introduction*, trans. P. Heath, New York: Harper and Row.
Moyar, D. (2011), *Hegel's Conscience*, Oxford: Oxford University Press.
Moyar, D. and Quante, M., eds (2008), *Hegel's Phenomenology of Spirit. A Critical Guide*, Cambridge: Cambridge University Press.

Nicolin, G., ed. (1970), *Hegel in Berichten seiner Zeitgenossen*, Hamburg: Felix Meiner Verlag.
O'Neill, J., ed. (1996), *Hegel's Dialectic of Desire and Recognition. Texts and Commentary*, Albany, NY: SUNY Press.
Pinkard, T. (1994), *Hegel's Phenomenology. The Sociality of Reason*, Cambridge: Cambridge University Press.
—(2000), *Hegel. A Biography*, Cambridge: Cambridge University Press.
Pippin, R. B. (1989), *Hegel's Idealism. The Satisfactions of Self-Consciousness*, Cambridge: Cambridge University Press.
—(2011), *Hegel on Self-Consciousness. Desire and Death in the Phenomenology of Spirit*, Princeton, NJ: Princeton University Press.
Rae, G. (2011), *Realizing Freedom. Hegel, Sartre and the Alienation of Human Being*, Basingstoke: Palgrave Macmillan.
Redding, P. (1996), *Hegel's Hermeneutics*, Ithaca, NY: Cornell University Press.
Rockmore, T. (1993), *Before and After Hegel. A Historical Introduction to Hegel's Thought*, Berkeley, CA: University of California Press.
—(1997), *Cognition. An Introduction to Hegel's Phenomenology of Spirit*, Berkeley, CA: University of California Press.
Rosen, S. (1974), *G.W.F. Hegel. An Introduction to the Science of Wisdom*, New Haven, CT: Yale University Press.
Russon, J. (2004), *Reading Hegel's Phenomenology*, Bloomington, IN: Indiana University Press.
Siep, L. (2000), *Der Weg der Phänomenologie des Geistes*, Frankfurt am Main: Suhrkamp Verlag.
Solomon, R. C. (1983), *In the Spirit of Hegel. A Study of G.W.F. Hegel's Phenomenology of Spirit*, New York: Oxford University Press.
Speight, A. (2001), *Hegel, Literature and the Problem of Agency*, Cambridge: Cambridge University Press.
Stern, R. (2002), *Hegel and the Phenomenology of Spirit*, London: Routledge.
Stewart, J., ed. (1998), *The Phenomenology of Spirit Reader. Critical and Interpretive Essays*, Albany, NY: SUNY Press.
—(2000), *The Unity of Hegel's Phenomenology of Spirit*, Evanston, IL: Northwestern University Press.
Taylor, C. (1975), *Hegel*, Cambridge: Cambridge University Press.
Vieweg, K. and Welsch, W., eds (2008), *Hegels Phänomenologie des Geistes*, Frankfurt am Main: Suhrkamp Verlag.
Westphal, K. R. (1989), *Hegel's Epistemological Realism. A Study of the Aim and Method of Hegel's Phenomenology of Spirit*, Dordrecht: Kluwer.
—ed. (2009), *The Blackwell Guide to Hegel's Phenomenology of Spirit*, Oxford: Wiley-Blackwell.

Westphal, M. (1998), *History and Truth in Hegel's Phenomenology*, 3rd edition, Bloomington, IN: Indiana University Press.
Williams, R. R. (1992), *Recognition. Fichte and Hegel on the Other*, Albany, NY: SUNY Press.

Other references

Aristotle (1951), *The Politics*, trans. T. A. Sinclair, revised by T. J. Saunders, Harmondsworth: Penguin Books.
Curley, E., ed. (1994), *A Spinoza Reader. The Ethics and Other Works*, Princeton, NJ: Princeton University Press.
Grene, D. and Lattimore, R., eds (1960), *Greek Tragedies*, 3 vols, Chicago, IL: University of Chicago Press.
Kant, I. (1929), *Critique of Pure Reason*, trans. N. Kemp Smith, London: Macmillan.
—(1996), *Practical Philosophy*, trans. M. J. Gregor, Cambridge: Cambridge University Press.
—(2000), *Critique of the Power of Judgment*, ed. P. Guyer, trans. P. Guyer and E. Matthews, Cambridge: Cambridge University Press.
McLellan, D., ed. (2000), *Karl Marx: Selected Writings*, 2nd edition, Oxford: Oxford University Press.
Nietzsche, F. (1969), *On the Genealogy of Morals* and *Ecce Homo*, trans. W. Kaufmann and R. Hollingdale, New York: Vintage Books.
—(1993), *The Birth of Tragedy*, ed. M. Tanner, trans. S. Whiteside, London: Penguin Books.
—(2003), *Writings from the Late Notebooks*, ed. R. Bittner, trans. K. Sturge, Cambridge: Cambridge University Press.
O'Connor, B., ed. (2000), *The Adorno Reader*, Oxford: Blackwell.
Price, S. and Kearns, E., eds (2003), *The Oxford Dictionary of Classical Myth and Religion*, Oxford: Oxford University Press.
Stewart, J. H. (1951), *A Documentary Survey of the French Revolution*, New York: Macmillan.

INDEX

absolute,
   freedom   9, 15, 24, 28, 45, 94, 162–4, 166
   knowing   12, 15, 21, 103–4, 185–9, 193, 201n. 93
   self-consciousness   170, 186
   spirit   172
absolute, the   4, 142, 144, 159–62, 173–4, 182, 186
abstraction   3, 11, 13, 36, 38, 41–2, 56–7, 71–3, 87, 93–4, 105–6, 124, 129, 135, 141, 150, 162, 177–9, 183, 188, 192
action (*Handlung, Tun*)   77–8, 91, 97, 116–17, 119, 121, 131–2, 134, 139–40, 142, 145, 147, 163–4, 166–71, 181, 185
activity   130–2, 134, 139–40, 152, 159, 161, 177, 181, 187
   of phenomenologist   11, 17, 23, 27–8, 36
actor   181
actuality   69, 78, 115, 121–2, 130, 138–41, 144–5, 150–4, 163–5, 167, 172–3, 178–9, 181–4, 186
   ethical   145
Adorno, Theodor W.   33, 192
Aeschylus,
   Seven against Thebes   149, 200n. 58
alienation   29, 100, 111–12, 136, 151–2, 156–8, 164, 192

also, the   47–8
alteration (of knowledge, object)   18–22
anatomy   129
animal   125–8, 174–6, 178–9, 183, 199n. 45
   functions   117
Antigone   148–9, 152, 155, 199nn. 56–7 *see also* Sophocles
appearance   66–9, 71–2, 75–9, 84
Aristotle   3, 48, 85, 124
art   177–8
   religion of   176–84
ascetic, the   119–20
assumptions   3–6, 195n. 15
   see also presuppositions

Bacchus *see* Dionysus
Battle of Jena   1
beautiful soul   170, 172, 186–7, 201n. 76
being   2–3, 5–6, 12–13, 31–2, 39–41, 43, 46, 51, 57, 66, 93, 98–9, 121, 124, 127, 131, 134, 139, 147, 186–8, 193–4, 195n. 15
   for-another   55, 58, 63
   for-self   10, 55, 58–9, 63, 93–5, 99–101, 103–4, 122, 175, 182
   in-itself   10, 17, 26, 32, 104
beyond, the   64–6, 70–2, 77, 81, 113–16, 120, 158, 161, 166–7

Bloch, Ernst   192
body   85, 87, 93, 131, 133, 139
Brandom, Robert B.   1, 193
brother and sister   147–8
Buddhism   174
Butler, Judith   1, 84

capacities   130, 137–41
categories   2–3, 10–11, 17, 57, 124, 196n. 23
Ceres *see* Demeter
change   18, 24–5, 29, 69, 72, 74, 78–9, 96, 125, 134, 138–9
  see also alteration
changeableness   109–16, 118, 120–5
character, characteristic   132–3
  determinate original   131, 139
  essential   54, 125–6, 199n. 45
Christianity   119, 174, 182–5
comedy   181
community   50, 142, 145–7, 150, 152, 159, 172, 183–4, 186, 201n. 90
comparison of knowledge and object   16–18, 37
complexity   21, 25, 27, 41–2, 47, 105–6
concept   2, 9, 11, 17, 32, 75, 79, 104–6, 114, 126, 186, 188, 196n. 3, 197n. 10
  of force   60, 63–5, 79
  of law   70–2
condition   11, 44–5
confession   172–3, 183
conscience   168–71, 173, 186–7
consciousness   6–9, 12, 16–18, 26, 32, 80–4, 87, 91, 113, 145, 185, 188, 197nn. 8, 10
  active   130–1
  actual   151–3

  natural, ordinary   5–8, 10–13, 15–16, 23–4, 30–1, 44, 89, 103, 109, 188–9
  pure   113, 151–3, 157–8, 162
contingency   108, 110, 122, 150–1, 156, 160
contradiction   29, 50–2, 54–7, 78–9, 82–3, 108–10, 129, 143
Cornuel, Madame de   201n. 77
Creon   146, 148–9, 199n. 56
criterion   16–18, 20, 50, 52, 106, 143
critique   2–5, 195n. 15
  immanent   37
cult   178–81, 183–4
culture   152, 157–8, 163

Daoism   174
death   9, 15, 28–9, 94, 98–9, 129, 135, 147, 149, 154, 164, 175, 183–4, 186
  fear of   98–102
  of God   183–4
deism   162
Deleuze, Gilles   193
Demeter   178–80
Derrida, Jacques   193
Descartes, René   8, 87
desire   84–8, 90, 93–4, 96, 114, 134
  for recognition   193
devotion   113–14, 116
dialectic   20, 25, 36–8, 42, 56, 77, 97–8, 102, 108, 191, 198n. 20
Diderot, Denis, *Rameau's Nephew*   157, 200n. 67
difference   49, 60–1, 63–76, 80–1, 111–13, 142, 162–3, 188
  organic   85

INDEX

Dionysus 178–80
divine, divinity 161, 169–70, 173, 175–86
  law 146–8, 150
  voice 169, 173
duty 22, 147, 165–71, 199n. 57
dynamism 56, 58, 65, 71–5, 77–9, 81

education 6, 15, 21, 36, 43, 152, 154
Einstein, Albert 198n. 17
enjoyment 80, 95–8, 105, 115, 117, 119–20, 135, 178–9, 198n. 21
enlightenment 28, 45, 158, 160–2
epic 180
Epictetus 105
epistemology 4, 11, 194, 197n. 11
error 4, 49–53, 159
ethical,
  actuality 145
  consciousness 142
  life 146, 149, 180
  substance 145–6
evangelical counsels 119
exclusion 38–9, 42, 47–50, 52, 61, 93, 148
Existentialism 102
experience 4, 9–12, 18, 20–1, 23–8, 38, 43, 45, 48, 51, 55–7, 83, 85, 92, 107
explanation 71–5, 80
expression 35, 46, 60–3, 73–4, 127–8, 131–3, 139, 155, 169, 172, 175
externality 126–8, 182

face 132, 139
faith 29, 151, 158–61, 173
family 146–9

fear,
  of death 98–102
  of error 4
feeling 114
feudalism 154, 156
Feuerbach, Ludwig 34, 191
flattery 155–7
force 22, 60–76, 79–80, 83, 85, 92, 125, 128
  concept of 60, 63–5, 79
forgiveness 172–3, 183
Foucault, Michel 193
Franklin, Benjamin 126
freedom 3, 5, 8, 91–105, 107–11, 119–20, 122, 126, 147–9, 162–4, 200n. 74
  absolute 9, 15, 24, 28, 45, 94, 162–4, 166
French Revolution 1, 3, 9, 28, 163–4
Fries, J. F. 191

Gadamer, Hans-Georg 88
Galileo's law of fall 68–9, 76, 198n. 15
Gall, D. F. J. 133
gift 115–16
giving up 43, 91, 109, 116–17, 119–20, 137, 172–3
God 159–61, 166–7, 173, 182–6, 201nn. 90, 93
  death of 183–4
gods (lower and upper) 179–80
Goethe, J. W. 157, 200n. 67
  Faust, Part One 199n. 50
  Wilhelm Meister's Apprenticeship 201n. 76
good, the 29, 106, 137–8, 152–3, 200n. 71

Habermas, Jürgen 192
Hagner, Joachim 48
Hamlet 201n. 87

hard heart 172
harmony of morality and
    nature 165–7
Harris, H. S. 193
Hegel, G. W. F.,
    *Encyclopaedia Philosophy of
    Nature* 2, 73, 198n. 15
    *Encyclopaedia Philosophy of
    Spirit* 2, 45, 196n. 23
    Lectures on Aesthetics
    77, 149
    *Outlines of the Philosophy of
    Right* 97–8, 149
    Phenomenology of Spirit 1–2,
    6, 8–10, 15, 20–1, 23, 28–9,
    31, 45, 67, 84, 97, 103, 123,
    191–4
    Science of Logic 2, 9–10,
    12–13, 33, 103, 197n. 10
Heidegger, Martin 30, 192
Helvétius, C. A. 160
here 37, 40
history 9, 24, 28, 31, 96, 174,
    183–4, 189, 192
human, humanity 112, 136,
    173–7, 180–6, 192
Hume, David 48
Husserl, Edmund 30
hymn 177–8, 181
hypocrisy, hypocrite 92, 167–8,
    171–3, 183, 186
Hyppolite, Jean 98, 193

I, the 30, 32, 37–8, 42, 84,
    87–8, 90, 93, 102, 108, 123,
    154–6, 158, 187
    that is We 90
idealism 97, 123–4, 192–4
identity 84, 94, 108, 129, 171–2,
    178–9, 183, 185–6
    of thought and being
    (or object) 5–6, 13, 21, 30,
    103–4, 113, 145, 186–8

immanence 7–8, 10–11, 17,
    27–8, 33, 37, 44, 48, 60, 82,
    182–3, 199n. 38
immediacy 5, 7, 21, 25, 30–5,
    37–9, 42–3, 46, 49, 51, 55,
    65, 110, 123, 127–8, 146,
    148, 164–5, 168, 197n. 2
'in so far as', the 53, 56
incarnation 112–13, 115, 121,
    182–4, 186
inclination 130, 166–7, 169–70
independence 59, 85–7, 90–3, 96,
    98–9, 102, 107, 119, 134,
    182, 193
indeterminacy 3, 13, 34–8, 41,
    105, 188, 195n. 15
indifference 35–7, 47–51, 71,
    73, 105
individual, individuality 6, 10,
    32, 111–13, 115, 117–18,
    120–1, 123, 131, 134–50,
    152–6, 162–5, 168–70,
    172–3, 186–7, 200n. 70,
    201n. 88
infinity 79–83, 85
inner,
    being 64–8, 70–2, 74–5,
    80–1, 170, 176
    and outer 78, 127–8, 131, 133
    self 131–3
inorganic (elements, nature,
    things) 126–7, 129
insight 151, 158–62
intelligible (object, unity, world)
    63–6, 68, 71, 75, 78–81, 125
inverted world 76–8
irritability 127–8
Islam 174

Jacobi, F. H.,
    Woldemar 201n. 76
Jesus Christ 182–4
joy 140–1

Judaism   174
judge, judgement   92, 112, 153, 157, 171–3, 183, 186

Kant, Immanuel   2–5, 16, 44, 48, 118, 123–4, 143, 166, 193, 195n. 15
  Critique of Practical Reason   166, 200nn. 71–4
  Critique of Pure Reason   1, 4
Kepler's laws of planetary motion   69, 198n. 15
Kielmeyer, C. F.   128
Kojève, Alexandre   1, 84, 98, 192–3

labour or work (*Arbeit*)   28–9, 96–7, 99–103, 105, 114–17, 119, 122, 131, 191–2
Lacan, Jacques   84, 192
language   16, 34–5, 44, 154–5, 157, 169–70, 172, 176–7, 180–1, 191
Lauer, Quentin   141, 193
Lavater, J. C.   132
law   68–78, 125–33, 137, 142–50, 152–3, 163, 171
  concept of   70–2
  divine   146–8, 150
  of gravity   70, 73–4, 198n. 16
  of the heart   135–7
  human   146, 148
  of inversion   78–9, 81–2
lawfulness   70, 72
Leibniz, G. W.   2
let, let go   11, 43, 109, 172–3, 183, 187
Levinas, Emmanuel   192
life   79, 84–7, 93–5, 98, 105, 119, 127, 129, 198n. 27
life and death struggle   28, 93–5, 98, 105, 110, 122
light-being   29, 174

Linnaeus, Carl   126
logic, logical   2–3, 5–6, 9–10, 13, 21, 25, 28, 31, 51, 56, 68, 76, 85, 88, 91, 94, 109, 122–3, 126, 133, 138, 147, 149, 164, 166, 172, 174, 185–9, 196nn. 23, 7, 199n. 38
  formal   3, 129
lord of the world   151, 166, 174
loss (of object, self, world)   8, 12, 25–6, 29, 36, 40, 42, 55, 62, 86, 108, 135, 157, 161, 170
Louis XIV   156
Lukács, Georg   192

Macbeth   201n. 87
McDowell, John   193
macro- and micro-transitions   24–7, 43–4
Marcus Aurelius   105
Marx, Karl   1, 96–7, 191–3
Marxism   102
mask   132, 181
mass   146, 152
master–slave relation   28, 95–103, 105–7, 110, 114–15, 191–3
materialism   162
matters   48, 59–63, 125–6
mediation   33, 35, 37, 66, 97, 118, 197n. 2
medium   47–8, 50, 52–3, 59, 85
Memnon Colossi   176
Merleau-Ponty, Maurice   192
metaphysics   2
minister   118–20
modern age   3
monarch   152, 156
morality   89, 165–8, 200n. 71
motionless tautology   84, 90

movement 11, 25–7, 59–60, 62–3, 65, 74–5, 78–80, 83–6, 90, 113–14, 133, 178, 180, 182, 188
mysteries 179–80

Napoleon 1
nature 126–7, 129, 147–50, 152, 160, 165–7, 174, 177–8, 199n. 49
  observation of 124
necessity 9, 11, 21, 23, 28, 31, 48, 68, 71, 73, 135–6, 197n. 8
  see also logic
negation 36, 41, 46–9, 57, 59, 64–5, 67, 84–7, 95–6, 105–9, 114, 122, 130, 134–5, 149, 152, 158–9, 164, 175
negativity 87, 98–101, 134
Newton, Isaac 28, 198n. 16
Nietzsche, Friedrich 65, 119, 180, 197n. 13
nihilism 65
noble and base self 153–6, 171, 200n. 65
now 21, 33–6, 39–41, 44, 197n. 5

object in phenomenology 17–27
observation 124–34, 139, 144, 199n. 45
ontology 2, 11, 44
opposites 55–6, 76
oracle 177
organic, organism 85, 87, 126–9, 199n. 45
other, the 83–4, 86, 90–1, 104
outrage 157–8

pantheism 175
passivity 11, 17, 48, 115, 124
perception 10, 21–2, 24, 26–8, 43, 45–59, 62–4, 78, 80–2, 107–8, 124, 128

person 150–2, 155
phenomenologist 16–17, 23–30, 36, 39, 43, 57–8, 62, 74, 82–3, 92, 95, 102–3, 109, 127
phenomenology 6–13, 16–18, 20, 23–4, 27–30, 33, 37, 44–5, 109, 119, 145, 149, 187–9, 192–3, 196n. 23
  of religion 174
philosophy 2–4, 6–13, 17, 30, 45, 109, 149, 185, 188–9
phrenology 133
physiognomy 132–3, 139, 155
Pinkard, Terry 84, 193
Pippin, Robert B. 193–4
plants 175
Plato 6, 48
Platonism 46
play of forces 62–72, 74, 92
pleasure 29, 135–6
pointing 39–42, 44
Polyneices 148
postulates 166–7, 200nn. 72–4
powerlessness 151, 156
presence 40–1, 123, 173
presuppositions 3, 8–12, 44–5, 188, 199n. 38
pretence 166–8
priesthood 159
properties 22, 27, 48–55, 58–9, 63, 124–5, 128, 197n. 10
psychology 130, 199n. 49
purpose 127, 146–7
pyramids 175

readers 23–4, 30, 36, 43
reason 121–40, 142–6, 172, 185–6
  instinct of 125
  law-giving 143–4
  law-testing 143–4, 146

recognition   88–9, 92–7, 122, 150, 152, 154, 168–70
  desire for   193
  mutual   89, 91–3, 147, 172
reconciliation   92, 172, 185–6
religion   15, 114, 158, 160, 173–4, 181–2, 185–7
  of art   176–84
  Egyptian   28, 175
  Greek   28, 174, 176, 181–2, 184
  Indian   175
  manifest   182–6 *see also* Christianity
  natural   29, 174–5
relinquishing, renunciation   115–17, 119–20, 122, 154, 172, 178–9, 183, 186–7
representation (*Vorstellung*)   104, 157–8, 180, 185
reproduction   127–8
resolve   3, 5, 8
ressentiment   65, 197n. 13
resurrection   183–4
revenge   76–7
reversal of consciousness   23, 26, 44
revolution   97, 163–4
Richter, Jean Paul   191
right   6, 142, 148–52, 155, 161
Robespierre, M.   160
Roman Emperor, Empire   105, 150–1
Rosen, Stanley   9
Rousseau, Jean-Jacques   3, 163

sacrifice   15, 117, 119, 137–8, 178–9, 183–4, 186
Sartre, Jean-Paul   84, 192
satisfaction   8, 42, 76, 87, 116–17, 141, 162, 198n. 21
scepticism   8, 29, 107–10, 122, 199n. 38

Schelling, F. W. J.   1
schema   118
Schubert, G. H.   191
science   1–3, 6, 8–11, 23, 44, 188, 195n. 6
  natural   60, 132
scientist   74, 126
sculpture   175, 178, 180–1
self-awareness   80
self-consciousness   45, 80–95, 98, 104–5, 114, 121–2, 126, 129–31, 134, 145, 150, 152, 159, 165, 173–87, 192–3, 197n. 8
  absolute   170, 186
  doubling of   88, 90, 92, 110, 134
self-identity   10, 50, 52–4, 57, 76, 84, 108–11, 124–7, 129, 143, 152–3, 157
self-negation   56–7, 87–9, 116, 175
self-will   101, 108
sense-certainty   10, 21–2, 24–8, 30–49, 51, 56–7, 80–3, 108, 124, 155, 191, 197n. 5
sensibility   127–8
shapes of consciousness   9, 11, 15, 20, 22–31, 41, 43, 45, 57, 123, 145, 188–9
Sieyès, Abbé Emmanuel Joseph   163
simplicity   3, 37, 41, 71–3, 75, 126
skull   133
slave   26, 29, 95–106, 114, 122
Socrates   8–9
solicitation   61–4, 79, 85, 92
Solomon, Robert   193
sophistry   56
Sophocles,
  Antigone   144, 146, 148–9
  Oedipus the King   149, 200n. 58

space 32, 35, 39, 71, 73, 112, 161, 183
speculative (logic, philosophy, thought) 2–3, 5–6, 8–9, 13, 29, 109, 145, 149, 185, 188, 199n. 38
sphinx 176
Spinoza, Benedict de 2–3, 201n. 93
spirit 45, 90, 134, 144–6, 148, 150, 155, 163, 165, 169, 172–3, 176, 182–4, 186, 192, 201n. 90
  absolute 172
  Holy 183, 185
spiritual animal kingdom 140, 144, 169
state, state power 146–50, 152–8
statue 160, 176
Stern, Robert 34, 193
stoicism 26, 29, 105–7, 110, 113, 121–2, 150, 186–7
substance 2–3, 12, 103–4, 145–6, 148, 150–1, 158, 165, 183, 185–8, 193, 201n. 90
  ethical 145–6
supersensible, the 65–8, 75, 77–8, 158
Supreme Being 160
surrender 11, 115–17, 178–9
suspicion 154, 164

terror 9, 164
thanking 116–17, 119
thing 22, 27, 48–60, 84, 93, 95–6, 99–100, 103, 120–2, 125–6, 128, 133–4, 157, 160, 162, 175–8, 197n. 10
  in itself 3, 5, 16
thinghood 47, 103, 124

this 32, 46, 57
thought 2–3, 5–6, 9–12, 21, 24, 27, 30, 60, 63, 103–8, 113–14, 129, 145, 154, 157, 165, 186–9, 193–4
time 32, 34–6, 39–40, 44, 68, 71, 73, 76, 112, 161, 166, 183
tragedy 77, 149, 180–1
transcendental philosophy 11, 45
Treviranus, G. R. 126
Trinity 182–3
true world 65
truth 16–17, 21, 25–6, 33, 35–6, 40–3, 45–6, 48–57, 65–8, 82–4, 91, 97, 104–6, 123, 143, 168, 187–8, 197n. 8

Unchangeable, the 110–20, 122
unchangeableness 107–11, 121, 123, 200n. 65
understanding 2, 4, 22, 28, 45, 57–83, 124–5, 128
  formal 10
  perceptual 57, 63
  proper 81–2
  superficial 77, 81
  true 79, 82
unhappy consciousness 25–6, 28, 109–22, 140, 173, 191–2, 200n. 65
unity 2, 48, 50, 53–4, 57–75, 79, 84–5, 110, 120–1, 123–4, 127, 129–30, 134–5, 148, 151, 155, 165–7, 179–80, 188, 195n. 15
  of being and doing 131, 139
  of opposites 55–6, 79
  undifferentiated 64–7, 70, 72, 74, 149, 162

universal, universality   10, 25–6,
      34–43, 46–51, 55–8, 60, 64,
      66–72, 79, 85, 101, 105,
      115, 120–1, 123–6, 129,
      135–44, 146–7, 149–56,
      158–9, 162–68, 170–2, 183,
      186, 201n. 88
   abstract   36, 38, 40–2, 56–7
   concrete   25, 42, 146
   conditioned, one-sided   55–8
   unconditioned   56–8, 60, 79
utility   160, 162, 200n. 69

vanishing   37, 62, 64–6, 72, 79,
      125, 165, 170
virtue   106, 137–8

Wahl, Jean   192
way of the world   137–8

we   23–4, 26–8, 33, 36, 39, 43–4,
      58, 74, 83–5, 90, 102–3,
      109, 173, 186
   that is I   90
wealth   152–4, 156–7, 163
Westphal, Kenneth R.   193
Westphal, Merold   193
what really matters   141–2
will   118–20
   general, universal   163–6
   pure   145, 164–5, 168
Williams, Robert R.   193
Word of God   182
work (*Arbeit*) *see* labour
work (*Werk*)   139–41, 163–4,
      176–7
writing   36, 132

Zoroastrianism   174

www.ingramcontent.com/pod-product-compliance
Lightning Source LLC
Chambersburg PA
CBHW070313230426
43663CB00011B/2115